I0819516

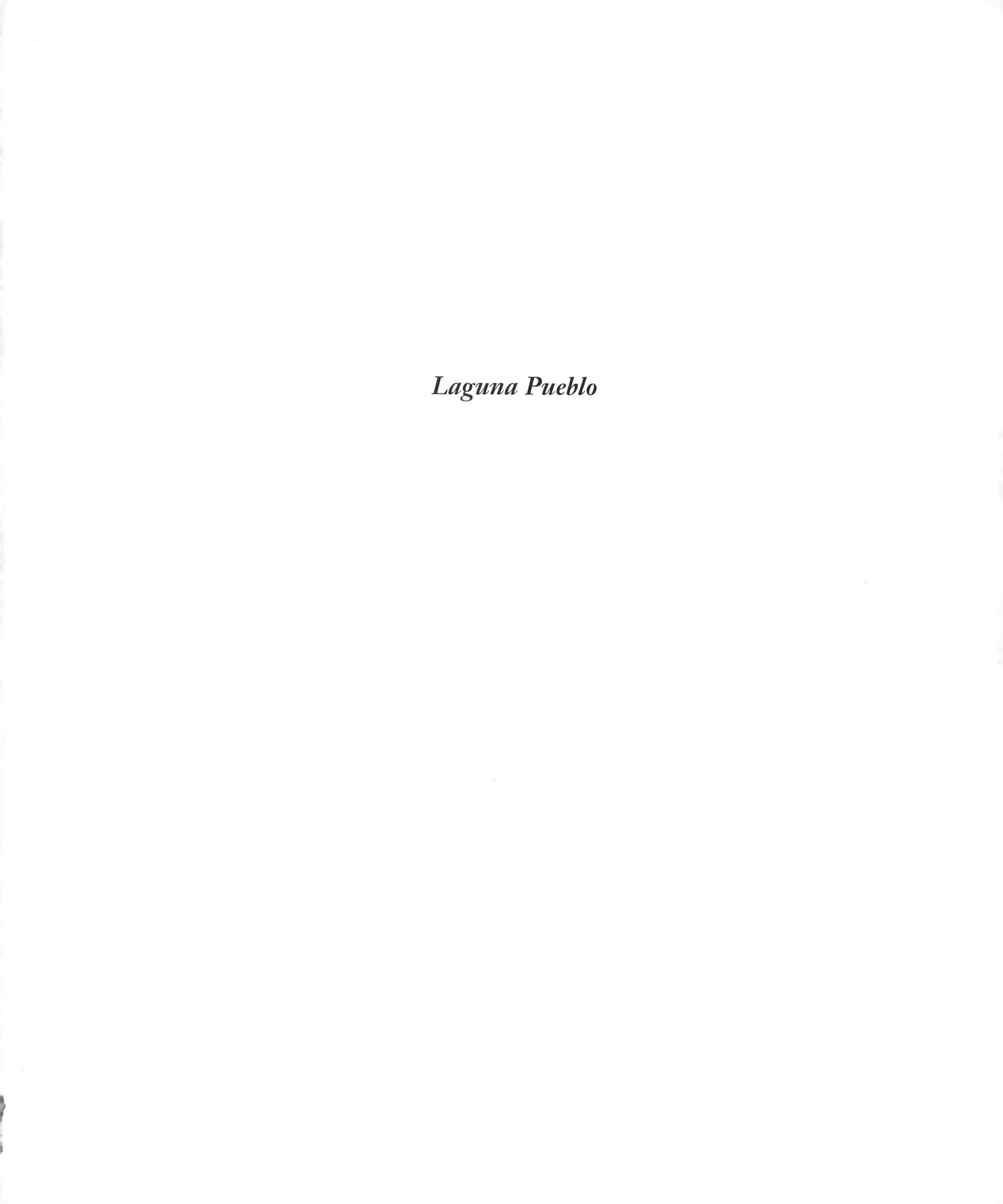

Laguna Pueblo

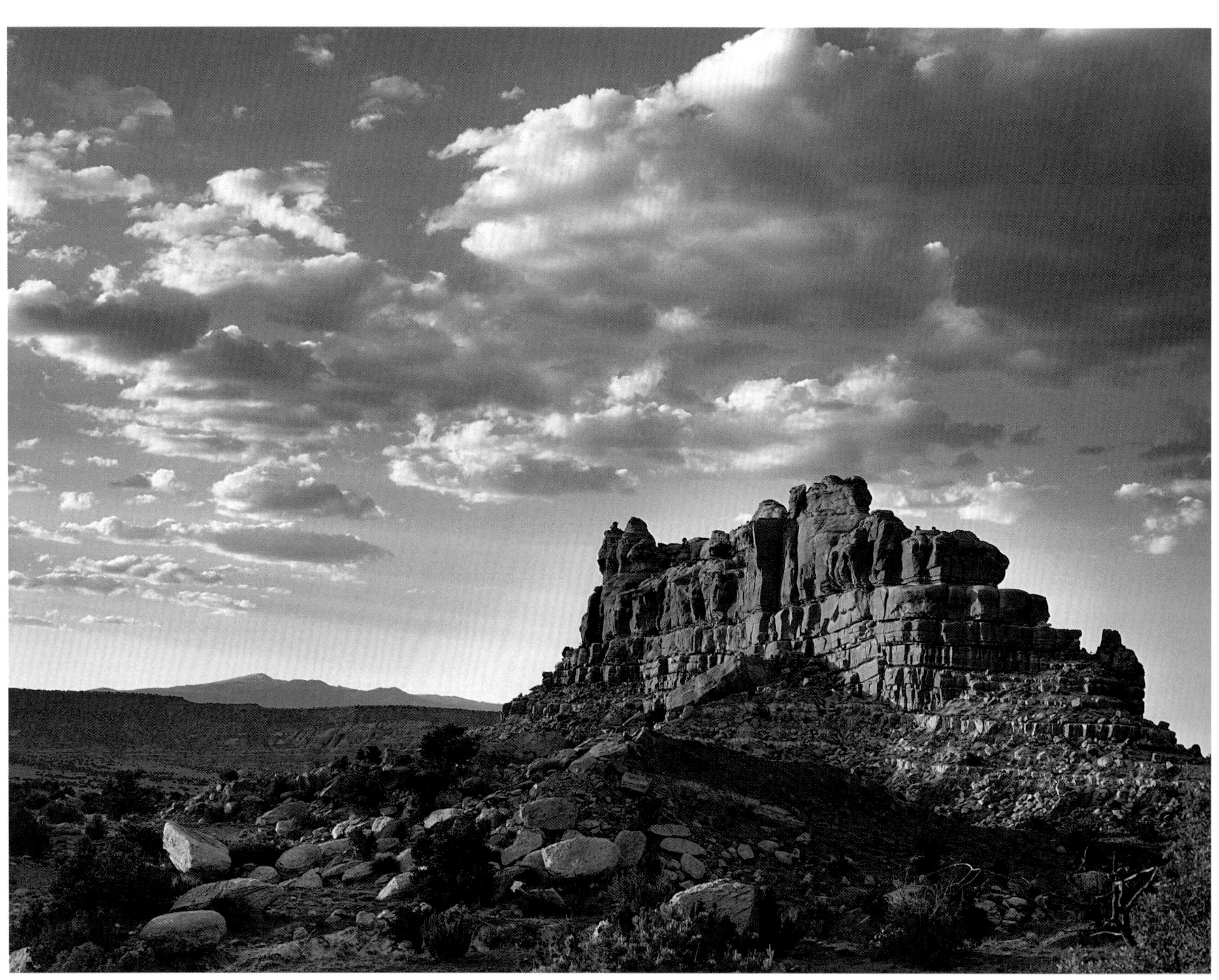

Laguna Pueblo

A PHOTOGRAPHIC HISTORY

Lee Marmon & Tom Corbett

UNIVERSITY OF NEW MEXICO PRESS • ALBUQUERQUE

Printed in China
20 19 18 17 16 15 1 2 3 4 5 6

Library of Congress Cataloging-in-Publication Data

Marmon, Lee.
Laguna pueblo : a photographic history / Lee Marmon and Tom Corbett.
— First edition.
pages cm
Includes index.
ISBN 978-0-8263-5535-5 (cloth : alk. paper) — ISBN 978-0-8263-5536-2 (electronic)
1. Laguna Indians—History. 2. Laguna Indians—Pictorial works.
3. Laguna (N.M.)—Pictorial works. I. Corbett, Tom, 1938– II. Title.
E99.L2.M35 2014
978.9'91—dc23
2014018325

Cover Photograph: *Clouds over the Malpais,* by Lee Marmon, 1985

The stark beauty of the Malpais (badlands) is accented in this photograph by the striking cloud formations and the rainstorm in the distance. Characterized by sandstone cliffs and valleys of lava rock, the area was once roamed by the Lagunas. They used the area for hunting, religious ceremonies, and as a place of refuge from enemies. The area is now managed by the National Park Service.

Lee Marmon photographs courtesy the Lee Marmon Pictorial Collection (Collection #2000-017), Center for Southwest Research, University Libraries, University of New Mexico.

Designed by Lisa Tremaine
Composed in Adobe's Janson Text, originally designed by Nicholas Kis, and Frutiger, designed by Adrian Frutiger

This book is dedicated to the Laguna people—past, present, and future.

With a special note to young people:

You are composed of parts from each of your ancestors
To know who you are, you must know who they were
To know where you are going, you must know where they have been

CONTENTS

PREFACE ix

ACKNOWLEDGMENTS xvii

INTRODUCTION xix

CHAPTER ONE *Geography* 1

CHAPTER TWO *In the Beginning* 7

CHAPTER THREE *The Conquistadores* 15

CHAPTER FOUR *The Laguna Mission* 19

CHAPTER FIVE *Tribal Government and the Lincoln Canes* 27

CHAPTER SIX *The Anglo Infusion* 33

CHAPTER SEVEN *The Railroad* 41

CHAPTER EIGHT *The Marmon Battalion* 51

CHAPTER NINE *Route 66* 57

CHAPTER TEN *The Jackpile Mine* 65

CHAPTER ELEVEN *Customs and Culture* 69

CHAPTER TWELVE *Portraits* 99

CHAPTER THIRTEEN *Landscapes* 153

CHAPTER FOURTEEN *Health Care* 175

CHAPTER FIFTEEN *Present Concerns and the Future* 183

NOTES 189

INDEX 195

When the manuscript for this book was in the final stages, we asked several family members and friends to read and comment on it. A unanimous suggestion was that we write a preface explaining our backgrounds, the driving force behind our friendship, and how we eventually came to coauthor this historical book.

We were somewhat surprised by this suggestion but were reminded that over the years, we have always been there to assist each other in a number of ways, even though we have greatly different backgrounds and personalities. One reviewer suggested that people may ask, "Why are these very different people such good friends, and why did they decide to write a book together?"

To tell who we are, we present the following biographies and history.

Lee Marmon

Most readers of this book will already know Lee Marmon as the premier Native American photographer of his generation and will be familiar with his famous image *White Man's Moccasins.* Since 1947, Lee has taken over one hundred thousand photographs documenting the history of the Laguna people and their tribal neighbors as well as the changes that have redrawn the contours of their culture over the past sixty-five years.

Lesser known about Lee is that he comes from a fascinating multicultural background. Born in Laguna Pueblo in New Mexico in 1925, he is the son of Henry Anaya Marmon and grandson of Robert Gunn Marmon, whose story is told in chapter 6, "The Anglo Infusion," and chapter 8, "The Marmon Battalion." Lee's mother, Lily Ann Stagner Marmon, was of mixed Spanish and German ancestry.

Lee grew up in Laguna Pueblo in the area adjacent to the main village. He loved books and began reading when he was four years old. He first attended school on the old Presbyterian compound. His mixed background exposed him to cultural conflicts, even early in life. Lee recalls,

> I was a pretty mean kid when I was growing up. I didn't care much for school, either. We all went to class in a one-room school. When I was

> about eight years old, my brother Polly and I would sneak out of class while the teacher wasn't looking. We would go rabbit hunting with the rifle I had hid in the bushes near the school. I guess that's why I'm not very good at math!
>
> One Sunday while we were in church, the pastor scolded us for talking. So that evening we got even by sneaking into the church when no one was around. We gathered up all the hymnbooks and burned them up in the wood stove!

Lee's rebellious nature, free-spirit grit, and zest for independence were evident at an early age. At age nine, he was sent to live with his Grandmother Stagner so he could attend school in Albuquerque. Upset one day because his grandmother did not have his favorite crackers, he decided to walk back home to Laguna, a distance of fifty miles. It was December, and by the time he got past Nine Mile Hill on the western edge of Albuquerque, it was getting dark and cold. Parts of the old Route 66 were still under construction at the time, and one of the construction workers from Laguna, as he was driving home, recognized young Lee in his light fall jacket and drove him the rest of the way back to the pueblo. If not for the construction worker, Lee might have frozen to death that night on the desolate West Mesa.

After graduating from Grants High School, Lee joined the army and served in the Aleutian Islands. While on the ship to Alaska, Lee admired the scenery and wished he'd had a camera to send photos home to his folks. This rekindled his childhood interest in and appreciation for photography. Upon returning home, he worked for his father at the Marmon Trading Post. It was during this time that his career in photography began to blossom. The rest of the story of his introduction to photography is told later in this book.

In 1966, Lee left Laguna to take a position in Palm Springs, California, as the principal photographer for the Bob Hope Desert Classic, a tournament that attracted top golf pros, including Arnold Palmer, Jack Nicklaus, Lee Trevino, and Johnny Miller—plus a host of dignitaries, executives, and celebrities, from Frank Sinatra to former presidents Ford and Nixon, and Bob Hope himself, all to support local charities.

In 1982, Lee returned to Laguna and has lived there ever since. He and his wife, Kathy, live in the old Santa Fe railroad station that has been converted into their home. An old outbuilding (previously used as a bathhouse for the Depression-era motor court built by his Grandfather Stagner) on the property serves as his photographic laboratory.

Tom Corbett

Born in Chicago in 1938 to parents of Irish and German heritage, Tom spent his early years in the upscale Chicago suburb of Wilmette. His father, forty-two years his senior, retired from his job as writer and editor for the *Chicago Tribune* when Tom was nine. His family then moved to rural Michigan, to six acres on a bluff overlooking Lake Michigan five miles north of the Benton Harbor–St. Joseph area.

It was there he learned to hunt and fish and to love the solitude of the outdoor world. He spent many hours walking the Lake Michigan shoreline and adjacent woods. It became his way of isolating himself from societal pressures.

Tom attended local high schools for three years and spent one year at Phillips Academy in Andover, Massachusetts. Ann Arbor was his second home while he attended the University of Michigan for undergrad, medical school, and subsequent professional training.

In 1964, the so-called doctor draft was still in effect. Twenty-six and single, Tom knew he was about to be drafted, so he enlisted with the U.S. Public Health Service for two years. His first assignment was at the Alaska Native Medical Center in Anchorage. While in Alaska, he also spent three months at the remote one-doctor, twelve-bed hospital in Barrow, plus completed a three-month tour with the United States Coast Guard as a medical officer aboard the USCGC *Chautauqua* stationed in Honolulu. While in the idyllic backdrop of Hawaii, he met Beverly, a student nurse at the Queen's Hospital. Later that year, she would become his wife.

His two-year assignment in Alaska was cut short with the untimely death of the physician at Laguna. Tom was transferred there to take his place in the early summer of 1965. His time at Laguna is chronicled in the following discussion of his relationship with Lee Marmon and in later pages of this book.

Friends for Fifty Years

Reporting to the area office in Albuquerque, Tom was instructed to find an apartment, report to the area office every weekday at 8 a.m., and then leave for the clinic at Laguna in a government car. He would arrive at Laguna about 9 a.m. and was to leave the clinic no later than 3 p.m. to arrive back at the area office by quitting time at 4 p.m.

After about a week of this routine, the young doctor announced to the area office that he was not able to adequately take care of five thousand Native Americans working six hours a day, five days a week. He volunteered to move to the reservation so that he could both convert the driving time to clinic time and make himself available for emergencies, reminding the area office that people don't get sick only from the hours of 9 a.m. to 3 p.m.

They said that it was not possible. When Tom asked why, the response was, "No one had ever done it before." Tom suggested he be the first.

The Bureau of Indian Affairs had constructed a small housing compound with about twenty rectangular two- and three-bedroom homes just east of the village of Laguna for the purpose of housing BIA employees, including teachers at the school. There were several vacancies, and he, along with several other non-BIA employees, took up residence there.

Lee Marmon, who ran the Marmon Trading Post, lived in the house next door. His family, including his first wife Virginia and daughters Leslie, Wendy, and Gigi, lived in Albuquerque during the week because the girls were going to school there.

Tom recalls his first meeting with Lee Marmon: "As I pulled up in front of my new home, I noticed a Jeep parked in front of the house next door. After taking several loads of boxes into the house, there was a knock on the front door. There stood a man in his midthirties, dressed in western attire, including jeans, well-polished cowboy boots, and a wide-brimmed hat. 'I'm Pitsy Marmon, your next-door neighbor,' he began. I had a feeling right off the bat that we would become good friends."

Lee would come over and invite Tom to go off-roading with him in his Jeep CJ-5. Sometimes they would go to the far reaches of the reservation. Pitsy (Lee's nickname used by friends and family) would always have his camera in the back and his pistol under the front seat. They would go on primitive two-tracks and make their own roads where there were none. Sometimes Lee would take him to Dripping Springs. Sometimes they would take the back road past San Fidel all the way up the back side of Mount Taylor. Everywhere they went on these remote journeys, Tom felt a sense of freedom and independence, and he felt that Lee did as well.

Other times Lee would take him to meet new people both on and off the reservation. Sometimes they would go to Grants, where characters out of the old Wild West still existed—characters like Old Gus Rainey, who eventually died in jail of a heart attack at age ninety-nine, while he was awaiting trial for murdering several people who trespassed on his property. Lee was an endless source of historical facts and events of the area, as well as a great storyteller.

One day soon after Tom arrived at Laguna, Lee showed him several of his photographs. It was then he realized that Lee was preserving the history of Laguna in photographs—documenting the history and changes of a tribe as the people were catapulted from an agrarian society into the space age. He had captivating portraits of the people and photographs of their environment and changing culture.

The portraits of the old people with their lined faces and elegant poses raised Tom's curiosity about how they lived. Lee was preserving in photographs a way of life that was slowly disappearing. Someday, Tom thought, he would have Lee tell him their stories. It occurred to him back then that these images and the stories behind them should be preserved for future generations in a book. Perhaps someday Lee would do it himself. If Lee did not, perhaps someday Tom could work with him to make sure the work was published. Lee was doing something no one had ever done before—record in photographs the history of a Native American tribe as it happened. What a wonderful story it would make if Lee continued the project throughout his lifetime!

Tom married the girl from Queen's Hospital in November 1965. When they returned to Laguna from Hawaii, Lee took them up to Mount Taylor to cut down their first Christmas tree. On the Fourth of July in 1966, always a huge celebration hosted by the Marmons, they all went camping at Dripping Springs, set off fireworks at the top of the mesa, and slept under the bright stars in the vast New Mexico sky.

Tom and his wife left Laguna in 1966 to return to Michigan. There, Tom began residency training at the University of Michigan Medical Center. About the time they left, Lee also left Laguna, by himself, for Palm Springs, California, where he became the official photographer for the Bob Hope Desert Classic and other high-profile assignments. When Tom found out Lee was leaving, he assumed that the long-term book project he had in mind would not be completed, and he dropped the idea from his plans.

By the early 1980s, Tom had finished his residency training, spent seven years in academia and research, and then entered into the private practice of anesthesiology. He and Beverly, often reminiscing about life on the reservation, spontaneously decided to take a four-day weekend and fly to New Mexico. They spent a day in Santa Fe and then decided to go back to Laguna to see if any of their old friends were still around and find out how they had fared in the ensuing years.

They were surprised to learn that Lee had returned to Laguna in 1982 and resumed his photography there. He was living in the old train station along with an increasing collection of photographs, and the idea for the book was resurrected.

Lee was gaining a local reputation, but Tom felt that he now deserved national recognition for his work. Lee had produced *White Man's Moccasins* posters, and they were becoming popular regionally. To increase Lee's exposure, Tom financed and produced posters using a small publishing company he had started as a side project to his medical practice. His company produced additional versions of *White Man's Moccasins*, as well as posters of Lee's color landscape *Engine Rock* and the cultural image *Buffalo Dancer*. They also introduced a line of T-shirts bearing Lee's images and started a website to sell the products.

The resurrected friendship gained momentum. The Corbetts began returning to Laguna on a regular basis—several times a year. In 1987, they sent their two oldest sons, Tom and Bob, to visit Lee for two weeks. He took them around New Mexico. They went with Lee while he completed a photographic assignment in Gallup. Looking back on the experience, Tom remarked, "It ignited in me a new awareness of what was possible, and it made me look at my own prescribed career path with a healthy, skeptical eye. It infused into my thinking a new awareness of the trade-offs associated with the highly structured, suburban life of a university-pedigreed career professional, and the unstructured but fiercely independent lifestyle that Pitsy enjoyed." Bob summed up the adventure this way: "Pitsy, through his own life and work, showed us that life can be lived on your own terms. I felt free out there."

Then in the early 1990s, Lee traveled to Ann Arbor to visit. Tom took the opportunity of Lee's visit to arrange for professionally recorded sessions of Lee's stories. Lee sat for hours in front of the microphone, relating the stories behind his photographs as Tom handed each one of them to him. The publishing company then produced Lee's first video, *Lee Marmon Gallery*, a collection of Lee's photographs with his narrations of the stories they had recorded. The main purpose of the video was to increase Lee's professional visibility. Several months later, Lee received word from the Smithsonian's National Museum of the American Indian that they had reviewed the tape and would like him to have a personal showing of his work there. Since that time Lee Marmon's work has received national and international acclaim, and he has given exhibits and lectures around the globe.

Several years later, the Corbetts' youngest son, James, who was studying photography, spent several weeks with Lee in and around Laguna and brought home hours of video he had taken of Lee relating stories and taking photographs. The most memorable clip was of a more elderly Lee Marmon walking slowly to his darkroom saying, "Now that I'm getting older, pretty soon it will be time for someone to take my picture." In 2005, using this fresh material, James produced a film for Flying Raven Productions titled *Lee Marmon—Life of a Southwestern Photographer.*

In 2006, for his fiftieth class reunion at Andover, Tom donated part of his collection of Lee's photographs to the school's Peabody Museum of Archaeology. That same year, the collection was put on display at the Oliver Wendell Holmes Library on the campus, and Lee gave talks and seminars to the Andover students.

In 2010, the book Tom had envisioned more than four decades earlier finally started to become a reality. That year he presented the idea to the University of New Mexico Press. The university had recently acquired Lee's collection of more than one hundred thousand photographs, and Tom proposed that it would be appropriate for that institution to be the publisher. The press, after reviewing the proposal, offered a contract that he accepted with the stipulation that Lee be coauthor. He emphasized his friendship with Lee over the years and that it was only fair to him, as they would be using his photographs and stories in the book. The two friends then signed on.

Why Are These Very Different People Such Good Friends?

The friendship Lee Marmon and Tom Corbett have shared goes much deeper than just their respect for each other's professions. Each has qualities the other admires yet doesn't possess. Over the years, the two men have used their opposite lifestyles and personalities to complement each other. At times they appear to live vicariously through each other.

Tom describes Lee Marmon as a "free spirit." He has perennially experienced a sense of personal freedom that most men only wished they possessed. To paraphrase Peter Fonda's character in the 1960s classic cult film *Easy Rider*, Lee "does his own thing in his own time." Lee's lifestyle has been typical of many great artists—unconventional, uninhibited, freewheeling, dismissive of widely accepted social norms, but often fraught with economic uncertainty. Lee sometimes wishes he had the economic and professional stability that has characterized the lifestyle of his long-time physician friend. Living on the reservation has inherent risks, such as relative isolation, including delays in medical appointments and the diagnosis of complex medical problems. Lee knows that whenever he has a problem, medical or economic, his friend the doctor is only as far away as the telephone or Internet, ready to offer personal advice or to buy another signed photograph for his collection.

Tom, who characterizes himself as quiet, studious, and introspective, lives in a professionally and economically stable, but highly regimented, world. He sometimes wishes he had the freedoms Lee Marmon innately enjoys. Yet he knows that if the pressures of living in his highly regulated, civilized world become extreme, all he has to do is call Lee and listen to his stories—or better yet, within hours he can join him at Dripping Springs, or on Mount Taylor, in his world of natural beauty where time seems to stand still and there are no boundaries and no rules.

ACKNOWLEDGMENTS

The authors wish to thank the people and institutions that made this book possible: Laguna oral historians and tribal elders Victor Sarracino and Irvin Shiosee contributed greatly to our knowledge of Laguna history. Using both photographs and tales of family history, Mr. Ron Fernandez contributed to our knowledge of Laguna in the early 1900s and the building of Route 66. We also thank the many other contributors too numerous to mention here.

We thank the providers of historical photographs prior to 1947, including the University of New Mexico Center for Southwest Research and Special Collections, the Palace of the Governors Photo Archives in Santa Fe, and Nevlyn and Lois Eckerman for the photographs from their family archives.

We appreciate the editorial suggestions of Clover McKinley, Thomas H. J. Corbett, and John Millrany, and the comments and suggestions of those Marmon family members and friends who reviewed the manuscript.

We especially appreciate the review and comments by New Mexico State Historian Rick Hendricks and Associate Professor Bruce Huckell, senior research coordinator at the University of New Mexico Maxwell Museum of Anthropology.

And finally, we thank our wives, Beverly Corbett and Kathy Marmon, for their patience, understanding, ideas, and editorial comments throughout the writing of this book.

INTRODUCTION

This book is a history of Laguna Pueblo. The idea for this book began almost fifty years ago when I first saw some of Lee Marmon's spectacular portraits of tribal elders. I soon learned that Lee was not only a superbly talented photographer but a gifted storyteller as well.

Lee Marmon has given us the opportunity to understand the history of Laguna Pueblo in photographs. He has documented through his own camera lens the people, customs, and cultural changes of the Lagunas since he began taking pictures in 1947. The Marmon family photo archives, containing images of Lee's family dating back to 1872 (see, e.g., the photo captioned "Robert G. Marmon in his living quarters" on page 32), supplement the history prior to 1947. Historical images from the University of New Mexico Center for Southwest Research and Special Collections, the photo archives of the Palace of the Governors in Santa Fe, and the photographic collections of Mr. Ron Fernandez and others complete the pictorial enhancement of this historical documentation.

Lee Marmon is also an ardent history buff and a wealth of information regarding not only Laguna history but national and world history as well. His library is filled with books on these subjects, and for most of his adult life he has been an avid reader. To supplement his own knowledge of the history of Laguna, we relied on numerous published sources contained in the endnotes of this book. Along with Lee Marmon's own oral history of the tribe, we also interviewed several other noted tribal elders and oral historians regarding certain customs, religious practices, and events of the late 1800s and early 1900s.

The entire work has been a labor of love. Of special note was the researching of the Marmon family history. Our ability to reach back in time and learn about the lives of Lee's ancestors, documented in this book, should be an inspiration to everyone curious about his or her own family history. Not only are physical characteristics inherited, but personality traits appear to be passed from one generation to succeeding generations. That being true, Lee Marmon seems to have inherited a unique combination of traits: the adventurous, independent, and rebellious spirit from his paternal grandfather Robert Gunn Marmon, who left Ohio in 1872 for the

West, married a Laguna woman, and lived an adventurous life; and the Laguna storytelling genes he appears to have inherited from his paternal grandmother, Marie Anaya Marmon.

As you read through the history, you will find the Laguna tribe cohesive, adaptive, and independent—all qualities that have allowed them to survive as a group through very difficult times. It is a fascinating story of group survival through severe natural and man-made adversities, including droughts, plagues, marauding tribes, foreign invaders, religious incursions, and Western cultural invasion. Through it all, the Lagunas have kept their identity and culture and have retained sovereign powers over their members and their territory.

Tom Corbett

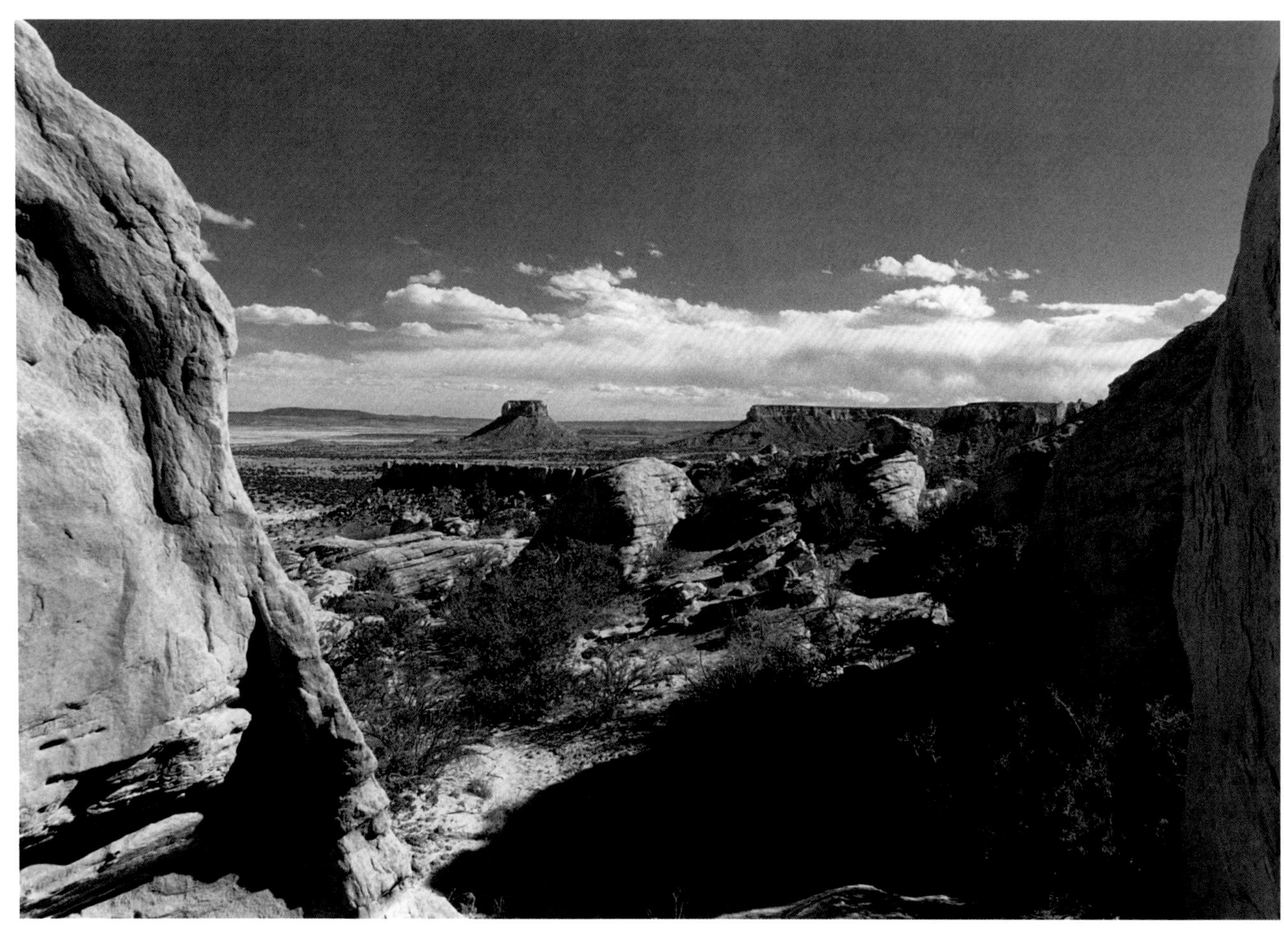

Patoche at Dripping Springs. Rising like a giant sandstone temple from the desert floor, this mesa typifies the geologic formations around Laguna Pueblo. Photo by Lee Marmon (1975).

CHAPTER ONE

Geography

Prior to the formation of the Laguna reservation by the U.S. government, the Laguna tribe inhabited a much larger land area. Stories passed on through many generations tell of living, hunting, and conducting religious ceremonies on land well east of the current Rio Puerco boundary, past the Rio Grande and extending to the Sandia Mountains. To the south, they inhabited and hunted lands in the Magdalena Mountains. To the north and west, their lands included most of Mount Taylor (their sacred mountain) and the villages of Seboyeta and Bluewater. Many of these claims have been confirmed by the finding of Laguna rock art and shrines—sacred places for religious ceremonies—in these areas.[1]

The Laguna reservation, located on the Colorado Plateau forty-five miles west of Albuquerque, lies in parts of four New Mexico counties—Cibola, Sandoval, Valencia, and Bernalillo—and has a total land area of 777 square miles. At an elevation of six thousand feet above sea level, the unique geography, topography, climate, and geology of the Laguna reservation has had profound effects on the Laguna tribe and culture.

Across and around Laguna land, there are grand vistas and vast landscapes with mountains one hundred miles distant. Giant sandstone temples rise from the desert floor. When the sun is high in the sky, the walls of these buttes and mesas are varying shades of yellow-brown and orange, constantly changing as the sun crosses from east to west or the occasional cloud passes overhead. As the sun begins to sink in the west, the walls become alive with more intense color. Some turn to gold while others become watermelon red.

Laguna Pueblo comprises six established villages: Laguna, Mesita, Paguate, Encinal, Seama, and Paraje. The village of Laguna is home to the tribal-government offices and law-enforcement facilities. When the railroad arrived at Laguna in the 1880s, the tracks were constructed along the

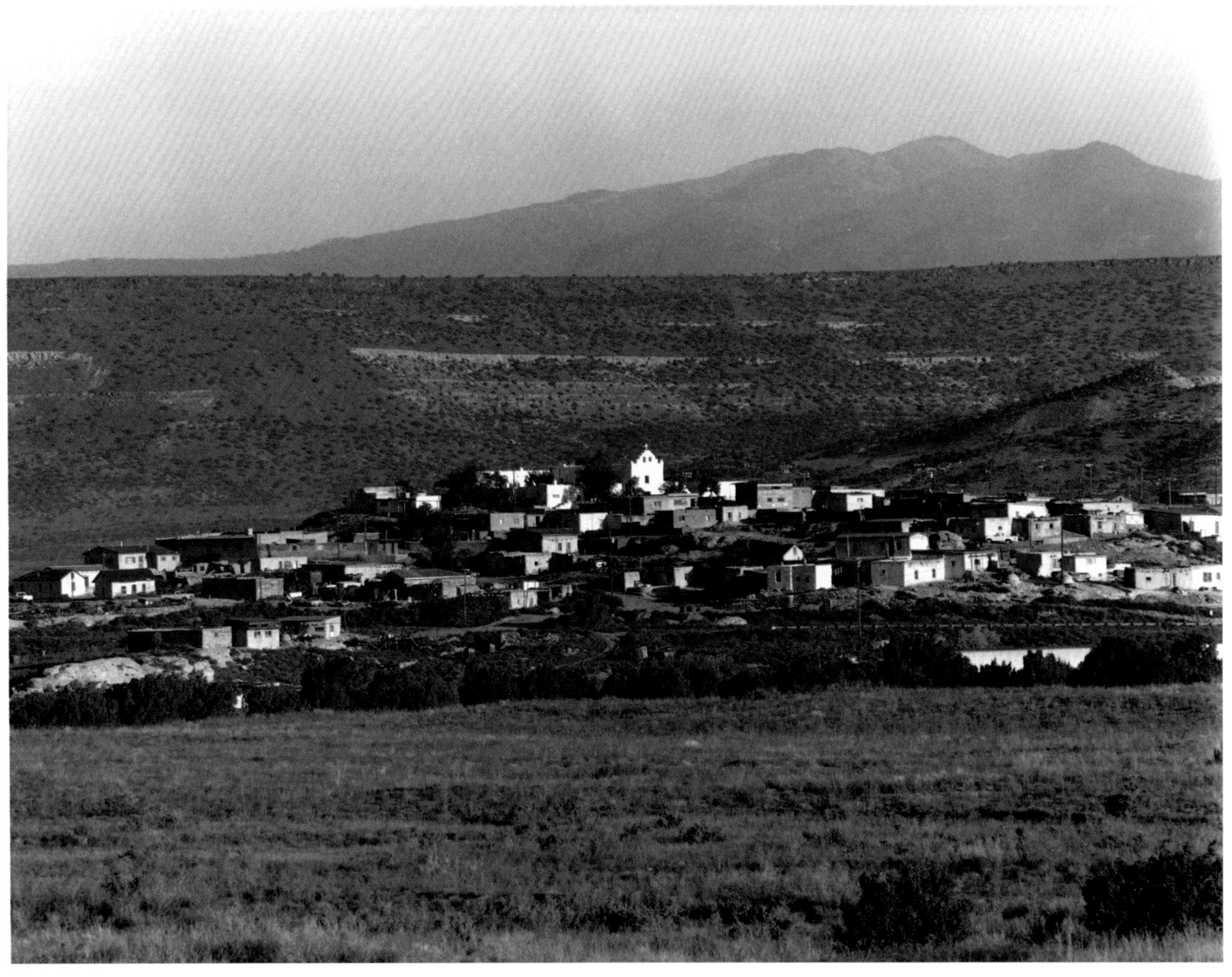

Old Laguna Village. The sacred Mount Taylor, provider of water, timbers, plants, and hunting grounds, hovers protectively over the village of Old Laguna. Photo by Lee Marmon (1985).

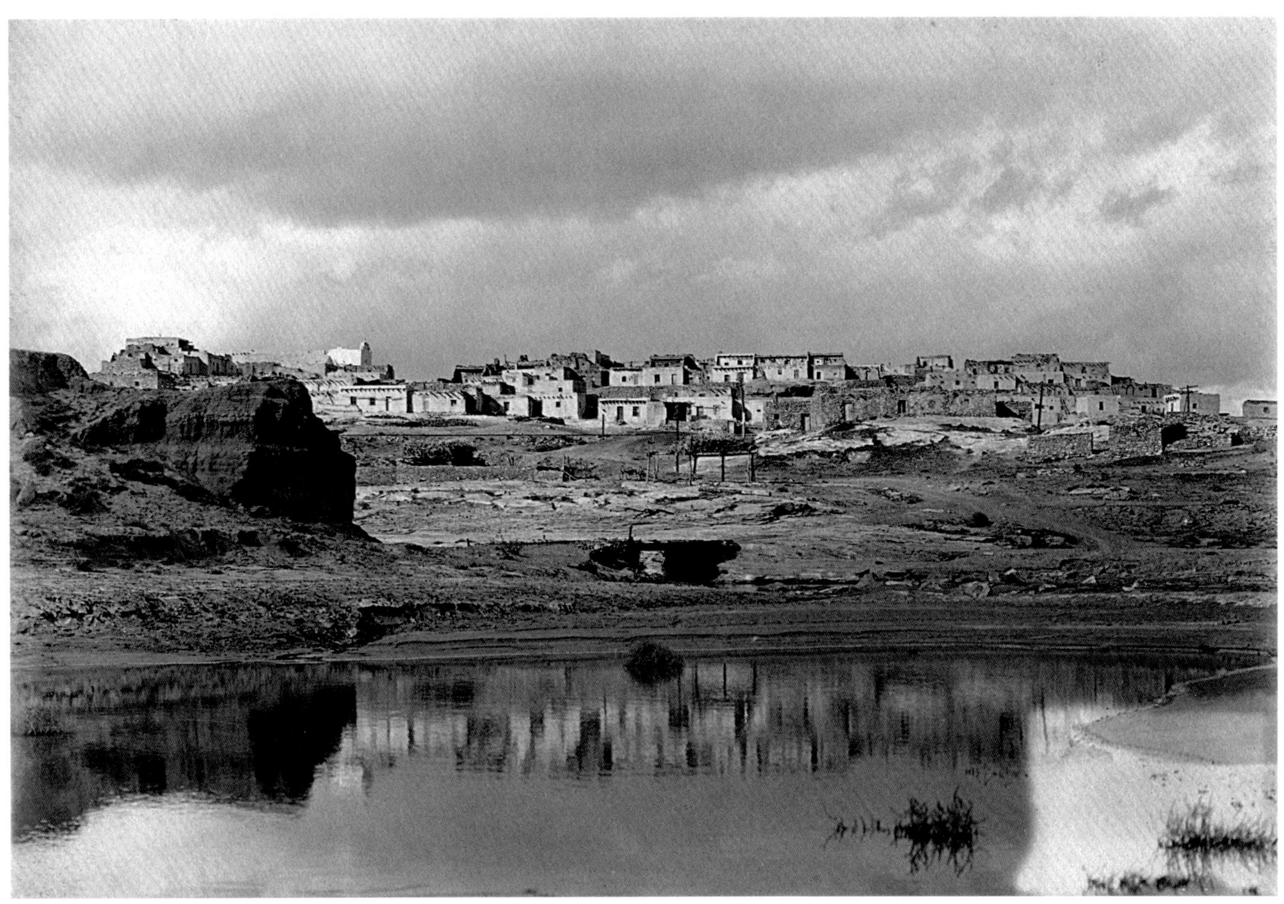

Laguna on the Rio San José, 1910. The village of Laguna is reflected in the calm waters of the Rio San José. The village lies on a gently rising hill with the San José de la Laguna Mission at the summit. This photo was taken from the Rio San José prior to construction of the Bluewater Dam west of Grants. The new Bluewater Lake greatly reduced the flow of water in the Rio San José and consequently reduced the amount of farmable land around Laguna. Photographer unknown. Courtesy of the Palace of the Governors Photographic Archives (NMHM/DCA), #2899.

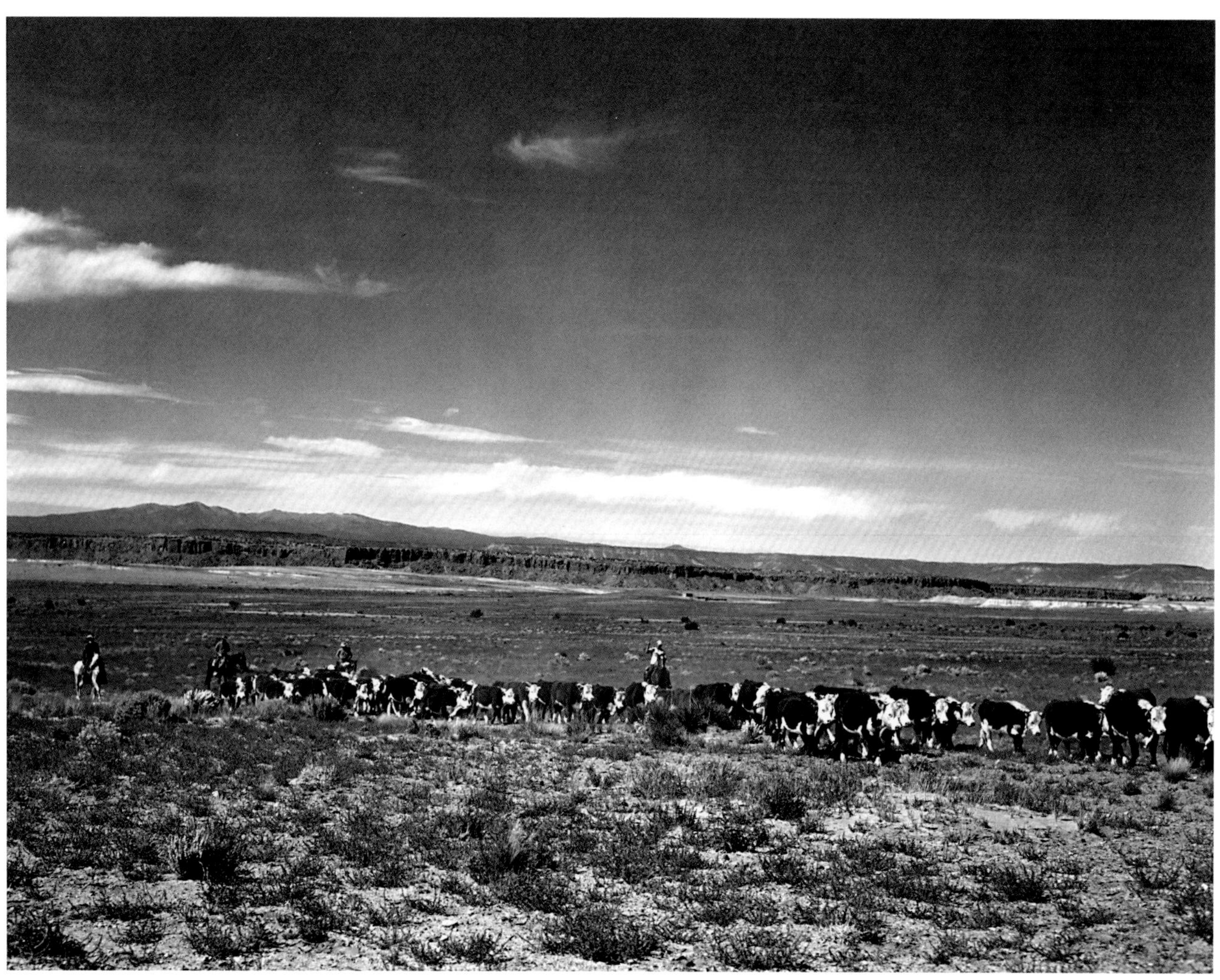

Grand Vista Across Laguna Land. This cattle drive across the Laguna reservation demonstrates the semiarid land and topography of the Colorado Plateau at six thousand feet. The scrubby vegetation on the valley floor, the mountains in the background, and the mesas between the mountains are typical of the area. Photo by Lee Marmon (1955).

south end of the village, parallel to the Rio San José. Historical Route 66, built in the 1920s, was routed through Old Laguna, and the present-day Interstate 40 is located just south of the village. The commercial center of Casa Blanca, located along Interstate 40, is just inside the western border of the reservation, while the tribe's new Route 66 Casino is located along the Rio Puerco, at the eastern border of Laguna land.

An 1864 census by Indian agent John Ward revealed the population of Laguna to be 1,143.[2] The population of Laguna, decimated by several epidemics in the late 1800s, was questionably estimated to be as low as 500 in 1905.[3] Federal census figures probably give a more accurate report for Laguna Pueblo over time. The thirteenth federal census reported the Laguna Pueblo population for 1890, 1900, and 1910 to be 1,140, 1,077, and 1,584, respectively.[4] The 1910 Indian population census reported the Laguna Pueblo population for the years 1871, 1881, 1890, 1900, and 1910 to be 927, 968, 986, 1,077, and 1,472, respectively.[5] The population of Laguna Pueblo has increased markedly since the 1910 census. The United States Census Bureau lists a population of 5,065 for Laguna Pueblo in 2000[6] and 5,374 for 2010[7].

More than any other pueblo, Laguna was catapulted into the mainstream of Western civilization by a series of events beginning in 1880 with the coming of the railroad. Rail commerce was followed by the building of highways across the reservation, and the discovery of uranium on reservation land resulted in the development of the Jackpile uranium mine.

CHAPTER TWO

In the Beginning

There is controversy regarding the origin of the Laguna tribe and the founding of the Pueblo of Laguna. The traditionalist view, in keeping with the oral history, is that the Lagunas had been settled in the area for at least centuries. The Lagunas, who had been living in smaller groups on the mesas near the lake, welcomed new arrivals from Acoma in 1697.[1] The two groups merged and began building the village on the hill rising from the Rio San José. The traditionalist version is supported by archaeological evidence of indigenous habitation of the area since 3000 BC.[2]

The modernist version states that in about 1697 members of several pueblo tribes who had earlier fled to the fortifications at Acoma for protection decided to return to their original tribes. As they traveled east and slightly north, they came to the Laguna area and, upon hearing that conditions were not well in their respective villages, decided to form a new settlement there along the lake.

The Emergence and the Migration: Laguna Oral History

For centuries the Laguna tribe has passed on by word of mouth the stories of their religious beliefs, culture, and customs. There was no written form of their Keresan language until 1883, when Adolph Bandelier composed a document of English words with a Keresan translation.[3]

Ethnologists Franz Boas and Elsie Clews Parsons collected stories and legends from Laguna oral historians and tribal elders from 1918 to 1921. In 1928, Boas published the work in two separate volumes, one in Keresan and the other in English. The stories include the Laguna version of their creation, the emergence of the Lagunas from the underworld known as Shi-bop, and the migration of the people from the place of emergence to Laguna. Also included are stories and legends of their customs and beliefs, supernatural beings, religious rites and prayers, and various cultural traits. Boas noted that he felt certain aspects of the stories had purposefully been omitted by the informants.[4]

The stories, collected from different oral historians, sometimes vary in detail, but the general theme is the same. One of Boas's informants, Ko'tʸe, whose Carlisle Indian School name was Robert Brown, was the grandfather of contemporary oral historian Victor Sarracino. In 2011, Mr. Sarracino told the stories of the emergence and migration of the Lagunas. He noted, after reading the books by Boas, that indeed certain parts of the stories had been omitted and that he would now fill in the missing links. The stories are lengthy, complex, and beyond the scope of this book. The stories of the emergence and the migration, narrated by Mr. Sarracino, are abbreviated here. He prefaced the stories by explaining that the several deities, the Creator, Mother-Father, Earth Mother, and Corn Mother, are one and the same, just as in the Catholic Church, the Father, the Son, and the Holy Ghost are one and the same. He began,

> The story I am about to tell you was told to me by my grandfather. It is a story that has been handed down by word of mouth, generation after generation. It is about the emergence and migration my people took from a place known as "Shi-bop."
>
> Shi-bop has been described as a place below the level of the sea, known as the "Fifth World." The people there were known as the Keresan tribe. They were the ancestors of the people of the Pueblo of Laguna. These people had contact with the supernatural world, in that they could communicate directly with the higher power who is the creator of all things. While in Shi-bop, the people were happy, obedient, and respectful of one another. They were provided with all necessary things, and hard work was not required. They prayed for each other and blessed each other religiously.
>
> Over a period of time the earth and all its components—the ocean, the land, the mountains, the sun and moon, the plants and animals—were assembled so that the people could emerge from the underworld and populate the earth. Other groups had emerged from the Fifth World prior to the Lagunas. Life for these groups was very demanding on the earth, so the Lagunas asked permission of Earth Mother to leave so they could be of help to the people already there.
>
> Permission was granted, so the Lagunas made many preparations

and received explicit instructions. Earth Mother chose two men to be the leaders of the group, Prayer-Stick Boy and White Hands. Two younger men, Maase'eewi and his brother Uyuuyeewi, were chosen as guides. The two young men memorized songs and prayers to guide the people on their long journey to a place by a lake at the base of a sacred mountain, which would be their home on Earth where they would prosper and multiply. The Lagunas were given seeds and eggs to nurture upon their arrival. They were told they must travel without deviating from the instructions, or suffer dire consequences. The people would lose their supernatural powers. They would have to work hard in order to live on the earth. They would suffer disease, hunger, and hardship . . . and death.

When the Lagunas were ready to leave, the surface of the earth opened in a circular fashion. A stairway appeared and the people climbed upward. As they came to the surface the people looked about and felt they were in a strange land. As they left the area, the circular opening from which they emerged sealed back up. It was the last time the people had contact with the underworld. The migration to the promised land of Laguna had begun.

The people traveled a long time and covered a great distance, at first obeying all the rules set down by Earth Mother when they left Shibop. But after a while, they grew tired. Prayer-Stick Boy insisted that the people were all too tired to continue and, contrary to the advice of White Hands, convinced the others to stop the migration and settle at a place they called White House. Everything the Lagunas needed was there—rain, good growing conditions, animals, and plants. So, instead of following the instructions to go to the land by the lake, they disobeyed Earth Mother. She became angry and created droughts and disease, and the people became hungry and sick.

After pleading for forgiveness, the Lagunas were allowed by Earth Mother to leave White House and resume their migration. She stripped them of their supernatural powers and divided the group into clans, each with specific functions, responsibilities, and restrictions. She shamed Prayer-Stick Boy by stripping him of his leadership and changing his name to Broken Prayer-Stick. Earth Mother then appointed White Hands as the sole leader. The group resumed their journey and finally arrived at the promised land by the lake. But because they had disobeyed Earth Mother, life was not as easy as originally promised. They had to work hard for everything.

The oral history gives no specific time frame for these events. But since their arrival at Laguna, the people have endured much hardship over the years. Despite the difficulties they have encountered, they continue to thrive and multiply.

The missing part of the story in the compilation by Boas is the account of the second group to leave Shi-bop and go to Laguna. This group followed Earth Mother's instructions explicitly and arrived at the promised land by the lake exactly as directed. These people were rewarded with eternal life and retention of their supernatural powers. They were allowed to live in a parallel world at Laguna, invisible to the human population but able to be called on to help their human counterparts through prayers and ceremonies. At special times, these spirits can, through certain rituals, become temporarily incorporated into the bodies of humans and take over a person until the needed function is performed. During that time, the spirit in that person is able to use the body and perform in a way that a normal human could not.

The existence and interaction of this second group is a major part of the Laguna religion and culture.

Archaeological Findings

15,000 BC–AD 500

During the last of the great ice ages more than thirteen thousand years ago, small bands of human beings began to inhabit the southwestern United States. They are thought to have originally migrated from Asia to North America across the Bering Strait. From Alaska, following game, they migrated across North America and eventually reached the Southwest. While some continued their migration southward into Central and South America, others remained on the Colorado Plateau. Archaeologists have found evidence of human habitation (Clovis spear points) in New Mexico dating to about thirteen thousand years ago. These early hunters roamed the area in search of mammoth, bison, and other game.

The early Paleo-Indians of the Southwest adapted to environmental change as the Ice Age gave way to more temperate climes. About 8,000 years ago, they relied on a mix of wild plants and animals for their subsistence; this was the archaic period. They moved across the landscape with the seasons, hunting and gathering in environments ranging from deserts to mountains. About 3,500 years ago, they developed agricultural techniques and ceramics, and from 1000 BC to 500 BC up to AD 500, they began living in villages made up of semisubterranean pit houses with wooden framework roofs covered with earth.

AD 500–AD 1500

In the second half of the first millennium these early Native Americans began to emerge from their pit houses in favor of aboveground, contiguous multistory buildings built of stone and clay mortar. They became less nomadic, growing crops and storing surpluses. They still celebrated many rituals in semisubterranean ceremonial chambers known as kivas but now performed other ceremonies and dances in aboveground community plazas.

These people were part of the ancient Pueblo culture at its peak from about AD 900 until AD 1300. They developed major population centers with roads and trade routes extending into Mexico. They constructed buildings—some up to four stories high—with as many as seven hundred rooms.

A pinnacle of their architectural achievement was Chaco Canyon, located in northwestern New Mexico about 125 miles from Laguna. Beginning in about AD 850, construction of Chaco Canyon continued for three hundred years. At its peak, Chaco Canyon contained nine building complexes, or great houses, four stories high, and a combined three thousand rooms. The two largest great houses are Chetro Ketl and Pueblo Bonito. Building the Chaco Canyon complex was an impressive undertaking in a desolate land. Sandstone blocks were cut from nearby mesas. Thousands of logs had to be transported more than fifty miles from distant mountains.

Chaco Canyon was originally thought to have been a trade center, but recent studies suggest it was a center of religious activity where people had great spiritual or supernatural powers. Recent observations have shown that the kivas and other buildings were placed in alignment with celestial cycles.

During the first half of the second millennium AD, whether due to disease, climate change, drought, warfare, religious strife, overexploitation of natural resources, or other factors, Chaco declined and the cities were abandoned. Many theories have been postulated regarding the decline of the ancient Pueblo culture, but the true cause or causes still remain a mystery. After AD 1275, the people left their major population centers, such as Mesa Verde in present-day southern Colorado, and moved into the upper Rio Grande, west central New Mexico, and adjacent parts of Arizona.

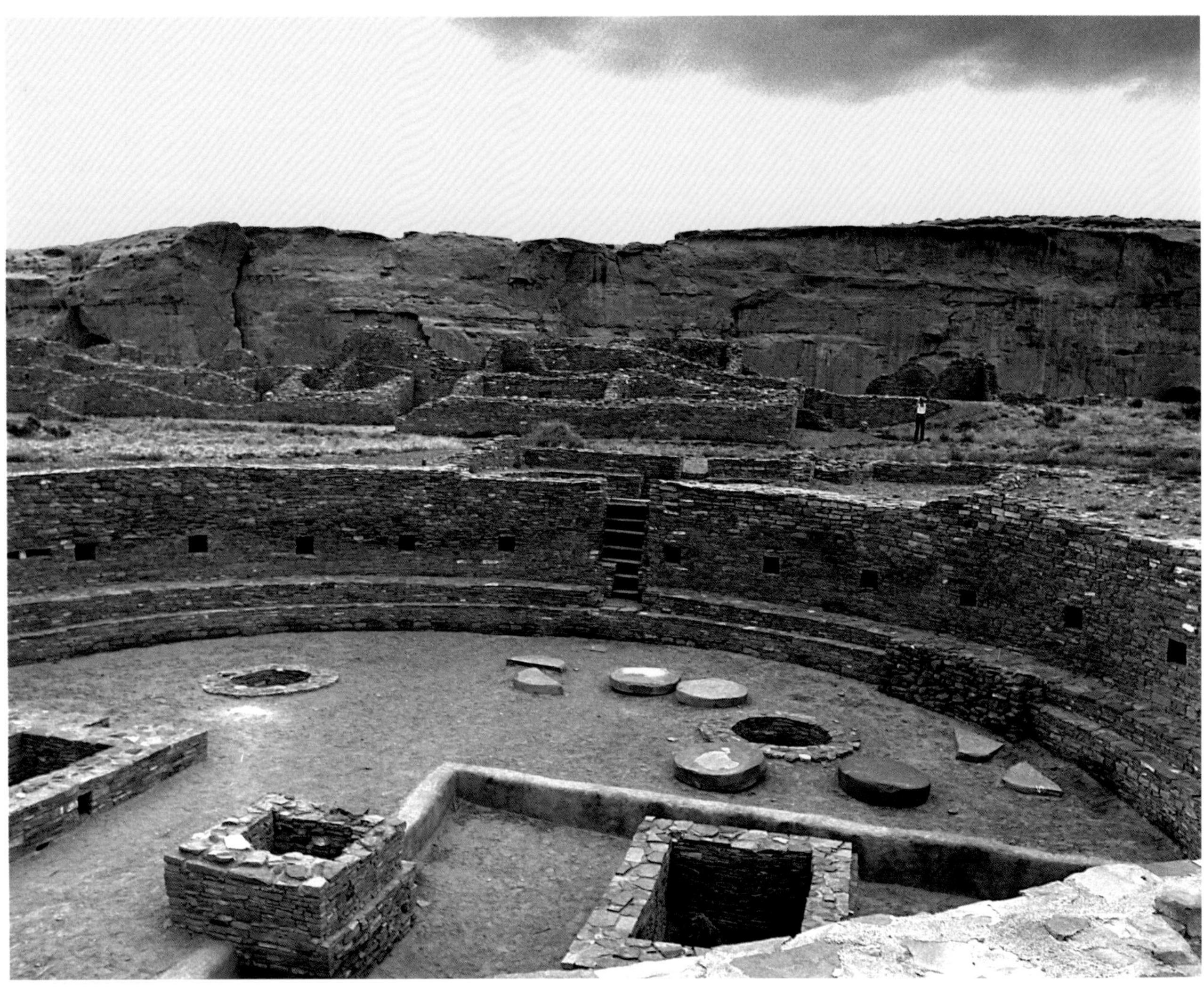

Great Kiva at Chetro Ketl. The great kiva at Chetro Ketl was excavated in 1936. This kiva is 55 feet in diameter and has a floor area of 2,350 square feet. Standard features of great kivas at Chaco include a stairway leading from the antechamber into the kiva, an encircling bench, a central firebox, paired masonry vaults, and wall niches. Large sandstone discs were used as supports for roof-supporting timbers (Linda Cordel, *Archaeology of the Southwest*, 2nd ed. [San Diego, CA: Academic Press, 1997], 309–18). Kiva roofs were built from massive beams covered with soil. Subfloor ventilation shafts, opening near the fire pit and extending underground beyond the kiva wall, then rising vertically to the surface, are a standard feature of Chacoan great kivas. Photo by Lee Marmon (1982).

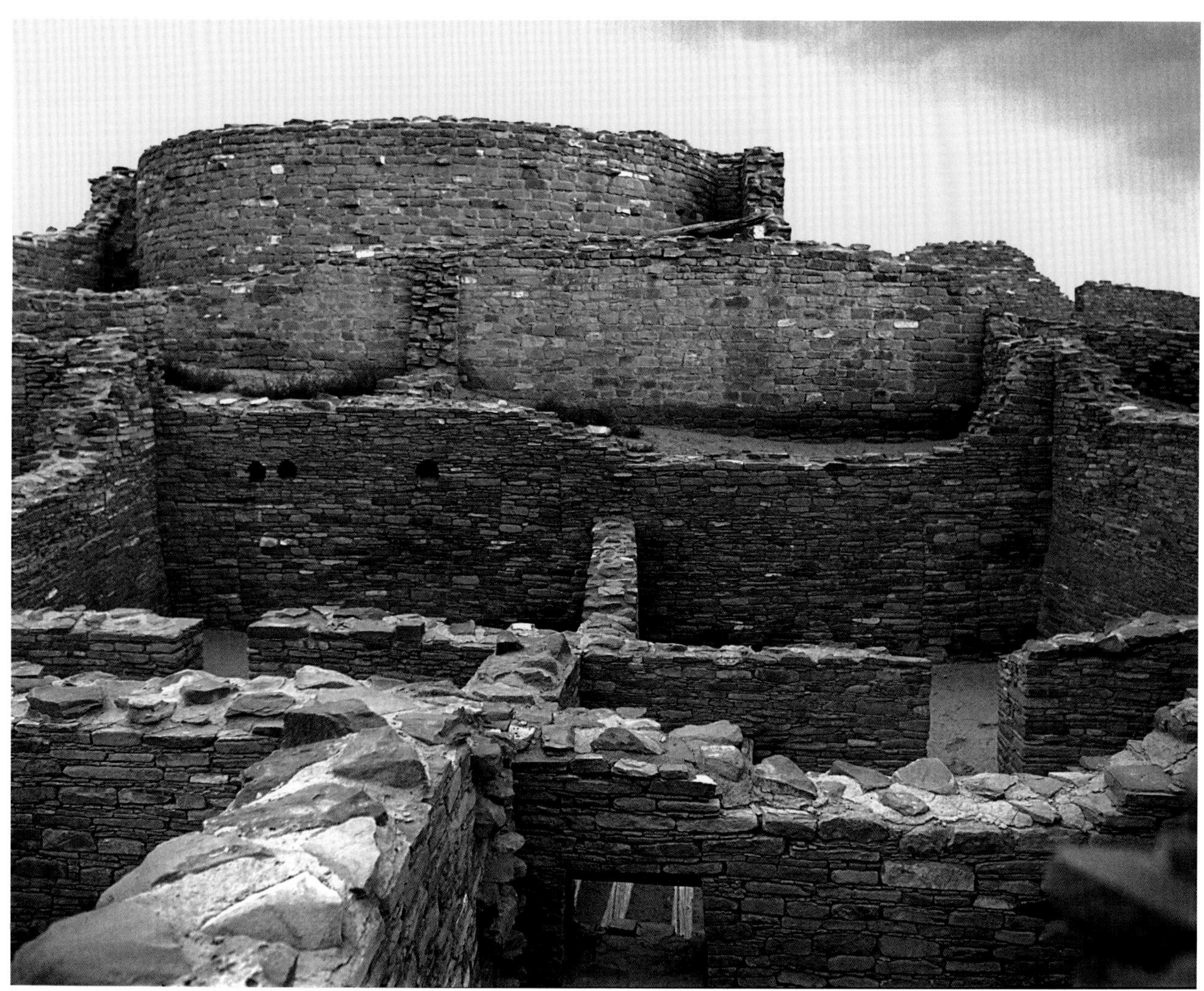

Ruins at Chaco Canyon. Ruins of one of the great houses at Chaco Canyon. There were nine great houses at Chaco Canyon, four stories high, with hundreds of rooms in each complex. Photo by Lee Marmon (1982).

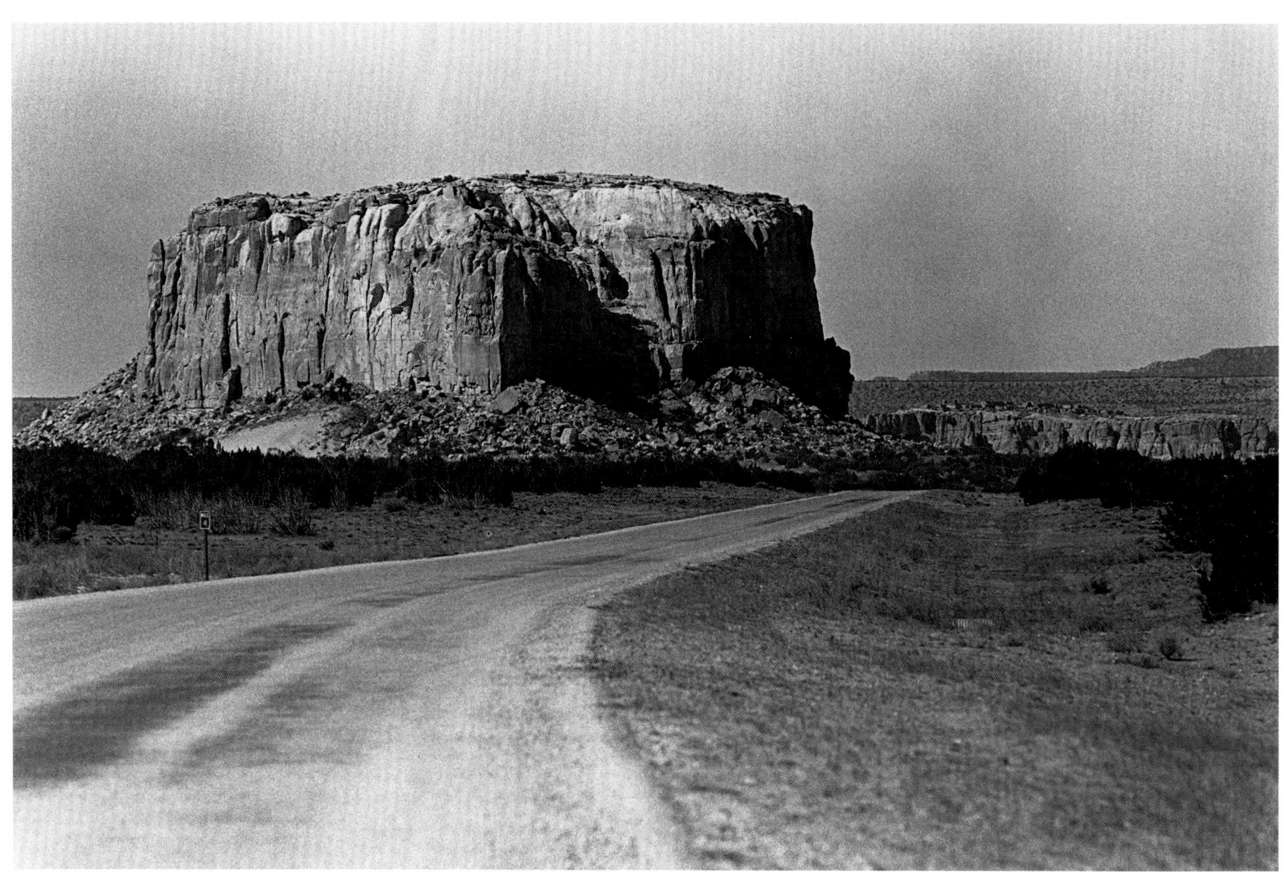

Road Past Enchanted Mesa. This road past Enchanted Mesa was constructed over the trail taken by de Alvarado and his small army in 1540 as they traveled from Acoma to the lake at Laguna. Photo by Lee Marmon (1950).

CHAPTER THREE

The Conquistadores

In 1539, don Antonio de Mendoza (1495–1552), the viceroy of New Spain (1535–1550), sent an exploration party led by Fray Marcos de Niza and Esteban, a North African slave, north to explore areas of New Mexico for gold and other riches to exploit and to pave the way for a later expedition led by Francisco Vásquez de Coronado. Esteban, born in the city of Azemmour in present-day Morocco and captured in 1513 during the Portuguese conquest of that city, was sold into slavery at age ten.

Esteban had been one of only four survivors of an ill-fated earlier Spanish expedition during which he gained considerable experience both being captured by and living with local tribes across Texas and northern Mexico. De Niza sent Esteban ahead to scout the unexplored territory, and after arriving at the Zuni pueblo of Hawikuh, he was killed by Zuni warriors. After learning of Esteban's death, Fray Marcos de Niza returned to Mexico with undocumented and exaggerated reports of the fabled Seven Cities of Cibola. His reports later proved false and he died in disgrace in 1558.

In 1540, a larger expedition led by Coronado set out for the area and contacted the populations along the Rio Grande and western pueblos. Upon reaching Zuni, Coronado led an attack against the tribe and, with his shining armor and plumed helmet, became the prime target of the Zuni warriors. During the Battle of Hawikuh, Coronado was severely injured and was saved from death by the heroic efforts of Captain Hernando de Alvarado.[1]

Unable to continue, Coronado sent de Alvarado, Fray Juan Padilla, and a body of soldiers on to explore the area east of Zuni. They arrived at Acoma and, impressed with the fortifications there, headed northeast a few miles where they found an attractive lake, surrounded by trees and fed by the Rio San José.[2] (The Rio San José starts at Mount Taylor, meanders in a southeasterly direction, through Laguna, and empties into the Rio Puerco south

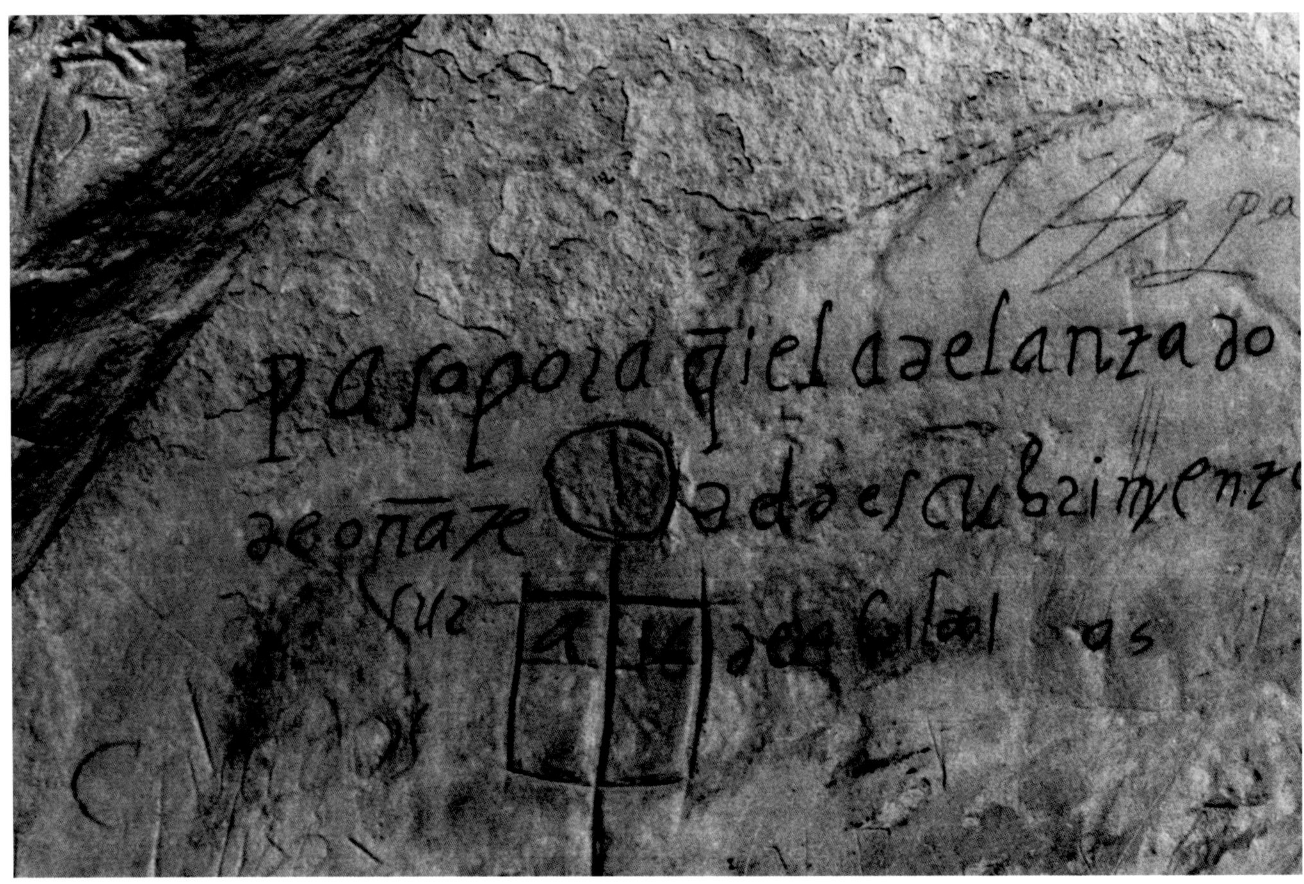

Inscription Rock. This ancient message board at the base of El Morro National Monument is seventy miles west of Laguna. For centuries, travelers have camped at the spring by the base of the mesa. The translated text reads, "Passed by here, the adelantado don Juan de Oñate, from the discovery of the Sea of the South, the 16th day of April, 1605." Photo by Lee Marmon (1950).

of Albuquerque.) The lake was described by de Alvarado as "formed by a flow of lava damming up a small stream."[3] The lake remained in existence until about 1850, when a beaver dam washed away and the lake was drained.

Following the initial exploration of the area by Coronado and his soldiers, the Spanish decided to send soldiers, missionaries, and settlers to the area. Their goal was to convert the Pueblo people to Catholicism, abolishing their "ancient religious beliefs" and making them into Spanish subjects. In 1598, don Juan de Oñate was selected to lead a colonizing expedition to the area. Prior to that expedition, Spain enacted the Royal Ordinances of 1573, which set humane rules for the "pacification" of the Native peoples of the Americas.[4]

The pacification program began without incident until December 1598, when a group of Spanish soldiers stopped at Acoma to demand food and supplies. A dispute ensued, and Oñate's cousin, Juan Zaldivar, and twelve of his men were killed by the Acomas. Despite the rules of the Royal Ordinances of 1573, Oñate retaliated with a brutal attack on Acoma. The battle lasted three days, during which the pueblo was plundered and burned. Hundreds of Acomas were killed or captured and severely punished. All men over the age of twenty-five had their left foot amputated, and all persons under the age of fifty were enslaved for twenty years.

Other instances of Spanish brutality occurred throughout the pueblos. Mission churches were built in many of the villages using forced labor. The churches were led by Franciscan friars who forced radical cultural and religious changes on the Indians and inflicted cruel punishment on those who resisted.

Tensions increased between the two groups, and by 1680 the Pueblo Indians successfully revolted against their occupiers. The Pueblo Revolt of 1680 was led by Popé, a medicine man from the Tewa Pueblo of San Juan. He conceived a brilliant plan to organize a coordinated attack on the Spaniards by more than three thousand warriors from the various pueblos at a time when simultaneous communication was nonexistent. They attacked the mission churches, burning all except the church in Acoma, and killed most of the friars. They killed entire Spanish families on surrounding farms, in haciendas, and in communities. Following a final stand at the Governor's Palace in Santa Fe, the Spaniards fled south in retreat. The revolt was successful, and the Spanish were driven from the area.

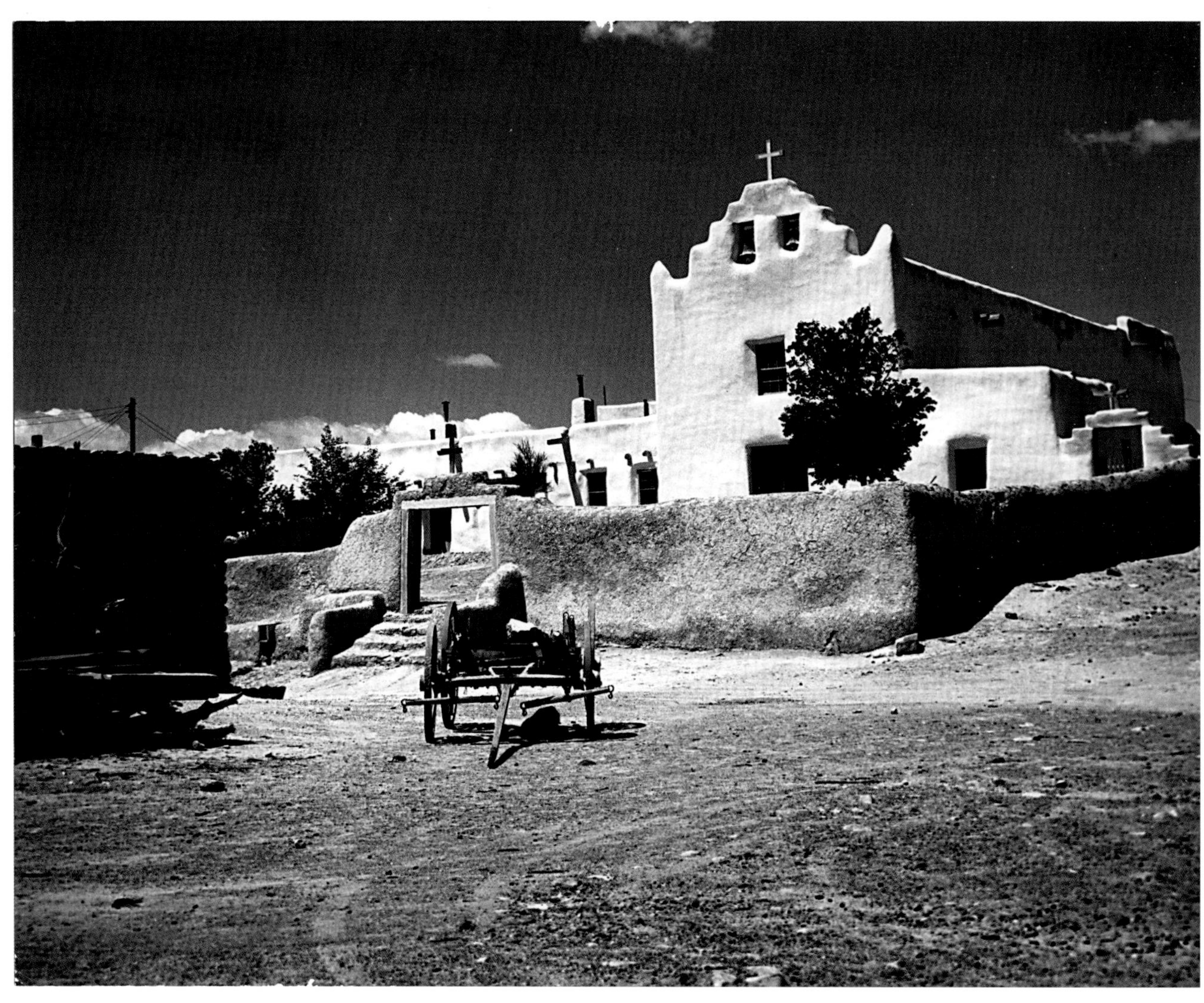

San José de Laguna Mission. Photo by Lee Marmon (1949).

CHAPTER FOUR

The Laguna Mission

Despite occasional small incursions by the Spanish, the Pueblo peoples regained and held their freedom and rights to their land from 1680 until 1692 when the Spanish returned in force. In 1691, Capitán General don Diego de Vargas was appointed governor of the New Mexico Territory. He had been assigned the task of reconquering and pacifying the region for Spain. By 1694, the Spaniards had reestablished their power and control over the Rio Grande pueblos, rebuilding the missions and replacing the friars.

Another Pueblo revolt occurred in 1696 but was unsuccessful. People from several northern and eastern tribes, including the Cochitis, Zias, and others, fled to the safety of Acoma prior to and during the revolt of 1696. The refugees sought protection from recurring subjugation by the Spaniards as well as from conflicts between rival pueblos. The high mesa of Acoma also provided protection from raiding Navajos, Utes, and Apaches. Hearing that the dangers had subsided, a group left Acoma to return to their villages along the Rio Grande but stopped at Laguna and settled there instead.

After de Vargas reestablished control over the Rio Grande pueblos, he then personally led an attack against the western pueblos. The Lagunas, hearing that the Spaniards were coming, placed all their women and children on a high mesa about three miles north of the lake and left the old men to guard them. The Lagunas repulsed the first attack by the Spaniards but eventually surrendered. De Vargas secured the services of both the cacique, whose Indian name was Kum-mus-tche-kush, and his war captain to act as guides for the expeditions to Acoma and Zuni.[1]

Following that campaign, de Vargas appointed the cacique, whom the Spaniards renamed Antonio Coyote, governor of the new pueblo at Laguna and presented him with a Spanish cane as his badge of office. The new

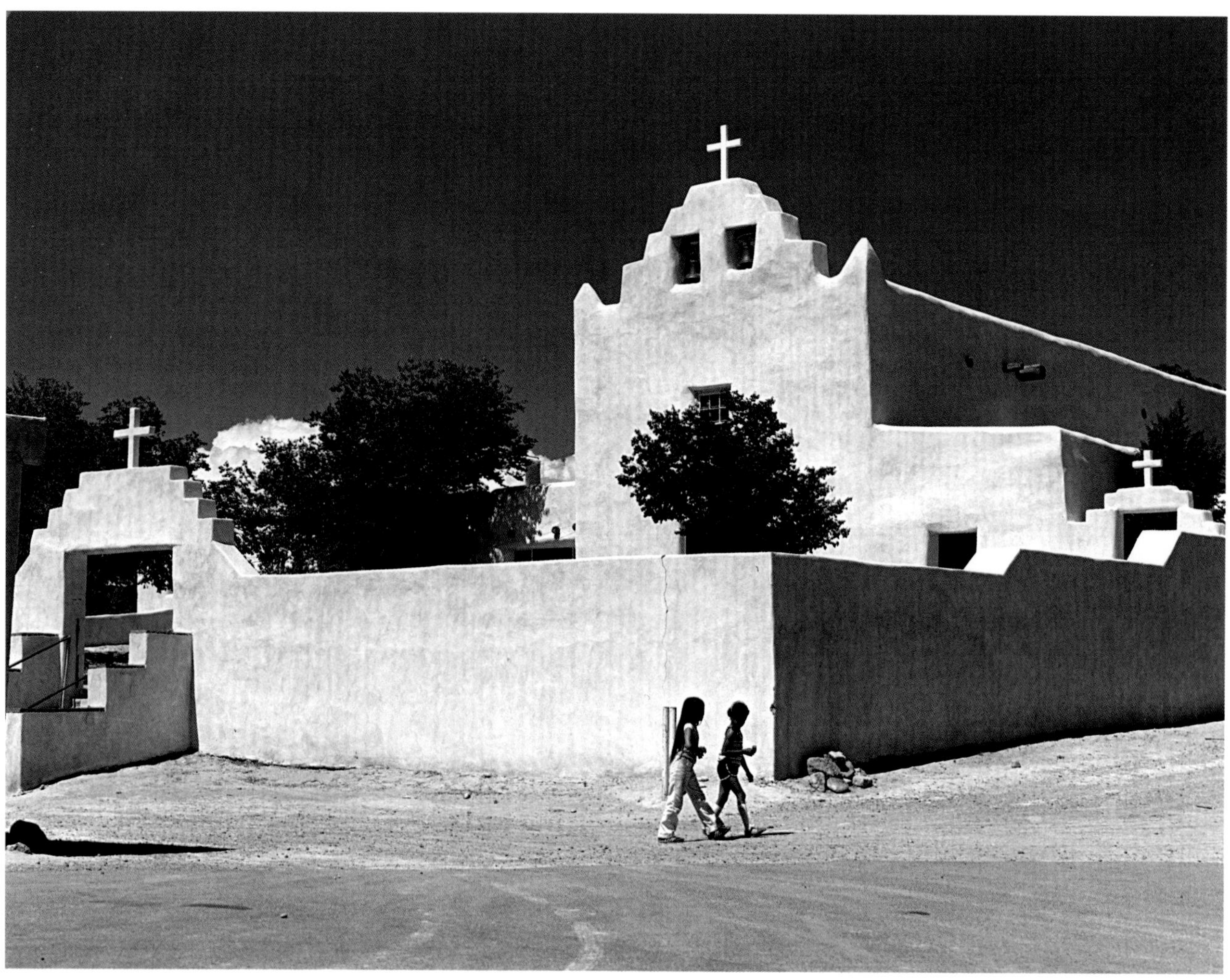

Morning sunlight shining on the Mission. Photo by Lee Marmon (1977).

governor was instructed to return to Laguna and build a church, to which de Vargas would send a priest.[2] The Laguna Mission was dedicated on July 4, 1699. The Lagunas subsequently developed a combination of Catholicism and their native religion that works to this day.

The Mission of San José de Laguna was built under the direction of Padre Antonio Miranda. The mission was constructed according to early pueblo architecture, but unlike other early missions, it was built of fieldstone, adobe, mortar, and plaster. The interior of the church measures 105 feet by 22 feet. The parapet supports twin bells, one bearing the inscription "1710." A walled campo santo (burial ground) was constructed in front of the mission.[3]

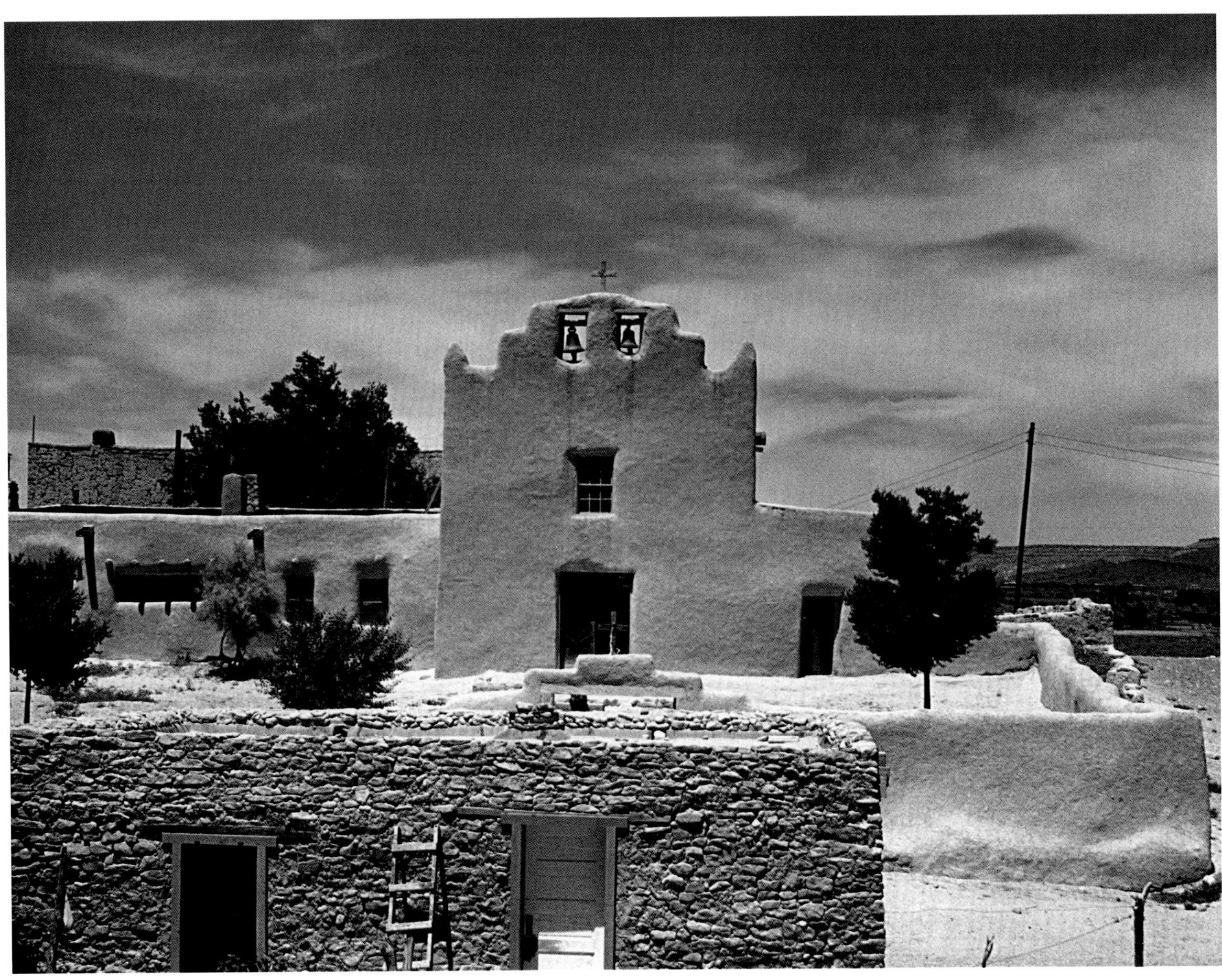

The Mission in 1947. The mission's convento (left) and courtyard (foreground) once used as a graveyard. Photo by Lee Marmon (1947).

The church was reroofed and underwent a general renovation in 1818. The convento was originally a two-story building, confirmed by photographs taken by Charles Lummis in 1890, but following a period of deterioration, it was remodeled into a single-story structure.[4] It was again refurbished in 1932. The mission acquired its distinctive white stucco exterior in 1977.

The walls of the mission are adorned with Laguna art and rare early Spanish paintings. The wooden doors are ornately carved. Red, green, yellow, and black murals decorate the white-plastered walls. The ceiling above the sanctuary is painted with Laguna symbols of a rainbow, the sun, the moon, and stars. The sanctuary itself has a beautiful eighteenth-century

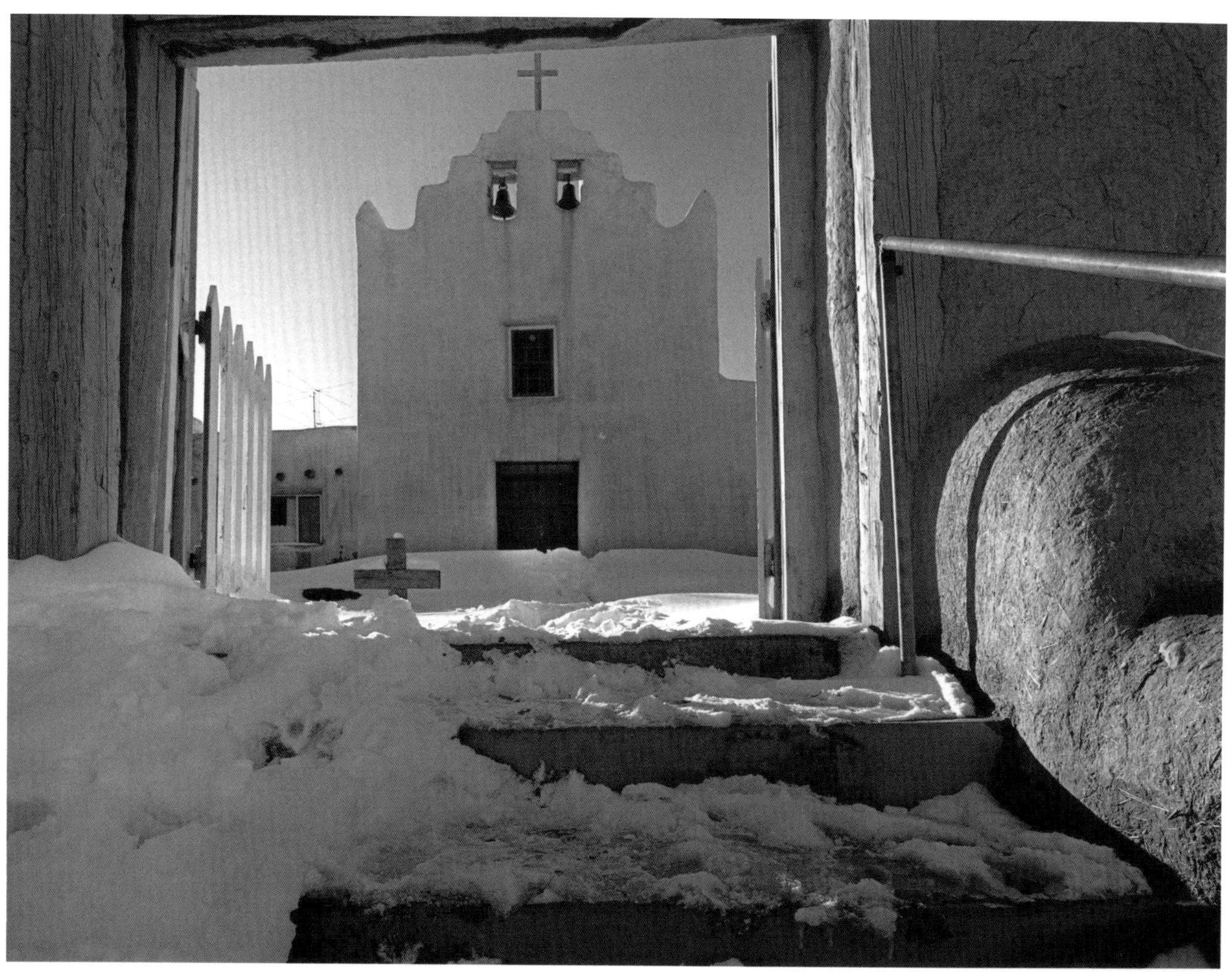

The Mission in Winter. The mission as seen through the door on the perimeter wall. Photo by Lee Marmon (1958).

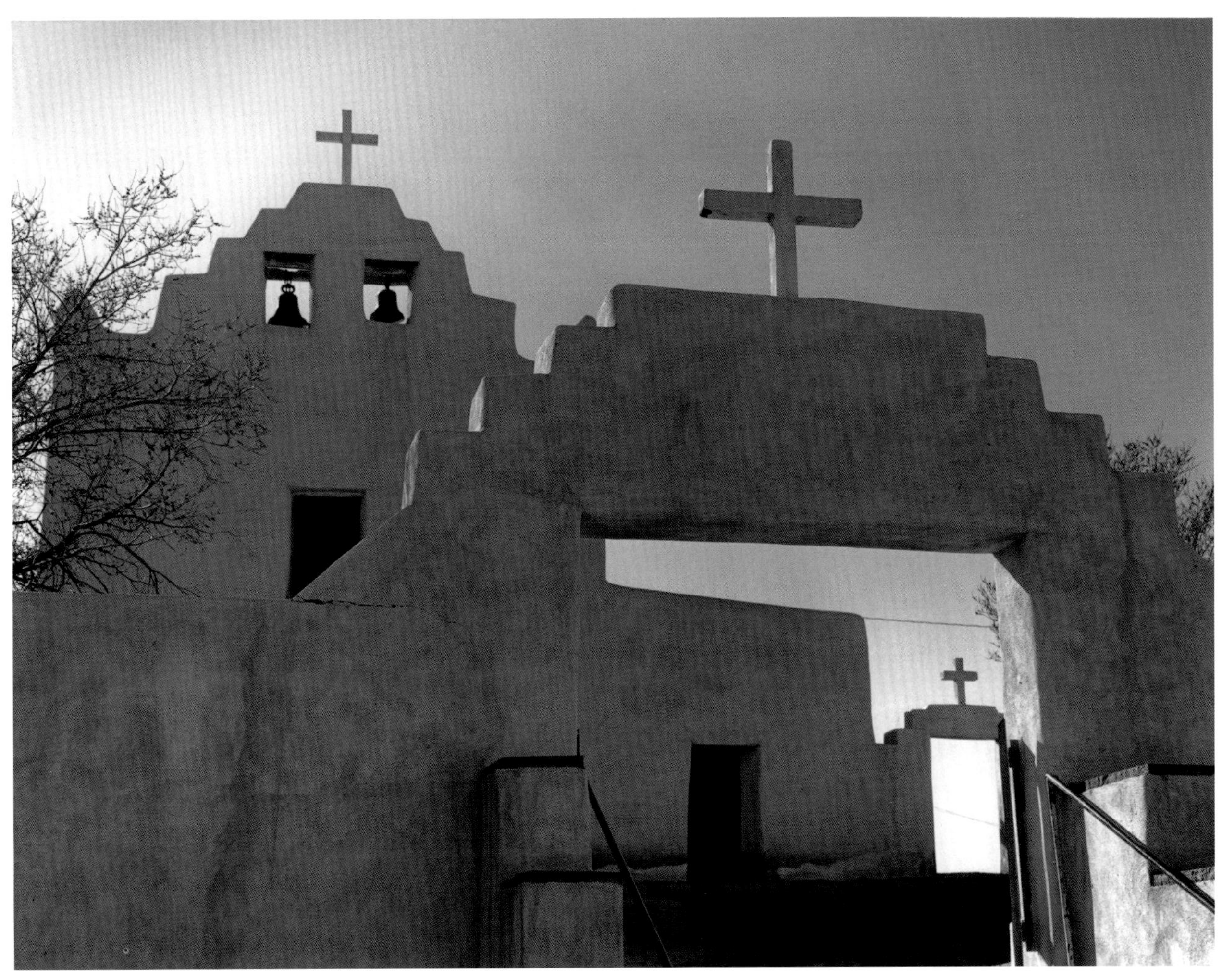

Laguna Mission with Three Crosses.
Photo by Lee Marmon (2002).

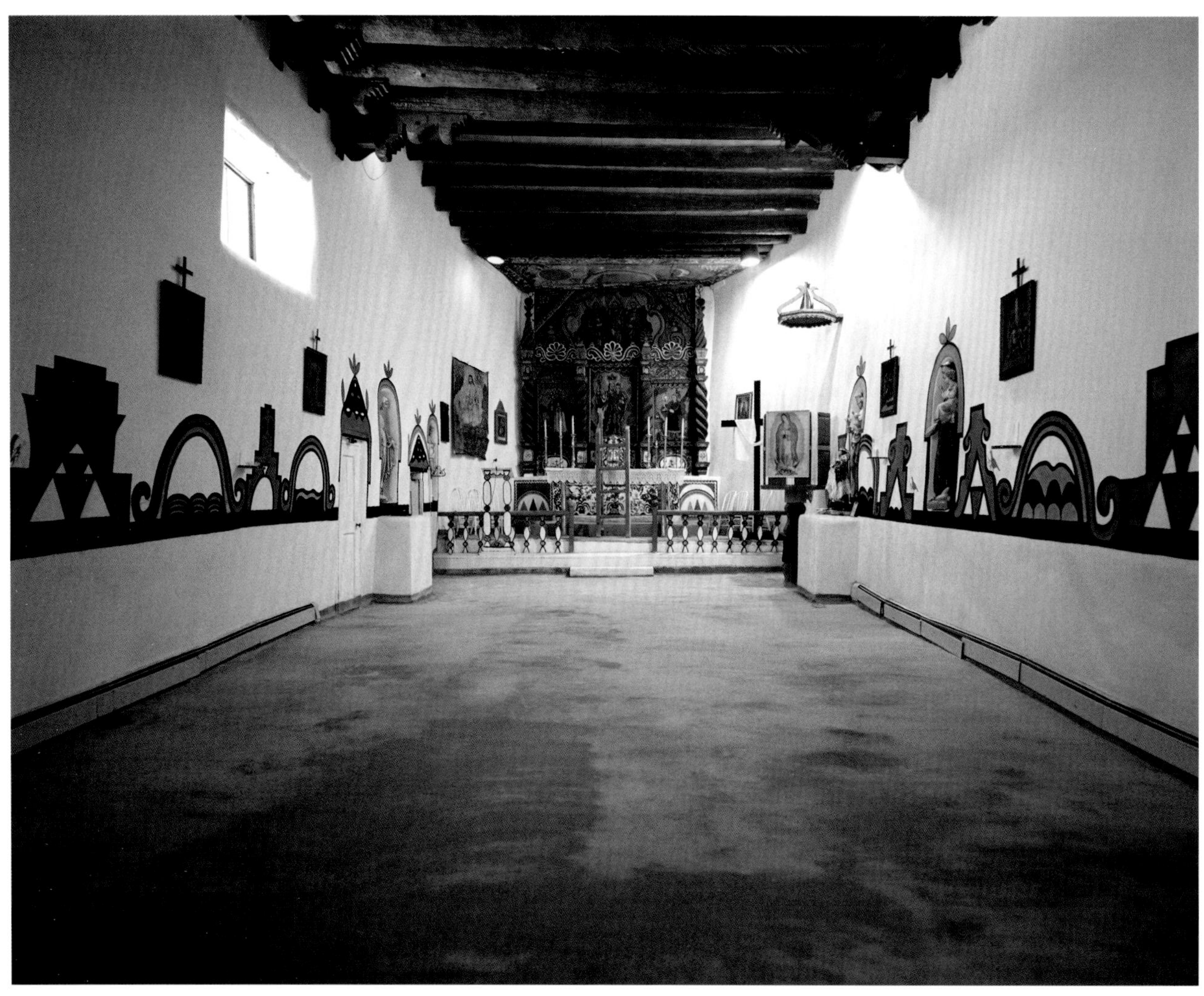

Interior of the San José de Laguna Mission. The ceiling of the mission has carved ornamental vigas interspersed with a herringbone pattern. The walls are painted sky blue and are decorated with Laguna religious murals interspersed with Catholic framed images. The packed-dirt floor is occasionally used by Laguna dancers celebrating certain religious events. Pews are brought in for Catholic services. Photo by Lee Marmon (1999).

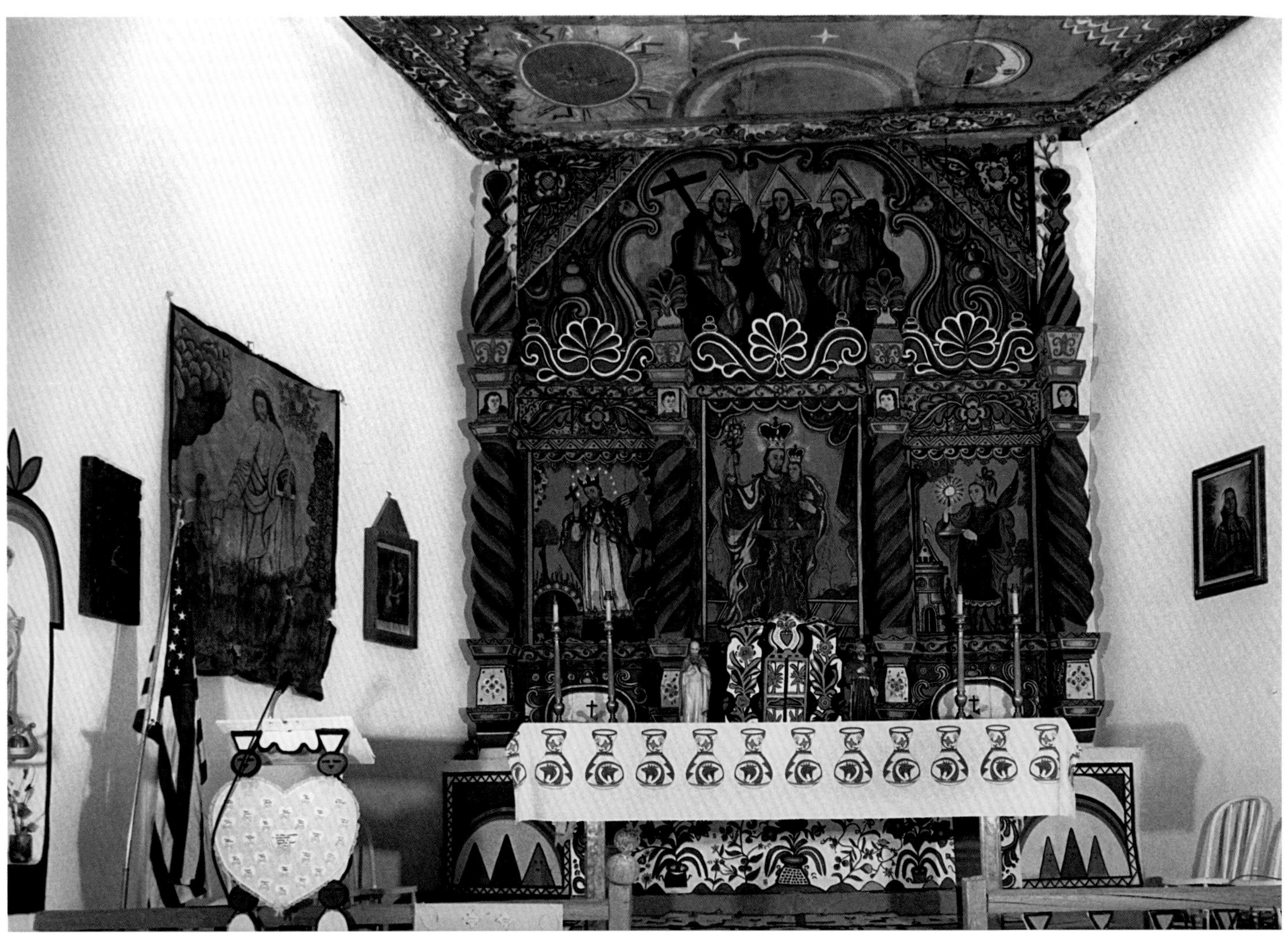

Mission Sanctuary. Photo by Lee Marmon (1999).

carved wood altar screen with spiral pillars painted red and black, a hand-carved pulpit and sounding board, and an adobe altar covered with a large animal skin adorned with multicolored designs. The sanctuary also displays a rare early seventeenth-century painting of San José on buffalo hide. The vigas supporting the latticed ceiling are elaborately carved.

A framed list of all the padres who have served the San José de la Laguna Mission since 1699 is located on the left wall as one enters the church.

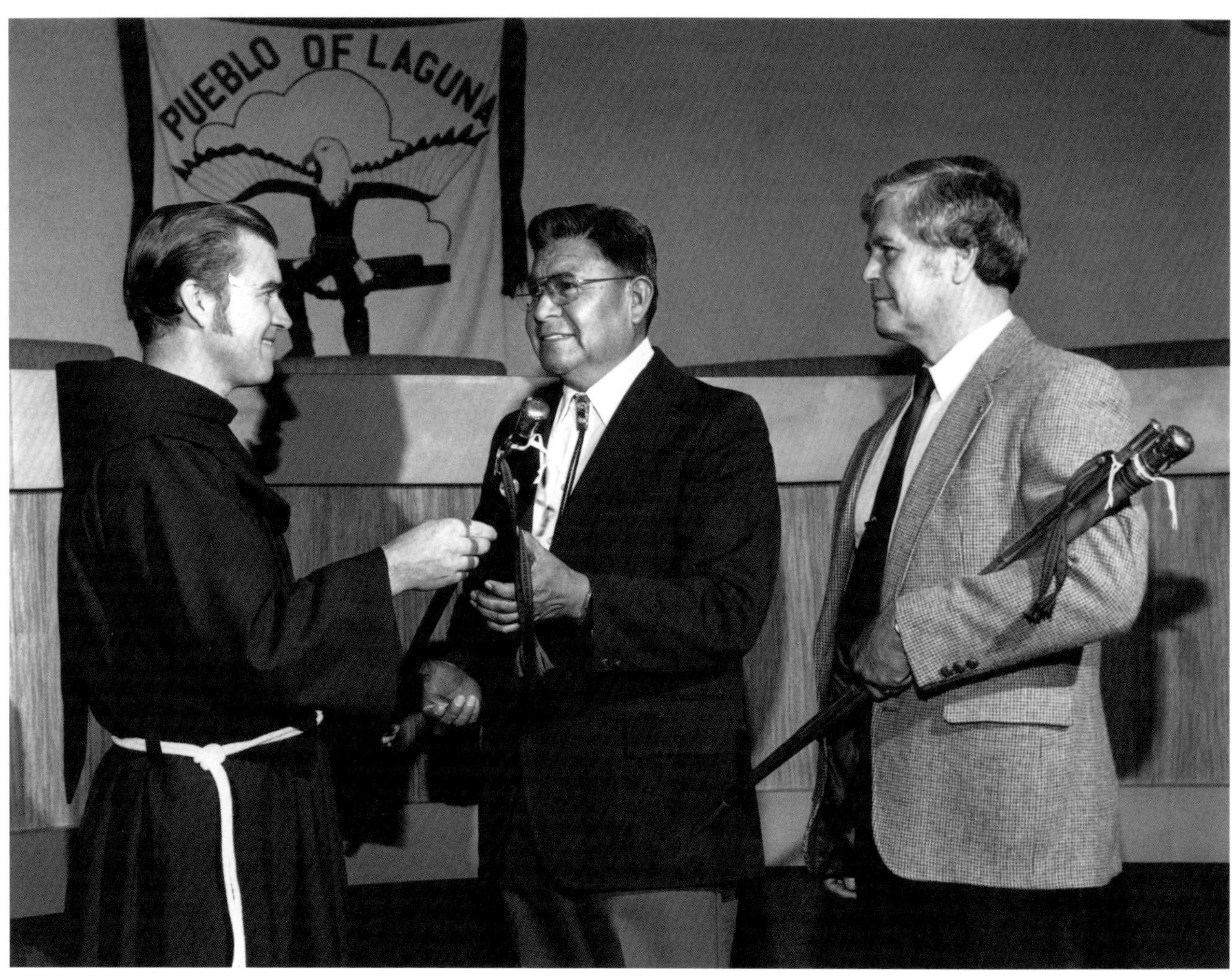

Presentation of the Canes, January 1, 1953. After blessing the Lincoln cane, the padre presents the cane to incoming governor Edwin Martinez. Lieutenant Governor Harry Early (right) holds the Spanish and Mexican canes. Photo by Lee Marmon (1953).

CHAPTER FIVE

Tribal Government and the Lincoln Canes

Laguna, along with the other eighteen pueblos, has survived independently while New Mexico has been under the control of larger nations since 1598. In that year, Spain began its rule with the arrival of Juan de Oñate, who had been awarded a contract by King Phillip of Spain to settle the area under Spanish rule.

New Mexico existed under Spanish rule from 1598 to 1680 and from 1692 until 1821. In 1620, the viceroy of New Spain (1612–1621), Diego Fernández de Córdoba, Marques de Guadalcazar and Conde de Posadas (1578–1630), decreed that the pueblos would elect officials. Each pueblo would elect its own leaders and was issued a cane representing its authority. The canes, interpreted by the Pueblo peoples as a symbol of sovereignty, would be passed on to each succeeding elected governor of the nineteen pueblos.

In 1821, when Mexico achieved its independence from Spain, New Mexico became a province of Mexico, and the Mexican government issued a second cane to each pueblo, again interpreted as a symbol of continuing sovereignty.

The United States gained control of the New Mexico Territory in 1846. In 1848, at the conclusion of the Mexican-American War, the Treaty of Guadalupe-Hidalgo ceded the Territory of New Mexico (and other lands) to the United States. The right of self-government of the Pueblo peoples (as had been the right of all Native American tribes) was recognized under the United States Constitution.

In 1863, Dr. Michael Steck was appointed superintendent of Indian affairs for the New Mexico Territory. Dr. Steck went to Washington, D.C., that year for Senate confirmation of his appointment. At that time he consulted with President Lincoln and obtained his approval to order and issue new canes as a symbol of the commitment of the United States to continue the Pueblo peoples' right of self-government.

The canes were made in Philadelphia and constructed of ebony with silver tips. "A. Lincoln" was inscribed on the tip along with the name of the pueblo, followed by the year "1863." Dr. Steck presented the canes to each of the nineteen pueblos in 1864. Since then, each year in January, a ceremony is performed in the mission, and the padre blesses the cane before the outgoing governor presents the cane to the new governor as he takes office.

Pueblo of Laguna Constitution

Laguna is the only pueblo of the nineteen to have a constitution. It was written and enacted in 1908 and unified the six villages of the pueblo. Amendments have been made over the years, instituting changes in government structure and adding new officer positions. It is a unique document, codifying the oral history and traditions that are the basis of Laguna culture. The constitution preserves the traditional laws, customs, and practices of the Pueblo of Laguna previously passed on orally for many centuries.

The preamble of the Pueblo of Laguna Constitution begins with recognition by Abraham Lincoln of the right of the Pueblo of Laguna to govern itself and the promise of the United States of America to protect that right. It states, "As evidence of said recognition, confirmation, and solemn pledge, our beloved President Abraham Lincoln gave the then Governor of the Pueblo a cane, which has in the course of years become the staff and symbol of the office of Governor of said Pueblo."[1]

Article III defines the governing body of the pueblo:

> SECTION 1. Council—The governing power of the Pueblo of Laguna shall be vested in the Pueblo Council. The Council shall be composed of the following persons:
>
> (a) One Governor.
> (b) One First Lieutenant Governor.
> (c) One Second Lieutenant Governor.
> (d) One Head Fiscale.
> (e) One First Fiscale.
> (f) One Second Fiscale.
> (g) One Treasurer.
> (h) One Secretary.
> (i) One Interpreter.
> (j) The representative or representatives of the respective villages of the Pueblo of Laguna who shall in the customary manner or as

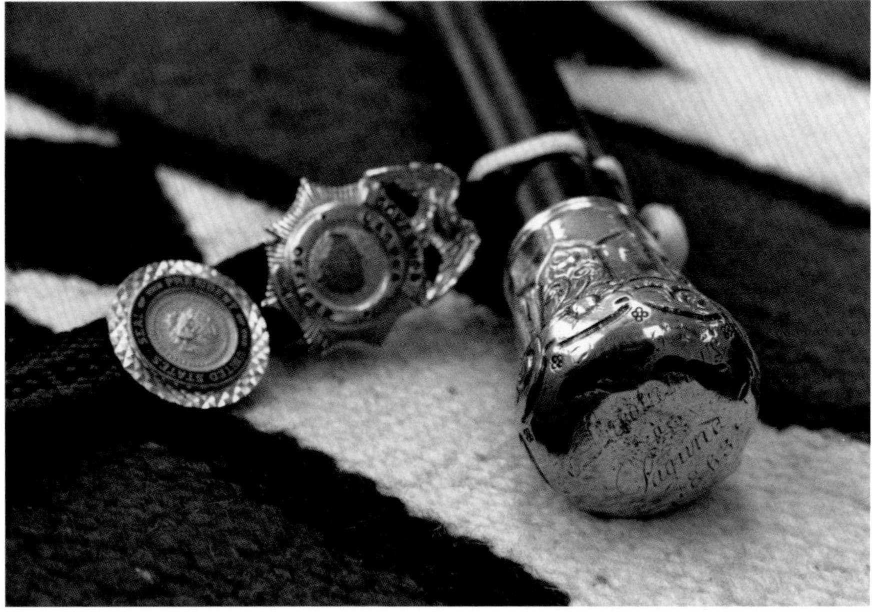

Lincoln Cane Inscription. The inscription reads "A. Lincoln, Pres" followed by "Laguna, 1863." Photo by Lee Marmon (1979).

provided by the Council be selected by said villages as representatives of each of said villages.

(k) Such other persons as the Pueblo Council may appoint or recognize as members of the Council.

SECTION 2. Other Officers—The Pueblo shall also have the following officers:

(a) One Captain of War
(b) One First Lieutenant of War
(c) One Second Lieutenant of War

Further details of the Constitution of the Pueblo of Laguna are beyond the scope of this book. The document is available online.

Pueblo of Laguna Elderly Code

The Pueblo of Laguna Elderly Code, adopted in 1993, states the following:

> Our Elders, preserving our past in their memories, influencing our present when we dare to listen, aiming us toward our future, rooted in their wisdom, deserve our respect, not our abuse. . . . Elders are valuable resources to the Pueblo and custodians of tribal history, culture and tradition and they are the best hope of the Pueblo to pass on the

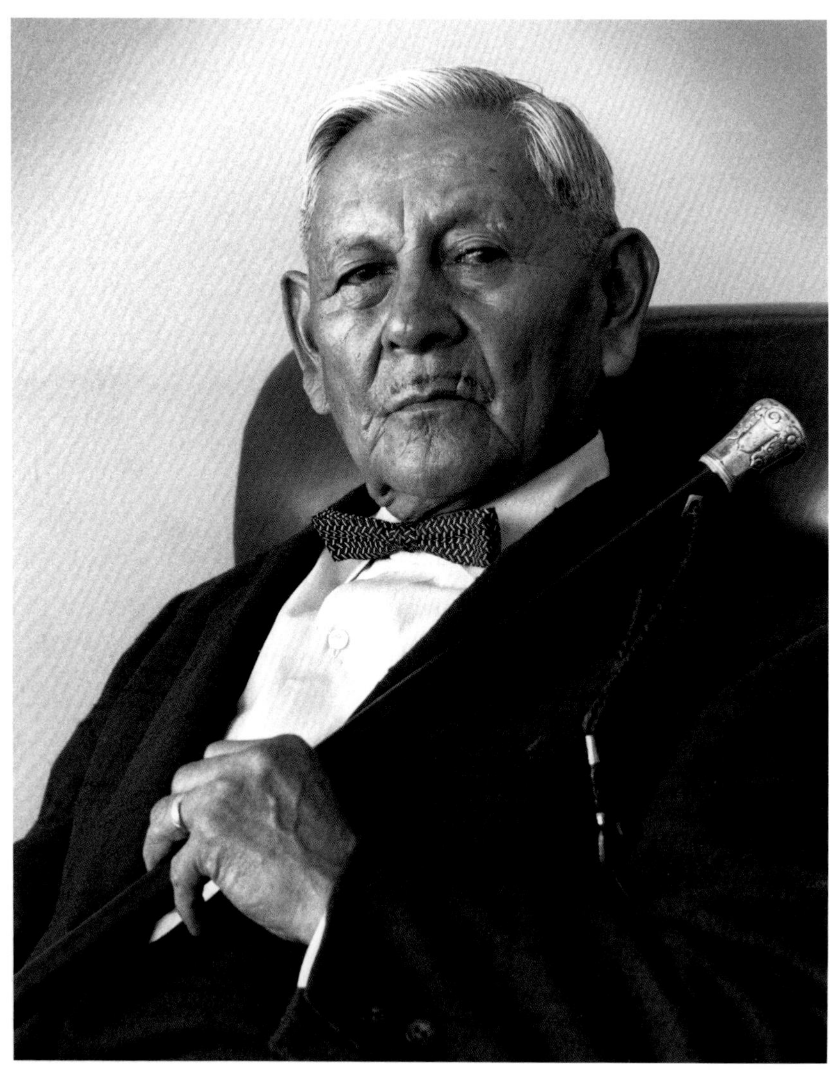

Governor Walter Sarracino with the Lincoln Cane. Photo by Lee Marmon (1963).

> Pueblo's history, culture and tradition to children of the Pueblo. . . . Anytime this code conflicts with customary or traditional law, the customary or traditional law shall control.[3]

The Elderly Code exemplifies the benevolent nature of the Laguna culture and the tribal determination to preserve its way of life.

Governor Walter Sarracino

Walter Sarracino (1890–1964) was elected governor for four terms of office, in 1935, 1937, 1951, and 1963. He attended the Carlisle Indian School in Pennsylvania, earning his degree in carpentry. Later, he displayed other

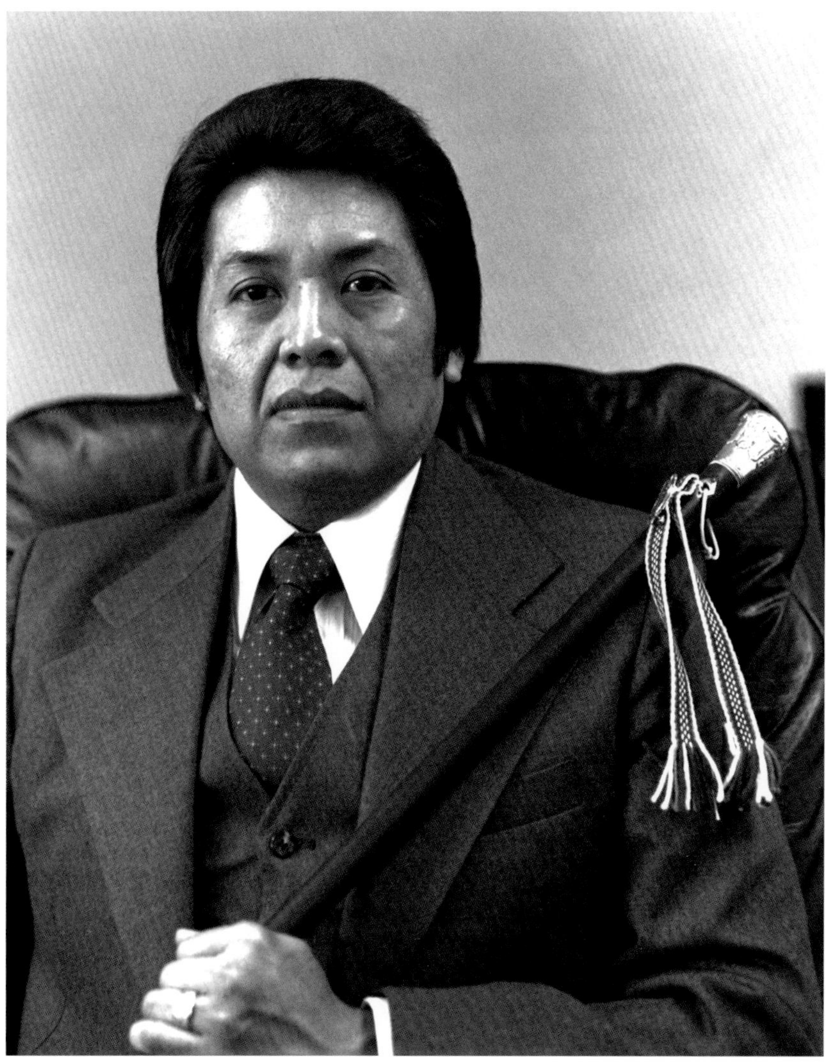

Governor Floyd Correa with the Lincoln Cane. Correa served as governor of Laguna from 1978 to 1979. Photo by Lee Marmon (1978).

talents in business, sports, and politics. He and his wife, Laura, built the Acoma Hotel in New Laguna in 1923. It was situated across from the Santa Fe station and was still in operation in the late 1940s.

He went to Washington, D.C., many times on tribal business. In 1953, Lee Marmon served as treasurer with Walter when the uranium mine opened near the village of Paguate. Walter also played professional baseball for a team in Albuquerque and was a champion rodeo broncobuster, performing once before the visiting king and queen of Belgium.

Walter's great-grandfather, Luis Sarracino, was presiding governor of Laguna in 1864 when the first Lincoln canes were presented on behalf of President Lincoln to the nineteen pueblo governors by Dr. Steck.

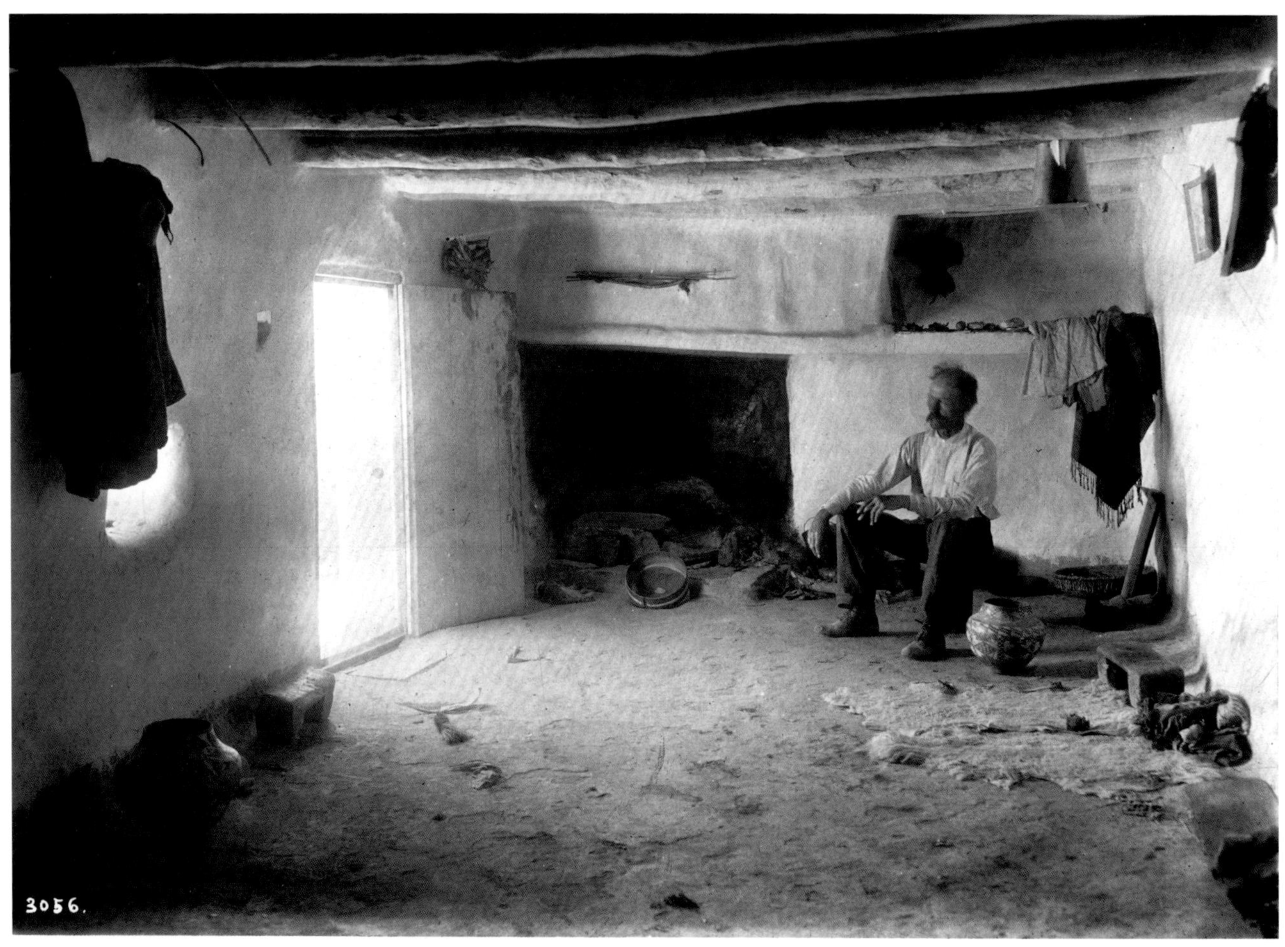

Robert G. Marmon in his living quarters while teaching at Acoma, 1872. Photo by William Henry Jackson. Courtesy of Lee Marmon.

CHAPTER SIX

The Anglo Infusion

The infusion of Anglo culture by a handful of Caucasian men from the Midwest was arguably the most influential factor in the adaptation of Laguna culture to Western civilization. These men married into the tribe and became involved in tribal affairs, infusing new cultural values. The transition was sometimes divisionary, rocky, and emotionally wrenching.

John Malcolm Gunn lived with the Lagunas from the mid-1870s until his death in 1938. He collected Laguna stories and legends and preserved them, along with the history of the time, in his classic book published in 1917, *Schat-Chen: History, Traditions and Narratives of the Queres Indians of Laguna and Acoma*.[1]

In his book, Gunn related the Laguna legend of She-ake, a powerful medicine man who made a number of prophecies, many of which have come true. She-ake would relay his visions of the future while lying flat on the ground, pounding the ground with his fists and commanding his audience to listen. Coronado also learned of She-ake, and in a letter to de Mendoza, viceroy of Mexico, wrote, "They declare that it was foretold among them more than fifty years ago that a people such as we are, should come, and the direction they should come from, and that the whole country would be conquered."[2]

She-ake foretold the coming of the Spaniards as bearded warriors with shirts of metal, predicting they would conquer and enslave the Indians. Then he prophesied the arrival of the people of light-colored hair, who would come from the East, conquer the country, and be the friends and champions of the Pueblo Indians. He foretold that these people from the East would build metal roads, and the Queres Indians would again be a prosperous, contented, and happy people.

She-ake's prophesy of the people from the East building metal roads was fulfilled by the coming of the railroad in the 1880s. She-ake's prediction of the coming of people with light-colored hair came to pass on both a regional and local level. An infusion of Anglo culture started shortly after the Treaty of Guadalupe-Hildalgo was signed in 1848. The U.S. government began sending parties of soldiers, surveyors, and settlers to the newly acquired New Mexico Territory. Notable individuals who had a significant impact on Laguna culture, in chronological order of when they first arrived in Laguna, include Rev. Henry W. Read, Rev. Samuel Gorman, Walter Gunn Marmon, Robert Gunn Marmon, George H. Pradt, Rev. John Menaul, John Malcolm Gunn, and Kenneth Colin Campbell Gunn.

Rev. Henry W. Read (1827–1910)

A contingent of U.S. Army soldiers went to Laguna in 1849, accompanied by Rev. Henry W. Read, a Baptist missionary from Cincinnati, Ohio. He introduced the Baptist religion to the Lagunas, but his stay among them was limited.

Rev. Samuel Gorman (1816–1880)

In 1851, the Baptist Missionary Society sent Rev. Samuel Gorman to Laguna to educate and convert the inhabitants to the Baptist religion. In 1857, he obtained a deeded parcel of land from the Lagunas. Located about a half mile east of the village, the land was used to start a Baptist compound. Gorman, using a $600 grant from the Baptist Home Mission Society in Ohio, constructed a twenty-by-forty-foot building, fourteen feet high, to use as a church. He built a home for himself, a store, and a mission school that also served as a meeting house for the tribal council.

While in Laguna, the reverend was accepted by the tribe and succeeded in converting a number of Lagunas to the Baptist religion. Gorman was called back to Ohio in 1861 at the start of the Civil War. He left behind a village divided among traditionalists who believed in the ancient beliefs, Catholics, and the new Protestant progressives.

When Reverend Gorman left, the Baptist Mission work was continued by local converts.

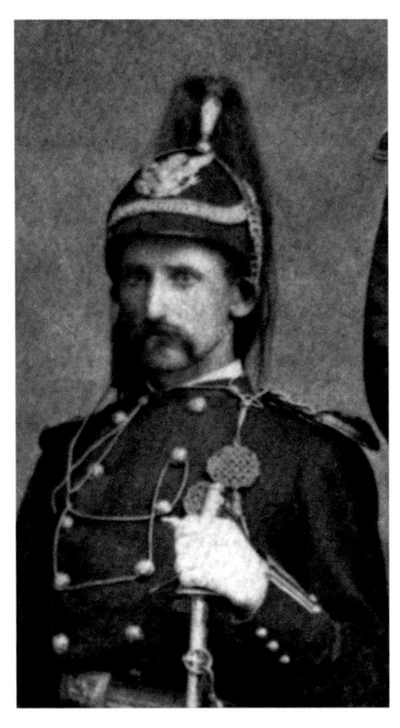

Colonel Walter Marmon, Age Thirty-Eight, Marmon Battalion, 1883. Photo courtesy of Lee Marmon.

Walter Gunn Marmon (1845–1899)

Walter Gunn Marmon, Lee Marmon's great-uncle, was born in 1845 in Logan County, Ohio. Orphaned at an early age, Walter and his brother Robert were reared by their maternal grandmother. The brothers studied engineering at Northwestern Ohio Normal School (Lebanon, Ohio). Walter enlisted as a private in the Union army when the Civil War started and was a first lieutenant in the 2nd Ohio Heavy Artillery at the end of the war.

In 1868, Walter went to New Mexico as a surveyor with Ehud N. Darling, who had a contract to survey the Navajo Indian reservation. In 1870, they made a preliminary survey for the proposed railroad from Albuquerque to the Arizona border. In 1871, Major William F. N. Arny, secretary of the New Mexico Territory, appointed Walter Marmon as teacher, doctor, and minister for Laguna Pueblo. He received salaries from both the government and the Presbyterian Church Board of Missionaries.

Walter became friends with Luis Sarracino, an influential Laguna tribal leader and powerful medicine man who had previously been friends with Reverend Gorman. Sarracino, educated in Durango, Mexico, spoke three languages. Sarracino had been influential in obtaining the land from the tribe that was used for the Baptist compound. Walter later married Sarracino's daughter, Mary Mollie Sarracino. Walter continued with his surveying career and opened a trading post with his brother, Robert. In 1877, Walter served on the Laguna Tribal Council.

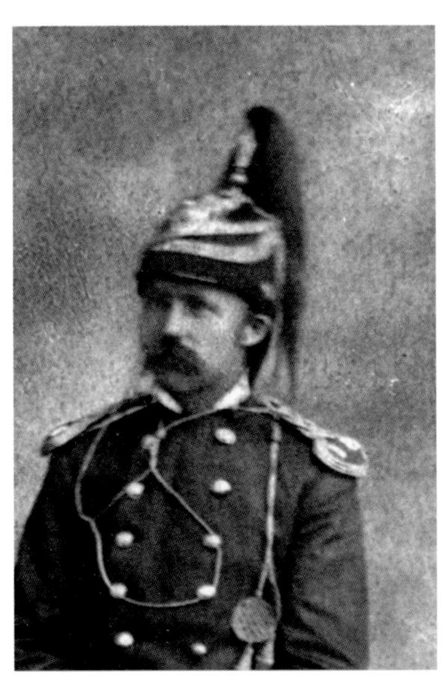

Captain Robert G. Marmon, Age Thirty-Five, Marmon Battalion, 1883. Photo courtesy of Lee Marmon.

Walter lived primitively in a room at the old Baptist Mission. In 1880, he and his brother purchased the mission from Reverend Gorman and his wife. The property became a compound for the Anglo population and their Laguna wives and a center for the Presbyterian ministry.

Described as "militant Presbyterians," the Marmon brothers established a Presbyterian mission at Laguna and continued to convert Lagunas to that religion. A major division occurred between the traditionalists and the new Presbyterian members of the tribe, and many traditionalists, determined to preserve and practice their own religion, left Laguna first for Isleta and eventually to Mesita to start their own settlement. After the traditionalists left, the two kivas at Laguna were destroyed by the progressives.[3]

In 1886, Walter Marmon was elected governor of Laguna. The Marmon brothers later drafted a constitution for Laguna, based on the United States Constitution. Walter died in 1899 after catching pneumonia while on a surveying job at Rama, New Mexico. It was November, and they were camping in the area in very cold weather. His associates brought him back, and he was buried not far from the old house.

Robert Gunn Marmon (1848–1933)

Lee Marmon's grandfather, Robert Gunn Marmon, was born on October 21, 1848, at Zanesfield, Logan County, Ohio. His mother, Annie Bell Gunn Marmon, died when he was four, and his father, Solomon Marmon, died four years later. His grandmother, Mrs. Isabel S. Gunn, took Robert and his older brother, Walter, to Kenton, Ohio, and Robert remained there with her until he was sixteen. He taught school in that vicinity for two terms, studied civil engineering at Northwestern Ohio Normal, and worked for two years as a surveyor.

In 1872, at age twenty-three, he traveled to the Southwest to locate his older brother, Walter, whom he knew to be somewhere in New Mexico. Along the way he met George H. Pradt, another civil engineer, who later joined the Marmon brothers in Laguna. Robert found his brother teaching school at Laguna and living in the old Baptist Mission built by Rev. Samuel Gorman.

Shortly after Robert's arrival, Walter went on a prospecting and surveying trip to Arizona and left Robert in charge of the school for three months. By the time Walter returned, Robert could speak the Laguna language even better than his brother.

On November 1, 1872, Robert Marmon was appointed teacher of a school newly organized at Acoma Pueblo southwest of Laguna. He held this job until the middle of January 1873, when he received an offer from Santa Fe to work as a chainman on a government survey.

In addition to performing intermittent surveying work, Robert opened a trading post in Laguna, ran cattle at Dripping Springs, later opened his home in the old mission building to visitors (an early bed-and-breakfast operation), and conducted tours of Acoma. A number of well-known people stayed with him, including Bandelier, early photographers Edward Curtis and William Henry Jackson, several prominent generals, including General Lew Wallace, who wrote part of his novel *Ben-Hur* within the building's walls, and the king and queen of Belgium. The notorious Billy the Kid, while a fugitive from justice, also stayed there for several weeks. The Laguna Post Office was established on January 24, 1879, with Robert Marmon appointed as postmaster.

The Lagunas accepted the Marmon brothers as members of the tribe and in 1880 elected Robert Marmon to the pueblo governorship. He was the first white man elected governor of a New Mexico pueblo and one of the few white men ever to hold that position. In 1886, his brother, Walter Marmon, was elected governor.

In 1880, Indians were permitted to enlist as regular members of territorial militia units. During the Apache campaigns of the 1880s, Robert Marmon was appointed captain of Company I, the first New Mexico Cavalry regiment, a company composed of only Laguna men.[4]

Robert Marmon's interest in educating the Lagunas continued, and he led several of the first groups of Laguna children to the Carlisle Indian School in Pennsylvania. He married Agness Anaya (1860–1891) on July 28, 1877. Following the death of Agness during childbirth in 1891, he married her younger sister, Marie Anaya, also known as Grandma A'mooh (1872–1962), in 1892. Robert had eight children, two with his first wife and six with his second.

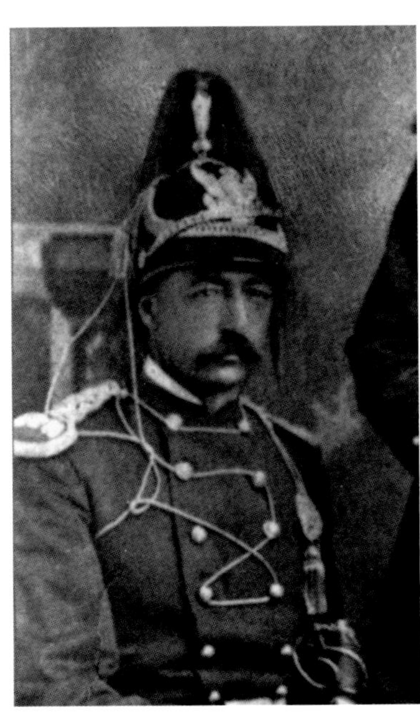

Major George H. Pradt, Age Thirty-Eight, Marmon Battalion, 1883. Photo courtesy of Lee Marmon.

George H. Pradt (1845–1927)

George H. Pradt was born in Pennsylvania in 1845. In 1869 he went to New Mexico as a U.S. deputy surveyor to make a survey of the Navajo Indian reservation. He and Robert G. Marmon met in Ft. Leavenworth, Kansas, when the latter was traveling from Ohio to New Mexico.

Pradt settled in Laguna in 1876 and helped the Marmons with religious reforms. A Civil War veteran, he served as an officer with the Marmon Battalion. He married Eulogia Miguel in 1877. They had ten children.

Rev. John Menaul (1833–1912)

In 1875, the government withdrew financial support for teachers on Indian reservations, ending support for Walter Marmon's efforts. Rev. John Menaul, sponsored by the Presbyterian Church, became the Presbyterian missionary and teacher at Laguna from 1875 until 1889. During those fourteen years, Menaul was instrumental in developing a positive attitude for Anglo education among the Lagunas. This progressive view toward education contributed to the success of partially integrating the Lagunas into Anglo culture and allowed them to develop economically and increase their standard of living more than any other pueblo. The 1890 federal census at Laguna revealed that of the 1,143 residents, 167 (14.6 percent) could read, write, and speak English. Of the 435 school-age children, 307 (70.6 percent) attended either day or boarding school.[5] These were extraordinary numbers for the pueblo populations at that time.

John Malcolm Gunn (1860–1938)

John Malcolm Gunn was born on October 6, 1860, in Hardin County, Ohio. Along with his brother Kenneth, he joined his cousins, the Marmon brothers, in Laguna in 1881. He was engaged in several business ventures there and spent much time collecting local history, stories, and legends of the Laguna and Acoma people. He contributed greatly to the preservation of the information through his writings. His best-known contribution is

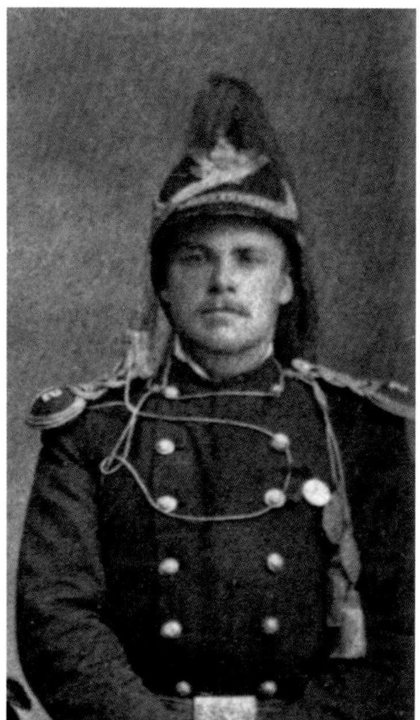

Lieutenant John M. Gunn, Age Twenty-Three, Marmon Battalion, 1983. Photo courtesy of Lee Marmon.

Schat-Chen: History, Traditions and Narratives of the Queres Indians of Laguna and Acoma, published in 1917.

Following the death of his brother Kenneth in 1920, John Gunn married his brother's widow, Meta Atsye Gunn, in 1923. He was sixty-three years old and she was fifty-four at the time. He died on August 6, 1938.

Kenneth Colin Campbell Gunn (1863–1920)

Kenneth Colin Campbell Gunn was born on February 7, 1863, in Kenton, Ohio. He joined his brother John and his cousins, the Marmon brothers, in Laguna in 1881. He opened a trading post there and was involved in several business ventures over the years. He married Meta Atsye in 1893 and had seven children with her. Kenneth died on May 21, 1920.

The Anglo Infusion

The Anglo infusion of the 1870s and 1880s brought many changes to the Laguna way of life. Some were positive while others were negative, at least temporarily. Introduction of new religions caused major disruption between Laguna believers in the new tenets and the traditionalists who continued to believe in the native religion and Catholicism. Education brought major positive changes but only after serious disruption in family life as some students were forcibly taken from their families and sent away to the Carlisle Indian School in Pennsylvania. Children spent as long as four years away from their homes and families, stripped of their cultural identity—their language, dress, and religion. Other students, whose parents saw the value of education in terms of coping with the invading Anglo culture, looked favorably on sending their children to Carlisle. In either case, the experience was emotionally wrenching for both students and parents.

The Anglo infusion also resulted in a change in tribal government. A new model of government, based on the United States Constitution, was passed, ending the rule by the cacique, or head religious leader. Laguna is the only pueblo to have changed its form of government.

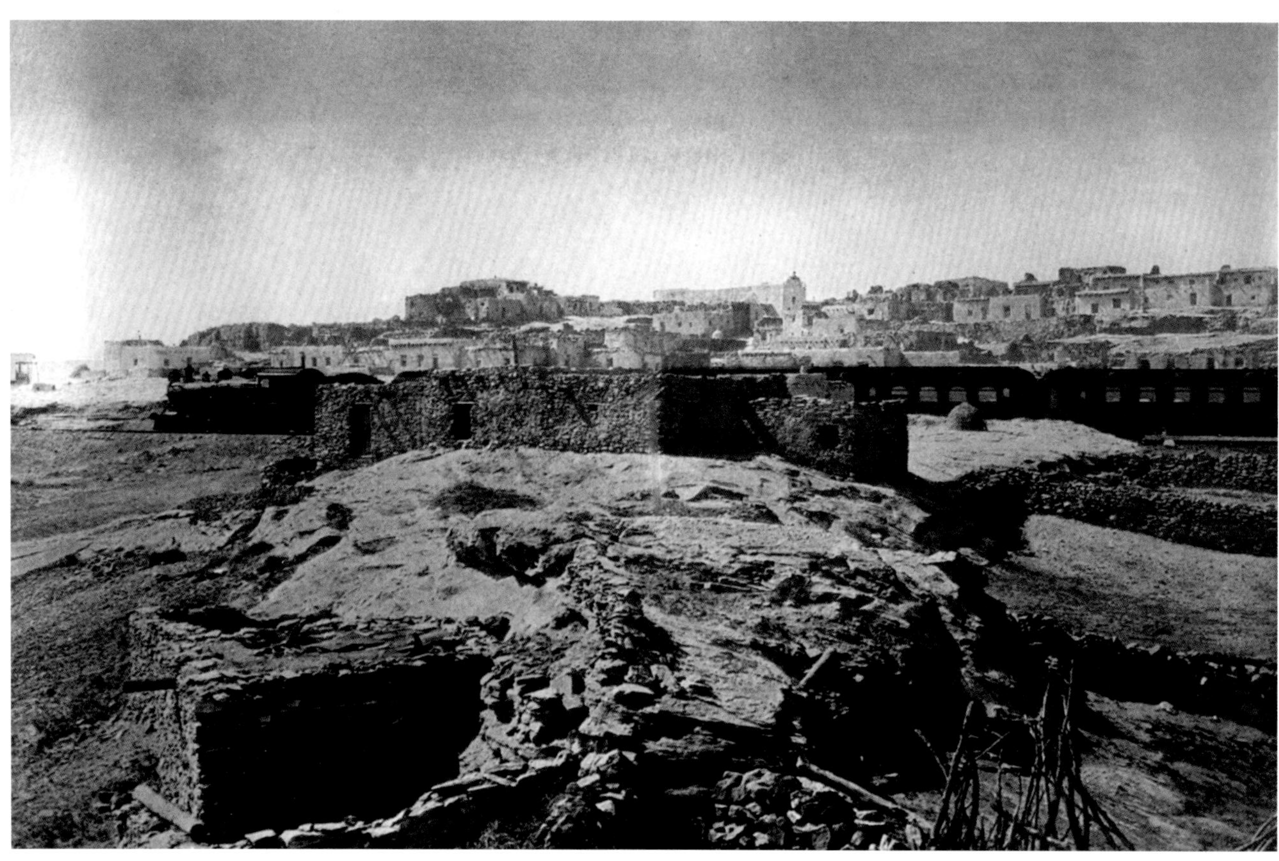

A train leaving the Laguna station and passing south of the village, circa 1890. Photographer unknown. Courtesy of the Palace of the Governors Photographic Archives (NMHM/DCA), #149714.

CHAPTER SEVEN

The Railroad

In 1862, Congress passed the Pacific Railway Act, authorizing the building of a transcontinental railroad. The Union Pacific Railroad would construct tracks west from Omaha, Nebraska, and the Central Pacific Railroad would extend its rail east from Sacramento, California. The project was finally completed on May 10, 1869, at Promontory, Utah, when the Union Pacific tracks from the West were joined with the tracks of the Central Pacific from the East.

Other transcontinental routes followed. The Atlantic and Pacific Railroad was commissioned to build a line from Isleta (Albuquerque), New Mexico, through Grants, New Mexico; Winslow and Flagstaff, Arizona; and Needles and Barstow, California, with a connecting link to Los Angeles. This became the main route for transcontinental service for the Atchison, Topeka and Santa Fe (AT&SF) Railway.

The section from Albuquerque to Grants required building the rail line across forty miles of Laguna land. In 1880, negotiations between the Lagunas and the Atlantic and Pacific Railroad resulted in a perpetual oral agreement sealed with a handshake. This historic agreement became known as the "Flower of Friendship" between the pueblo and the railroad. For many years, Laguna tribal representatives met annually with officials from the railroad to reaffirm the oral agreement, a meeting that became known as "Watering the Flower."

In exchange for the rights to lay the tracks through the ideal topography of the reservation and to use Laguna water from the Rio San José to power the steam engines, the railroad agreed to provide on- and off-reservation employment for Lagunas, free housing for railroad workers and their families, and free rail passes for tribal members. Other considerations included installing several pipes from the river to the village above to pump water so the Lagunas would no longer have to carry their water uphill to their homes.

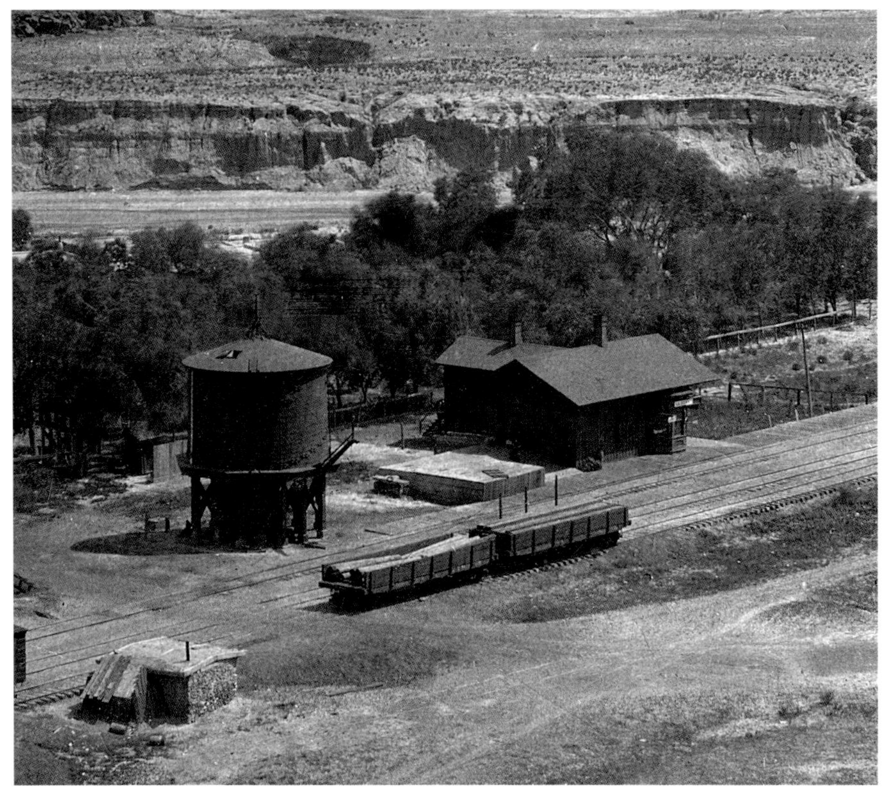

(*top*) Close-up of the water tower and the original train station, 1897. The train station to the right of the water tower burned shortly after this photo was taken. The new train station was constructed on the site and is now the home of Lee Marmon. Cobb's Studio, Albuquerque (1897). Photo courtesy of Lee Marmon.

(*bottom*) Close-up of a coal car being loaded from the Laguna coal chute, 1897. Note the early locomotive with the funnel smokestack between the coal chute and the boxcars. The coal car is being positioned to be refilled from the coal chutes. Cobb's Studio, Albuquerque (1897). Photo courtesy of Lee Marmon.

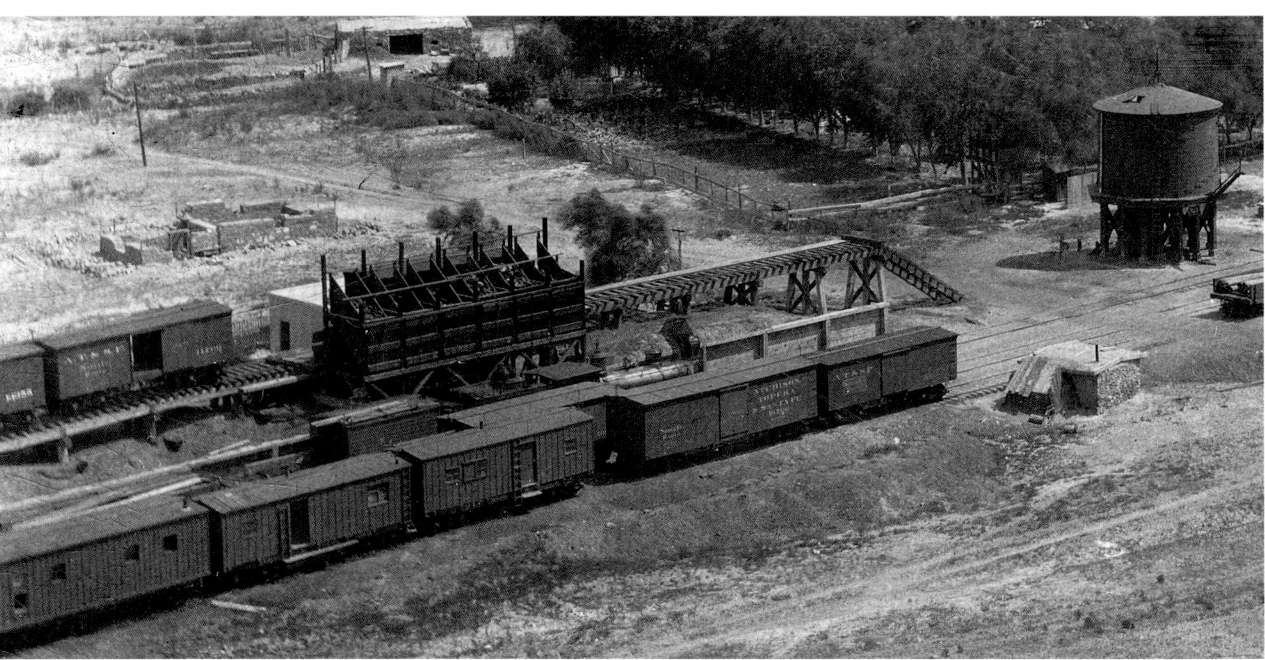

The railroad, employing Laguna men, began building and maintaining the track across the reservation. At Laguna, the tracks coming from the East were initially constructed parallel to the Rio San José, turning northwest at the southernmost point of Laguna and creating a semicircle around the village. The water tower, station, and coal chutes were constructed adjacent to the old Baptist Mission area. On August 21, 1883, the first train passed through Laguna on its way from Kansas City to San Francisco. Lee Marmon relates the early days of the railroad.

When the train would come from the East, Old Laguna was a stopping point for coal and water and for picking up freight and passengers. The conductor would tell the passengers they could get off the train and walk through the village and the train would pick them up on the other side of town. After refueling, the engineer would pull the train around and toot the whistle. At the signal, the passengers would reboard the train. And vice versa, when the train would come from the West. The train would stop and offload on the west side of the village and let the passengers off and then pick them up on the east side. This was from about 1885 until the early 1900s. Early on, people who were interested in the Indians could come from back east, get off here at Laguna, and they were right here at a pueblo. Then they could get from here to Acoma. It was the only pueblo in New Mexico where you could do that. Of course that held until the advent of the motor car; then tourists could go to Santa Fe and Taos.

In the early 1900s, the railroad straightened out the track and bypassed Old Laguna, citing too many curves in the track. The residents of Old Laguna had complained that the train was too close to the village. The smoke and noise bothered the villagers and the animals. When the railroad rerouted the tracks, they built the station where New Laguna is now. The town then built up around the station. Nothing existed there before that, and that's how New Laguna got its name.

One of the first structures built in New Laguna was the Acoma Hotel in 1923 to accommodate the tourists. It was convenient for the people who got off the train and wanted to go to Acoma. Someone would escort them from the hotel to Acoma and also to Old Laguna. They had a curio store in the hotel.

A number of important people came through Laguna, including early photographers Curtis and Jackson and some of the generals. In the early days, they stayed at Old Laguna but switched to New Laguna

Laguna women selling pottery to tourists disembarking from the train at the Laguna station. William Henry Jackson original. Detroit Photo Co. (1888). Courtesy of the Palace of the Governors Photographic Archives (NMHM/DCA), #41729.

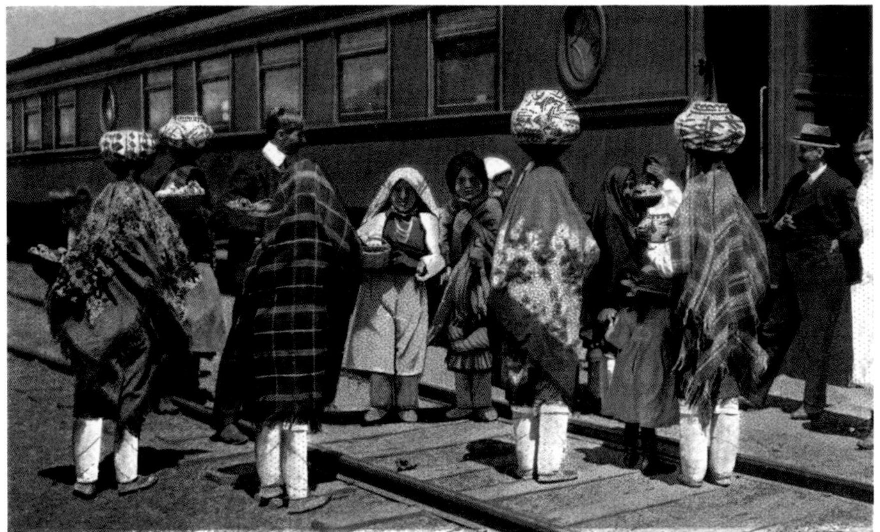

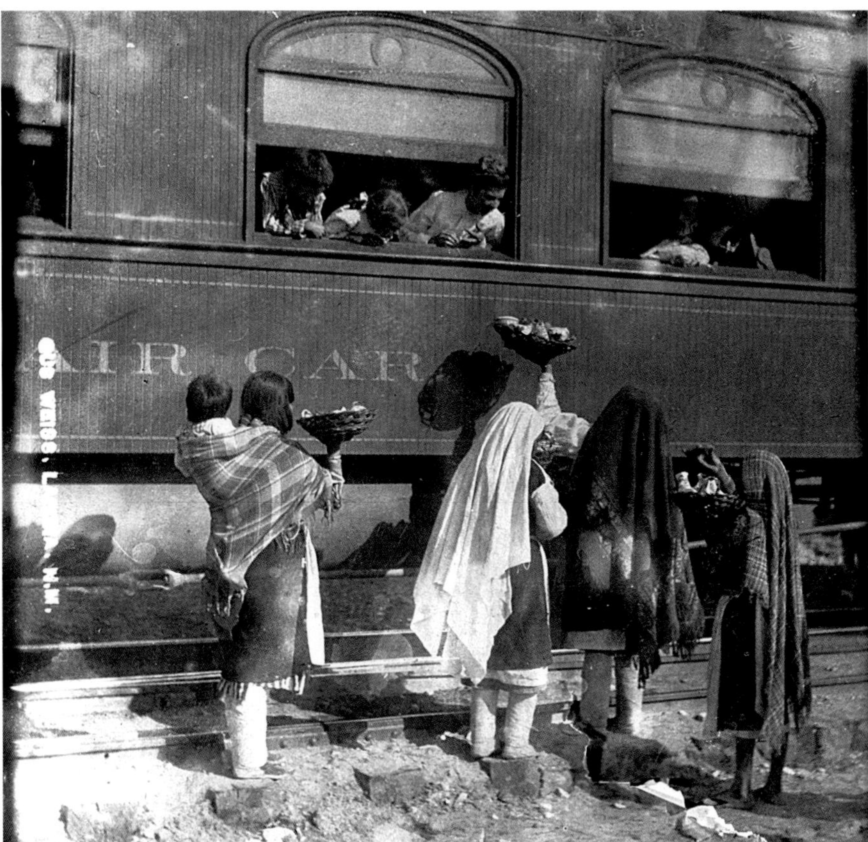

Laguna women selling pottery through the passenger car windows at the Laguna station, circa 1890. Photo by Gus Weiss. Courtesy of Ron Fernandez.

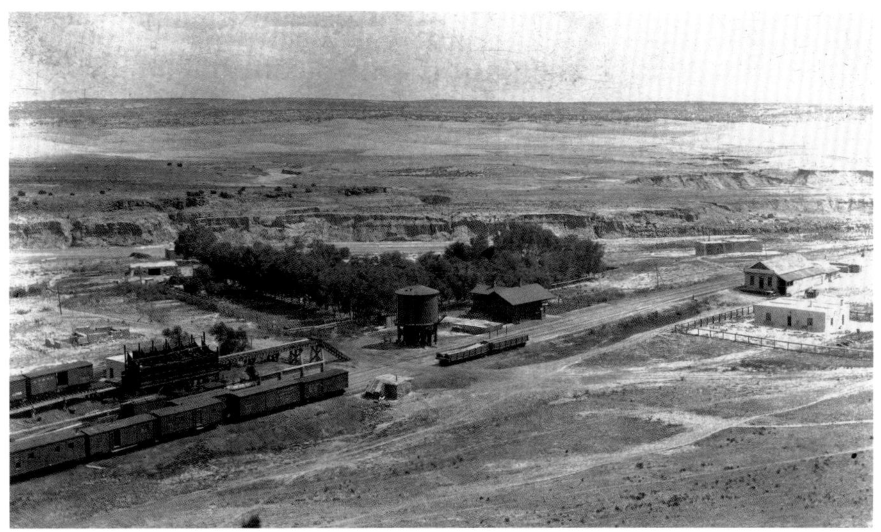

AT&SF Laguna complex. This photo shows the entire AT&SF Railway Laguna complex from left to right, including the coal chute, water tower, and train station. The two structures on the right, the white house with a fence around it, and the larger building in back of it belonged to Robert G. Marmon. He rented the larger building to the Bibo family for use as a trading post and the house to Gus Weiss, Bibo's son-in-law who worked at the trading post, as a residence. The Rio San José is seen crossing the middle of the photograph, flowing along the base of the cliff and behind the trees. Cobb's Studio, Albuquerque (1897). Photo courtesy of Lee Marmon.

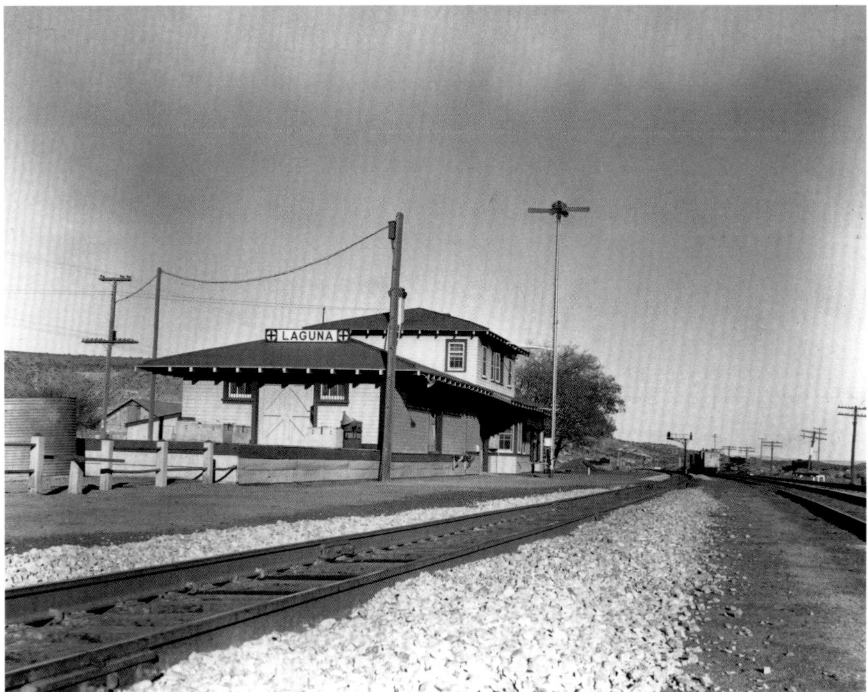

Train Station at New Laguna. Photo by Lee Marmon (1949).

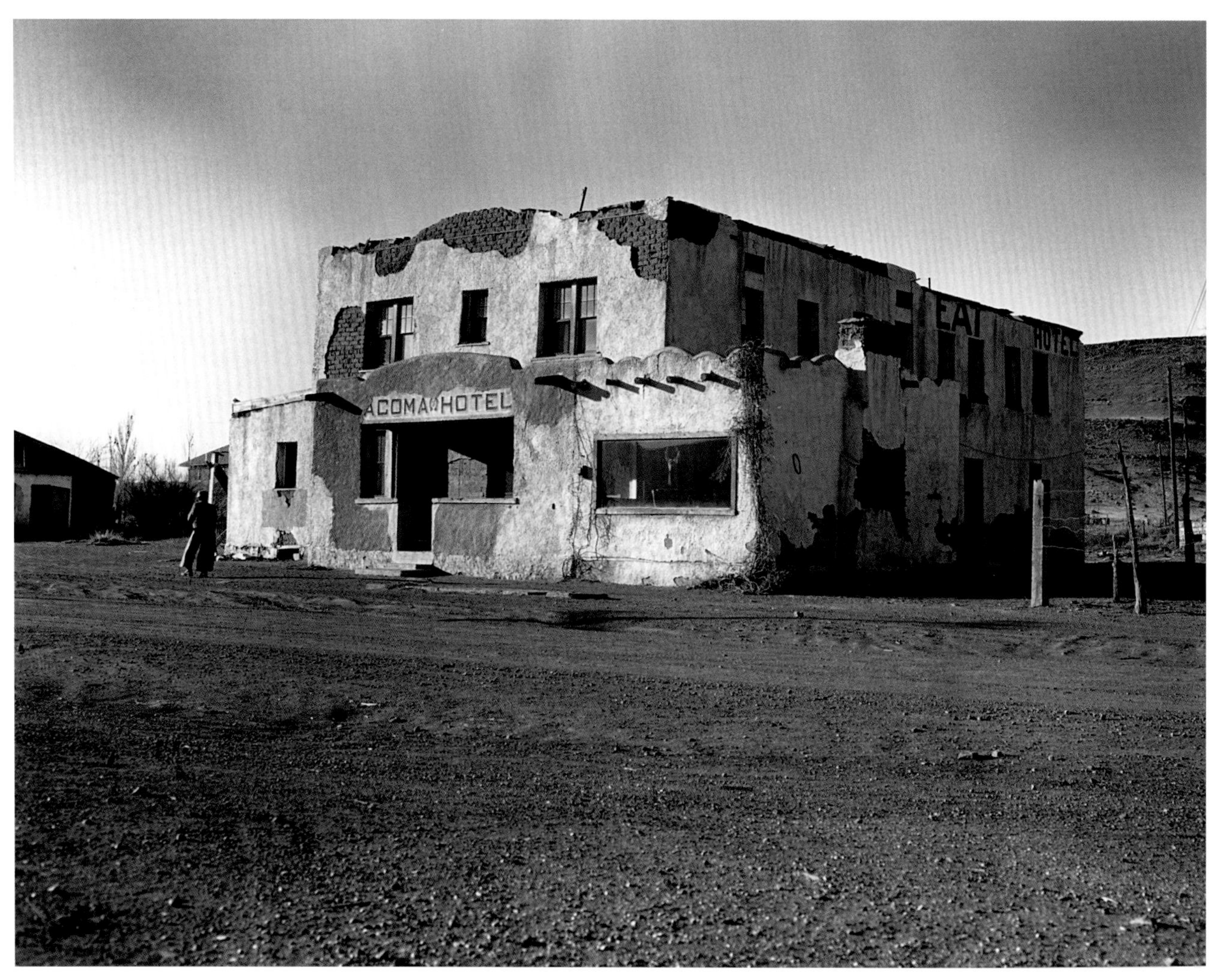

Ruins of the Acoma Hotel at New Laguna. Constructed in 1923, the Acoma Hotel was a convenient facility for passengers who came to visit Acoma. Hotel guests included Willa Cather and other noted authors, photographers, historians, and other public figures. Photo by Lee Marmon (1949).

after the hotel was built. Willa Cather stayed there almost a week because the roads to Acoma were too muddy. She was doing research for her novel *Death Comes for the Archbishop.* The hotel and railroad station are gone now. The younger people in the tribe have never seen these buildings.

Prior to the building of the railroad, Laguna men were permanent residents on the reservation, engaged in farming, sheepherding, and other agriculturally related activities. The railroad radically changed the lives and the economy of the Lagunas. There was now easy access to new goods brought by the trains. Many people left the reservation to work on the railroad. They went to Gallup, New Mexico; Winslow, Arizona; and Barstow and Richmond, California.

As the years passed, Laguna men continued working on the railroad, and Laguna colonies were founded at Albuquerque, Gallup, Winslow, Barstow, Richmond, and Los Angeles.[1] The Laguna tribal government recognized these colonies as satellite villages. The railroad provided "boxcar colonies" for the families. Boxcars were set up in rows, partitioned into rooms with windows, and provided with wood-burning cook stoves for each kitchen. Restrooms were communal for many years, and later, showers and toilets were installed in each unit. Living together in these boxcar communities provided the Lagunas with privacy and the opportunity to maintain their cultural identity. Children, however, did attend local Catholic or public schools, which provided a higher-quality and more diverse education than did the schools on the reservation. They became known as "boxcar kids." Many continued their lives outside the pueblo, attending high school and college.[2]

The trains no longer stop at Laguna. The tracks now run north of the village. Long freight trains and Amtrak trains can be seen crossing the reservation by drivers on Interstate 40.

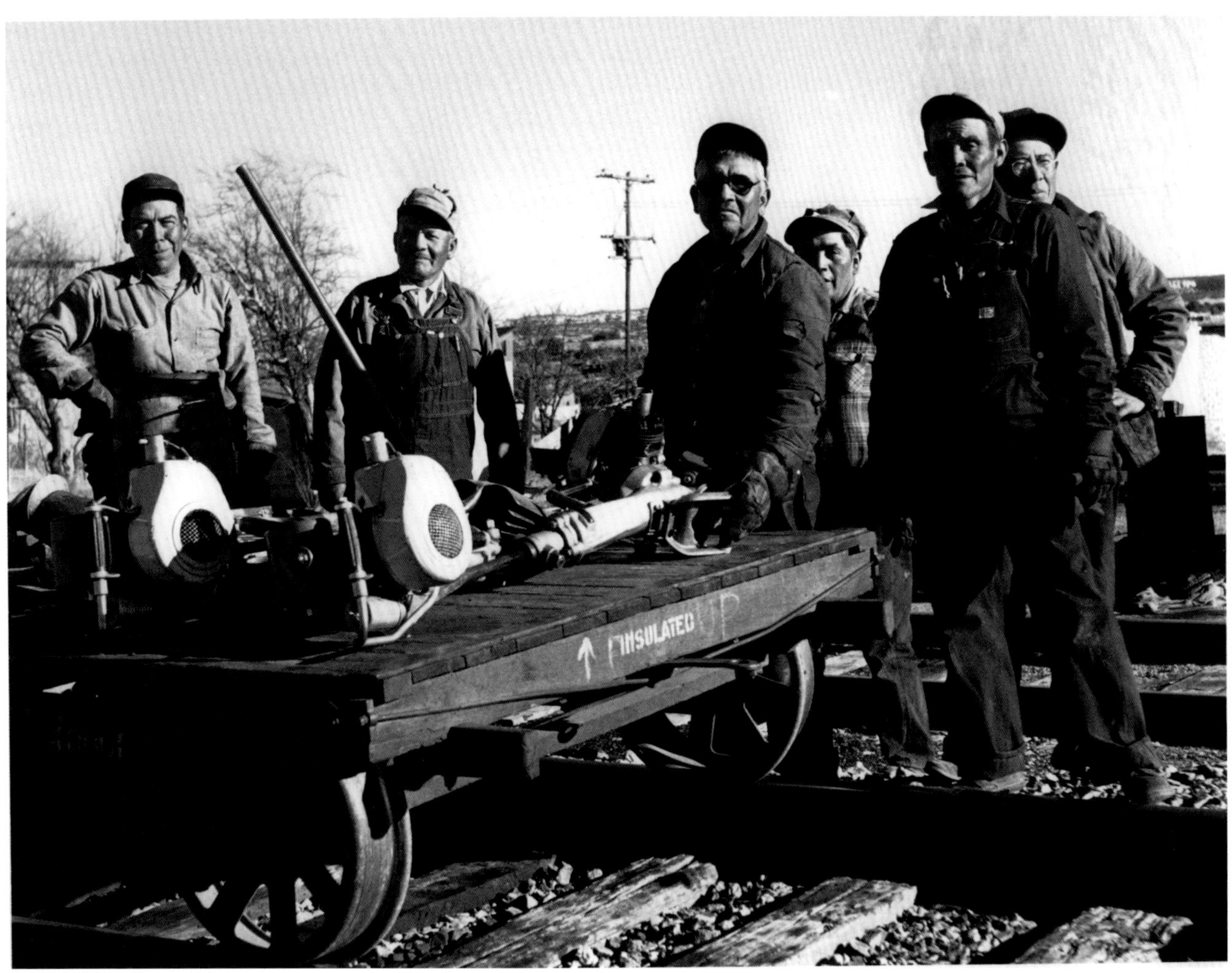

Laguna Section Gang. Laguna men working for the Santa Fe Railroad on the section gang around quitting time. Very few pictures exist of the old Laguna section gang. Photo by Lee Marmon (1948).

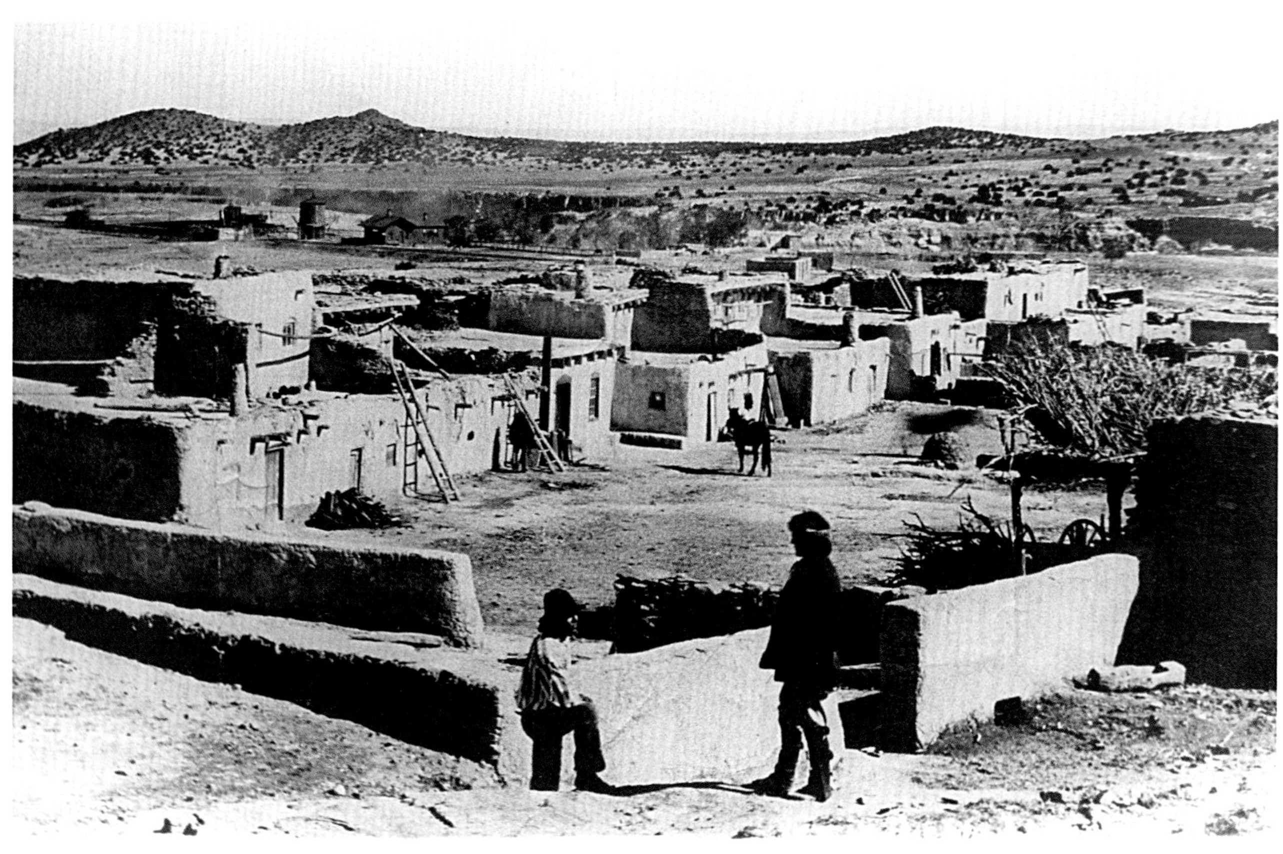

View of Laguna looking east from the mission. The AT&SF Railway compound is situated east of the village. The water tower and original train station (a wood-framed building) are clearly visible in the upper-left quadrant of the photograph. The station burned to the ground in 1898 and was replaced with a larger adobe structure. Photo by Ben Wittick (circa 1898). Courtesy of Ron Fernandez.

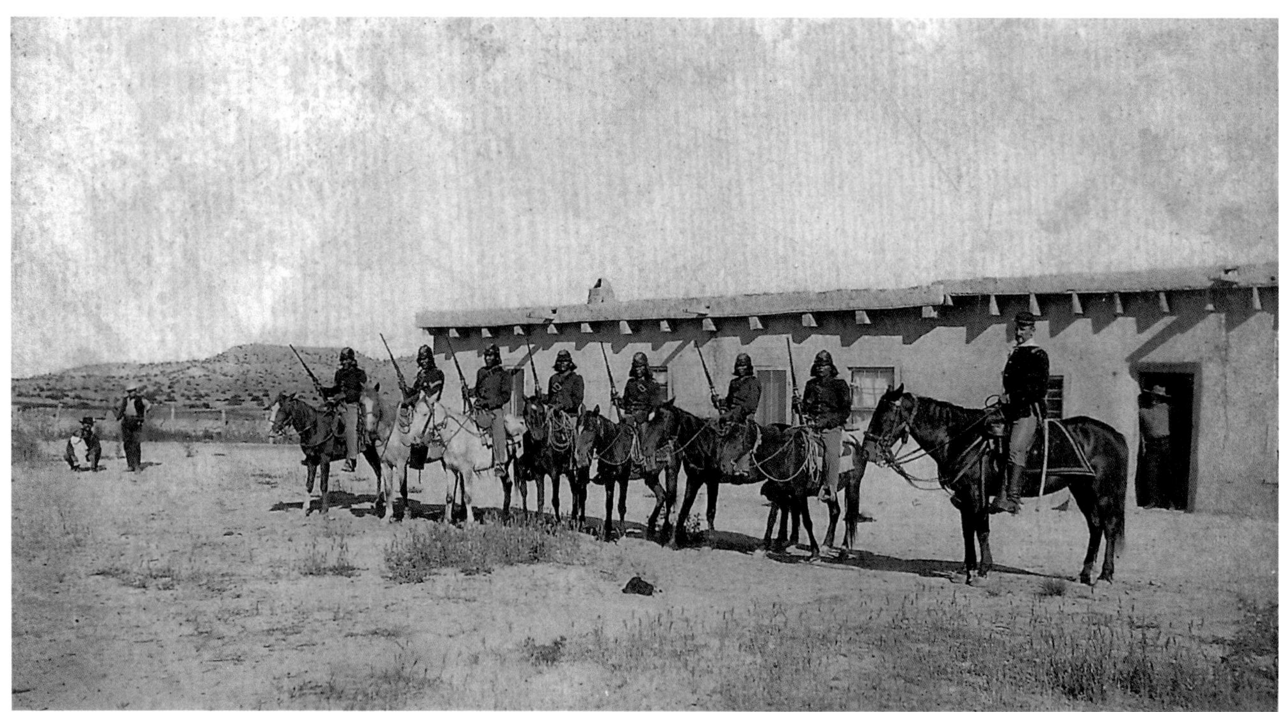

The Marmon Battalion in uniform and on horseback, 1886. Colonel Walter G. Marmon is on the far right. Photographer unknown. Courtesy of Nevlyn and Lois Eckerman.

CHAPTER EIGHT

The Marmon Battalion

Pueblo villages had been the targets of both Apache and Navajo raids since at least the beginning of the seventeenth century. The settled pueblo villages, engaged in farming and ranching, were prime targets for the nomadic and predatory invaders who stole crops and livestock and took women and children as slaves. As the Spanish, Mexican, and later the Anglo settlers moved into the New Mexico Territory, they, too, became prime targets of the raiding parties.

These raids were one of the motivating factors for the Lagunas to ally with the Spanish in the late 1600s. Lagunas fought in cooperation with the Spanish soldiers, and together, they were able to fortify their defenses against the raiders. From 1821 until 1848, when Mexico ruled the territory, the Lagunas continued their military alliance with the Mexicans.

The Treaty of Guadalupe-Hidalgo, signed in 1848, ended the Mexican-American War and gave title of the New Mexico Territory (and other areas of the Southwest) to the United States. James S. Calhoun, who in 1849 was appointed Indian agent for the newly acquired New Mexico Territory and later, in 1851, became governor of the territory, made urgent requests to the United States government that a militia be organized for the protection of the inhabitants and to pursue the invaders. He also advised that Pueblo Indians be allowed to form auxiliary units.[1] His requests were denied. However, in the late 1850s, General McCook established a military camp at Laguna and recruited a company of Laguna Indians to act as scouts in a campaign against the Apaches.[2]

At the beginning of the Apache campaigns of the 1880s, Indians were finally permitted to enlist as regular members of territorial militia units. In December 1882, Walter G. Marmon, who had previous military experience fighting in the Civil War, was granted permission by the territorial governor to form Troop F of Company I. In 1883, his troop was reorganized

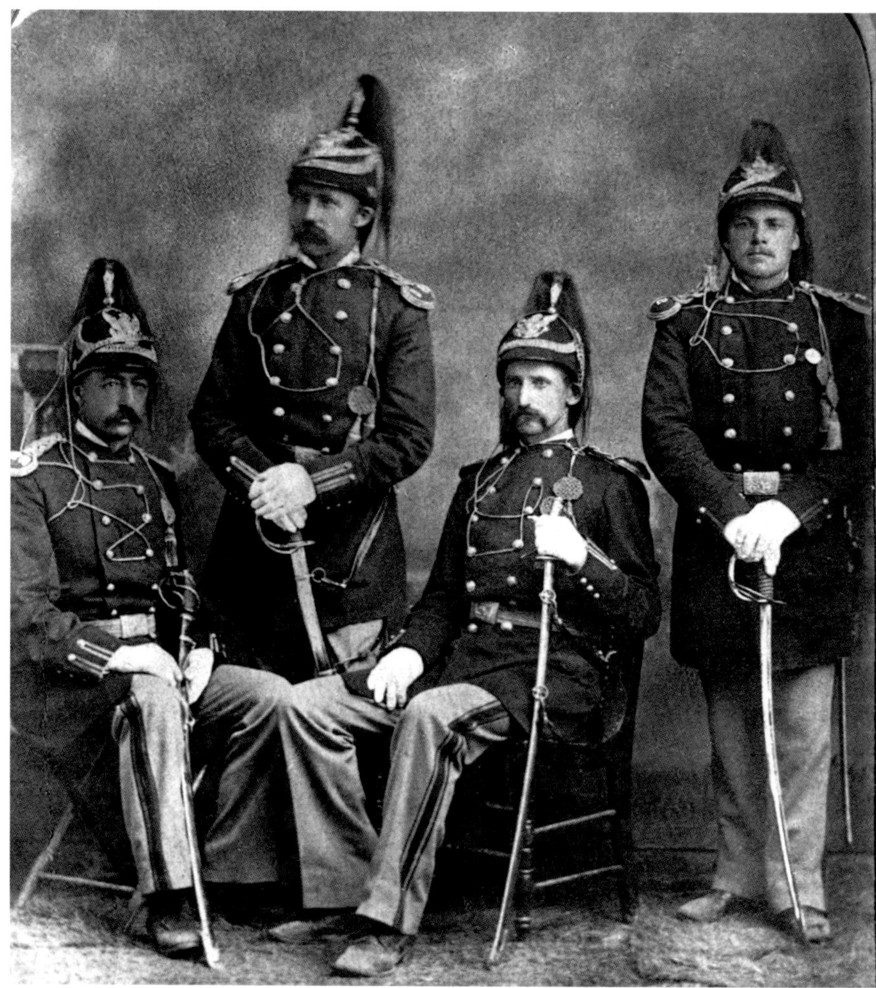

The Marmon Battalion officers at the Tri-Centennial Marksmanship Competition in Santa Fe, New Mexico Territory, 1883. Left to right: Major George H. Pradt, Captain Robert G. Marmon, Colonel Walter G. Marmon, and Lieutenant John M. Gunn, Company I, First Cavalry, New Mexico Volunteers. Photographer unknown. Courtesy of Lee Marmon.

and given cavalry status. The militia would assist in the chase after raiding Navajos, Apaches, and Utes. Troop F consisted of Pueblo men commanded by the Marmon brothers, their cousin John M. Gunn, and Major George H. Pradt, who also had military experience in the Civil War. The territorial government provided rifles to the troops, but each man would have to provide his own horse and food. Each volunteer was promised financial compensation by the government.[3]

The Marmon Battalion held regular drills in their native language, Keresan, rather than English, and learned to become skilled marksmen. The company developed a reputation for marksmanship and competed with other units in Santa Fe in 1883, placing second in overall competition.

The Laguna troops drilled for weeks before the annual marksmanship competition. Lee Marmon recalls his grandaunt Susie Marmon (1877–1978) telling how, when she was a little girl, she watched the Marmon brothers and Troop F holding their target practice down by the San José River that flows adjacent to the pueblo and near their home.

The Marmon Battalion was involved in several campaigns against the Apache raiders, sometimes patrolling as far away as southern New Mexico and being gone thirty or forty days at a time. At other times they were strategically positioned along the Atlantic and Pacific Railroad as it traveled through areas vulnerable to raiding parties.

The final Apache campaign for the Marmon Battalion ended in late June 1885. Geronimo surrendered the following year, and the Pueblo peoples were beginning to feel secure enough to venture away from the main villages and settle in the surrounding countryside. However, sporadic raids continued to occur as late as 1908, according to Marie Marmon (1872–1962), widow of Col. Robert G. Marmon.

The battalion remained in active status until 1917. Following the Apache campaign, the unit continued in active pursuit of the small bands of renegades that continued to plunder the area. They also went after train and bank robbers and other lawbreakers.

Although the Laguna scouts were promised financial compensation by the territorial government, they received none. The pay allowed during active duty was \$0.45 per day (\$13.50/month) and \$2.00 per day (\$60.00/month) for the care of privately owned horses. Officers received considerably more, from \$2.60 to \$5.18 per day (\$77.50–\$155.35/month). Instead

No. 74 OFFICE OF ADJUTANT GENERAL. \$155.00

TERRITORY OF NEW MEXICO.

CERTIFICATE OF INDEBTEDNESS.

Santa Fe, N. M., July 1st, 1885.

This is to certify that there is due to Capt Robt G. Marmon, *the sum of* One Hundred and fifty five $\frac{x}{100}$ *dollars, from the Territory of New Mexico under the militia law of 1880, Compiled Laws, Title XXV. This claim for services during the Apache Indian raid of May and June, 1885. Having been properly made, examined and allowed by the Governor and Adjutant General; and not paid in Territorial warrants, for the reason that the appropriation was not sufficient to meet all this class of claims.*

In Testimony whereof the Governor of said Territory, and the Adjutant General have hereunto subscribed their names, and affixed the seal of the Adjutant General's office.

Edward L. Bartlett
ADJUTANT GENERAL OF NEW MEXICO.

Edmund G. Ross
GOVERNOR OF NEW MEXICO.

Certificate of Indebtedness issued by the New Mexico Territory. This certificate was issued to Captain Robert G. Marmon, July 1, 1885. None of the certificates issued to the officers or troops were ever honored. Photo courtesy of Lee Marmon.

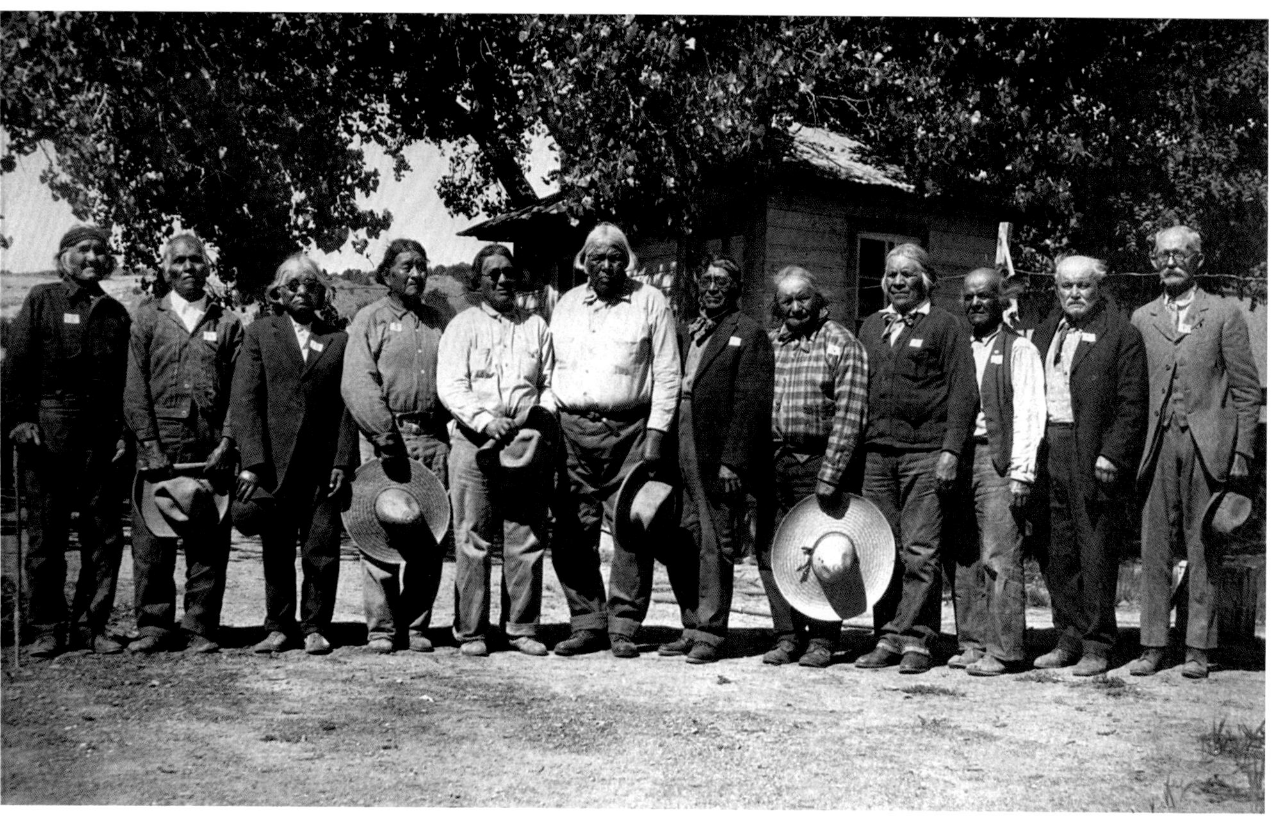

Surviving members of the Marmon Battalion. The surviving officers are John Gunn (second from right) and Robert G. Marmon (far right). Photo courtesy of *Mountain View Telegraph* (1928). Reprinted with permission.

of money, they received certificates of indebtedness from the territorial government.

The men also had to provide their own uniforms—at considerable expense—and wore them proudly. Eventually, the men requested their paychecks, but the government never honored the certificates of indebtedness. Colonel Marmon, feeling responsible for his men, bought many of the issued certificates from them, expecting that he would be able to redeem them at a later time. But the colonel was never able to redeem the certificates, and several still are among the Marmon family's genealogical records.

The battalion was ceremoniously disbanded with an emotional meeting of the surviving eleven members in the fall of 1917. Col. Walter G. Marmon had died in 1899, but his brother, Col. Robert G. Marmon, and his cousin, Lt. John M. Gunn, were present.

Lee Marmon recalls:

> The Apache raids affected our family personally. My maternal great-great-grandfather was with a group moving sheep from Laguna

Pueblo to Isleta Pueblo to trade for corn and melons. Just west of Albuquerque, they were attacked by a band of renegade Apaches about three o'clock in the morning, and my great-great-grandfather was killed.

My grandfather worked tirelessly through the 1920s and early 1930s to get a pension for each one of the scouts. My mother drove my grandfather around the reservation getting statements from the men and their families to send with the applications. He finally managed to get a small pension for each of them. Several families later told me that if it weren't for that pension, during the Depression they would have starved to death. My grandmother, even into the 1950s, was still getting a pension check for the Indian Wars.

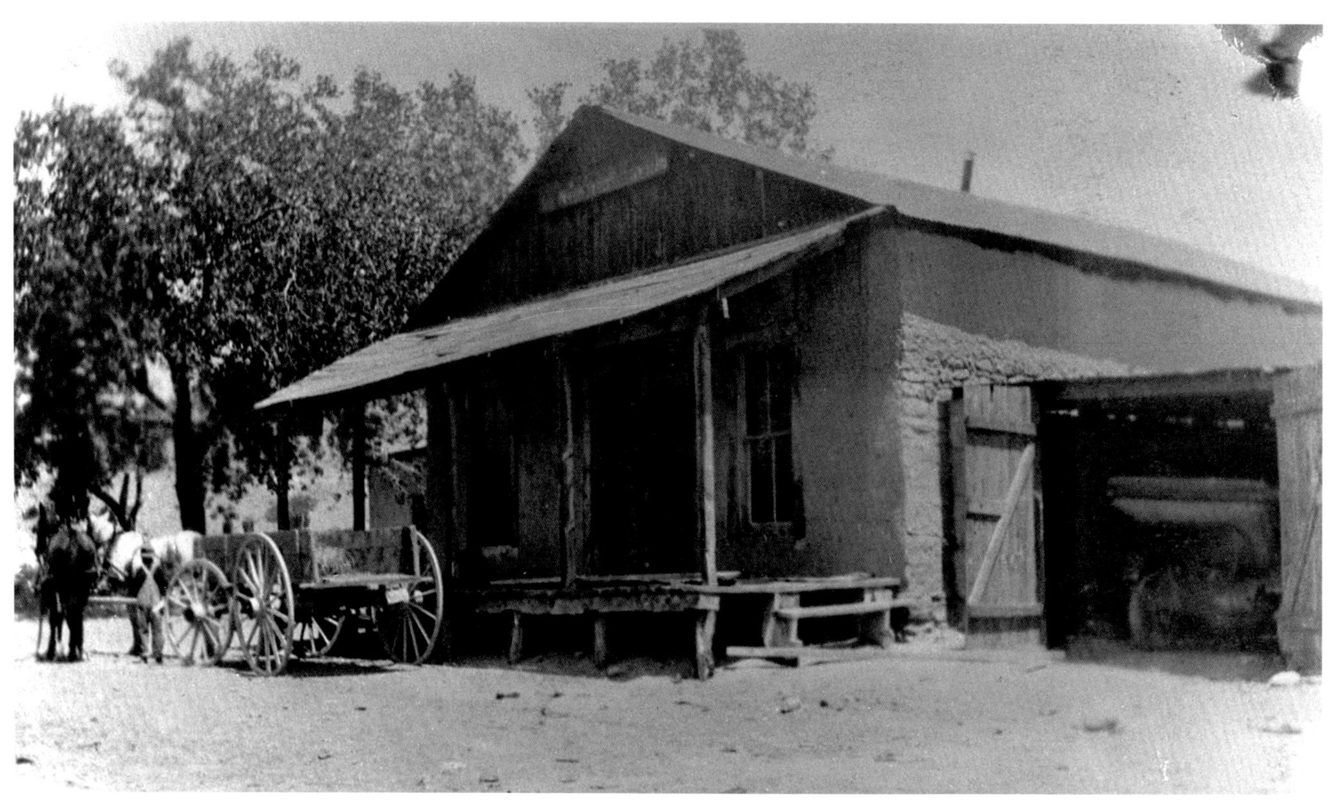

Gunn Brothers Trading Post, circa 1915. Photographer unknown. Courtesy of Ron Fernandez.

CHAPTER NINE

Route 66

Intertribal trade was common in the Southwest long before the Spanish invasion in the 1500s. Trade routes dating back a thousand years have been discovered all the way from Chaco Canyon to Mexico.

Trade routes between the Rio Grande pueblos and the western pueblos followed the courses of the Rio Puerco and the Rio San José. Additional trade routes appeared with the formation of Spanish settlements. The Albuquerque-Wingate and Beale Wagon Roads were carved across Laguna land in the 1860s and 1870s. Additional wagon roads were developed, including one between Los Lunas and Laguna.[1]

Trading posts began to appear along trade routes in the mid to late 1800s, bringing both economic and social exchange between the Pueblo and Anglo cultures. New goods, brought to Laguna from Albuquerque by wagon via the road from Los Lunas, became available to elevate the local standard of living.

Following the Civil War, Laguna Pueblo experienced an influx of Caucasians. The Gunn brothers, Marmon brothers, and George H. Pradt all settled in Laguna and started businesses or trades, including trading posts, milling operations, surveying, and other businesses in the area. Kenneth and John Gunn opened one of Laguna's first trading posts. In 1893, Kenneth Gunn married Meta Atsye, a Laguna woman from the village of Paguate. She had attended the Carlisle Indian School in Pennsylvania. Descendants of the Gunn family continued trading-post operations for over one hundred years. In 1917, Kenneth Gunn's daughter Jessie married Seigfried Abraham, one of several Jewish merchants who migrated to New Mexico after immigrating to the United States in 1913. Abraham partnered with the Gunn brothers and later took over the store and enlarged the operation. Descendants of the Marmon family intermittently operated similar businesses until 1978.

In 1893, John Gunn constructed and operated a flour mill on the banks of the Rio San José. Several years later, the mill was destroyed in a flood and he then constructed a new mill next to the Gunns' trading post. Both businesses were located along the wagon trail from Los Lunas and across the street from the AT&SF water tower. Also in 1893, Simon Bibo, who along with his brothers had opened several mercantile stores in the territory, established a branch store in Laguna adjacent to the railroad tracks.

The advent of mass automobile production in 1901 followed by the introduction of the Model T Ford in 1909 created both the need and demand for improved roads throughout the United States. During the early 1900s Congress passed a law claiming eminent domain over Pueblo lands for public use, such as railroad and highway rights-of-way. This law gave federal and state governments authority to improve or construct roads through Indian reservation lands without tribal consent. The law was not repealed until 1975.

Automobiles were not driven to Laguna until about 1915. The only roads were wagon trails. Lee Marmon recalls:

> I remember my dad telling the story of one of the first cars to come to Laguna. Gus Weiss, who ran one of the trading posts, won a new 1915 red Buick in a contest run by the *Albuquerque Journal.* Gus drove the car from Albuquerque to Laguna. In those days, the only way to get here was to drive from Albuquerque south to Los Lunas, then take the old wagon road from Los Lunas to Laguna. The road was pretty rough, and there was no bridge across the Rio San José. People had to drive through it, and that's one reason wagons had such large wheels. Well, the car got stuck in the river, and people from the village, who had all been waiting to see Gus's new car when he arrived, had to pull it out of the river with a team of horses.

Increasing demand for better roads throughout the country led to the planning and construction of Route 66 from Chicago to Los Angeles. The new highway opened in 1926 and was rerouted several times over the years. Early construction of Route 66 west of Albuquerque went south to Los Lunas, west to cross the Rio Puerco, and then northwest to Laguna, a distance of about seventy miles. Across the Laguna reservation, the road passed by the villages of Mesita, Old Laguna, New Laguna, Paraje, and Casa Blanca.

At the village of Laguna, the 1926 version of Route 66 was constructed over the wagon road from Los Lunas. Approaching the village from the

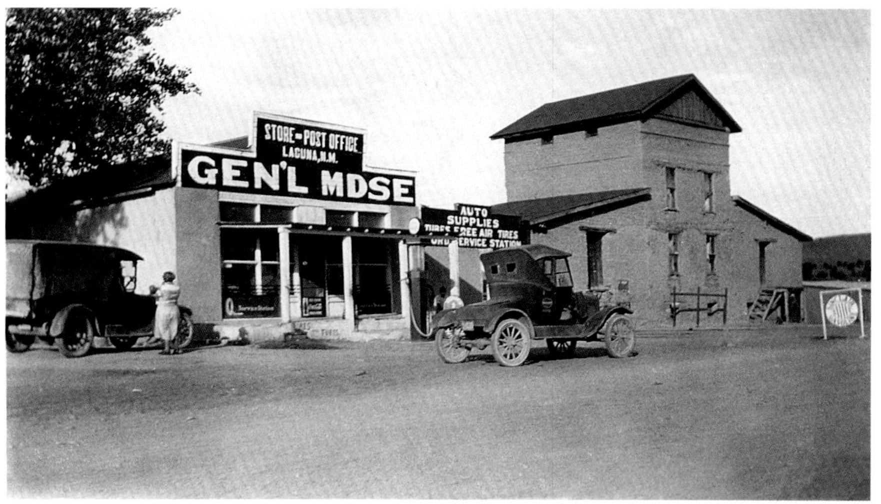

Laguna trading post and flour mill run by the Gunn brothers and Siegfried Abraham, circa 1920. John Gunn constructed the first flour mill at Laguna in 1893. It was near the banks of the Rio San José and was destroyed by a flood later that decade. He later opened the second flour mill, pictured here next to the trading post. Note the gasoline pump in front of the trading post and that Laguna now has a post office. Photographer unknown. Courtesy of Ron Fernandez.

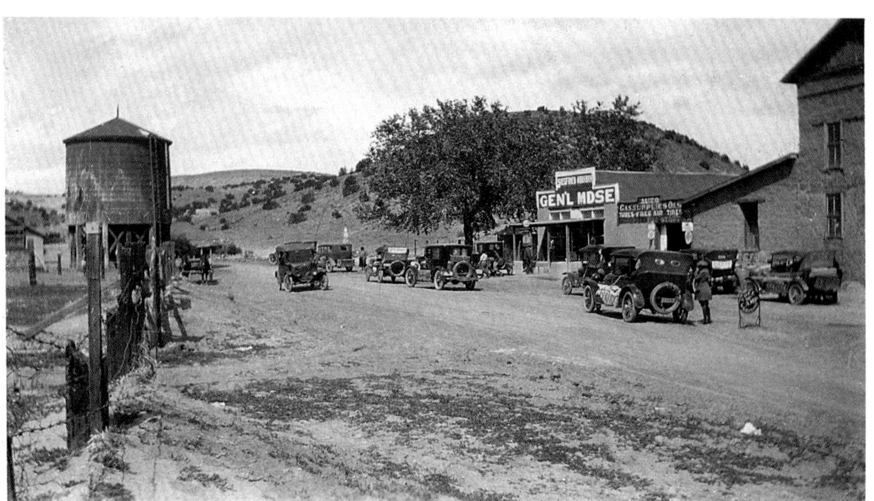

The original U.S. 66 entering Laguna from the south (looking north), circa 1926. The flour mill is still next to the trading post, now owned by Siegfried Abraham. Although the railroad tracks were removed years earlier, the AT&SF Railway water tower is still in place. Photographer unknown. Courtesy of Ron Fernandez.

south, the new highway crossed the Rio San José bridge, passed the flour mill and Gunn Trading Post to the railroad trackbed and the AT&SF water tower, and turned west to follow the old railroad trackbed around the village.

The Lagunas complained that the traffic near the village was dangerous and disruptive and petitioned to have the route changed. By the end of the decade, the Pueblo leadership successfully petitioned to have the road moved north of Laguna.

In 1934, Route 66 was rerouted about one hundred yards north of the trading post. Seigfried Abraham abandoned the original Laguna trading post, opened a Conoco gas station, and started construction of a trading

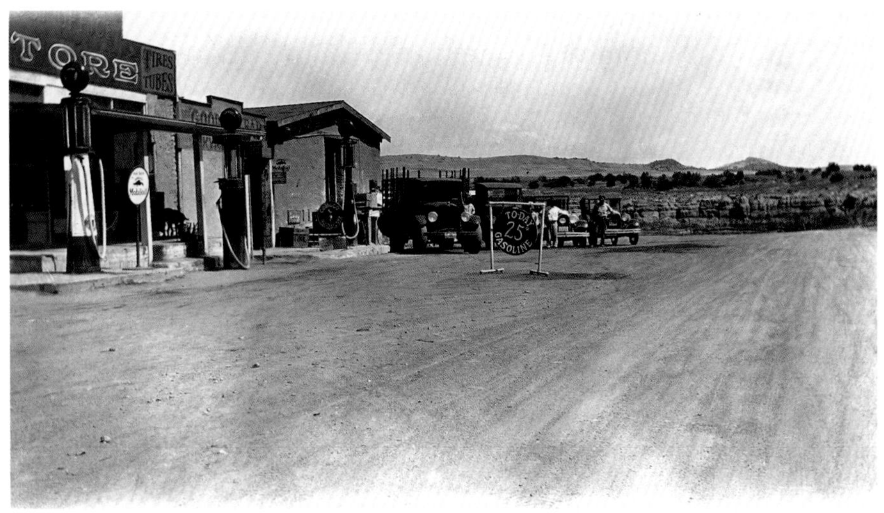

An expanded gasoline service station with two pumps in front of the trading post, circa 1929. Route 66 had opened three years earlier. Gasoline was twenty-five cents a gallon. The flour mill has now been dismantled. Photographer unknown. Courtesy of Ron Fernandez.

post adjacent to the new gas station. At the time, the new Route 66 was still a dirt road. Both facilities closed with the death of Sigfreid Abraham in 1938. They reopened in 1945, operated by Joe Fernandez and his wife, Rebecca Abraham Fernandez (Sigfreid's daughter). They made a number of improvements and upgrades, including adding a butcher shop, walk-in refrigerator, self-service, and a wider line of products. Following Joe Fernandez's death in 1972, his sons Ron and Arnie took over the operation.

Route 66 was realigned in 1937 so that the highway bypassed Los Lunas and went directly west from Albuquerque, up Nine Mile Hill, across the Rio Puerco, and past all the villages on the reservation except Old Laguna. The rerouting across New Mexico lowered the total road distance across the state from 507 to 399 miles.

Route 66 played an important role during the Depression years. Lee Marmon explains:

> Route 66 was the main highway for people who had lost their farms during the Dust Bowl times and the Depression of the early thirties. They came from Texas, Oklahoma, and Kansas, heading for California. It was like a scene from the movie *The Grapes of Wrath.* Families would come through in old jalopies with all their kids, and grandma or grandpa, along with their dog or cat—even chickens. Their cars were filled with as many possessions as they could stuff in them. They would pass through Laguna with no food and no money, and they would be running out of gas. They were mostly honest, hardworking people

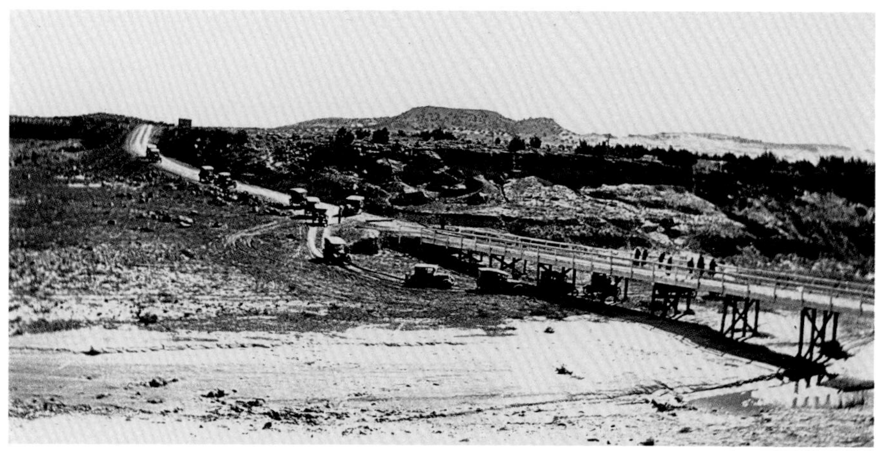

U.S. 66 wooden bridge over the Rio San José, circa 1928. As part of the new highway system, wooden bridges were constructed over the Rio San José. Occasionally, an auto accident on a bridge would cause the structure to catch fire and stop traffic for several days until a new bridge could be built. Here, cars are detoured under the wooden bridge and must ford the Rio San José to get to Laguna. Photographer unknown. Courtesy of Ron Fernandez.

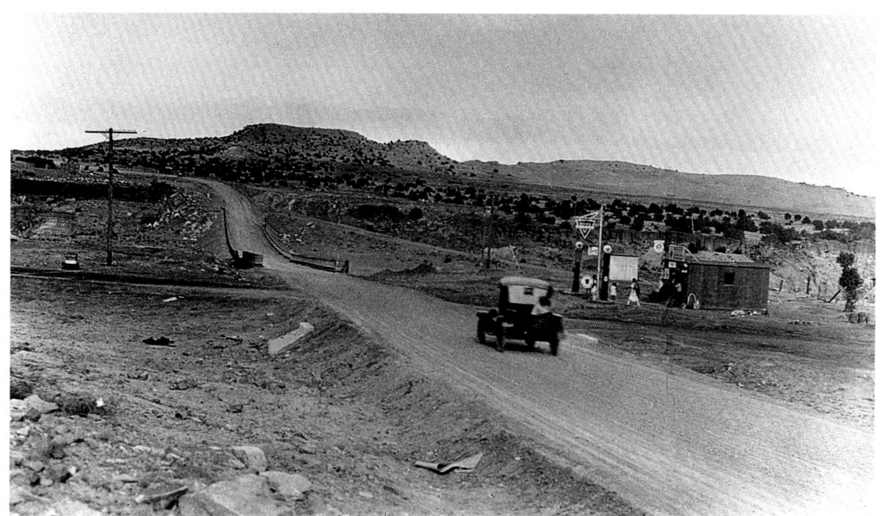

Siegfried Abraham built the first Laguna gas station on Route 66 after the highway was rerouted away from the village in 1934. Note the wooden bridge over the Rio San José and the still unpaved road. Photographer unknown (circa 1935). Courtesy of Ron Fernandez.

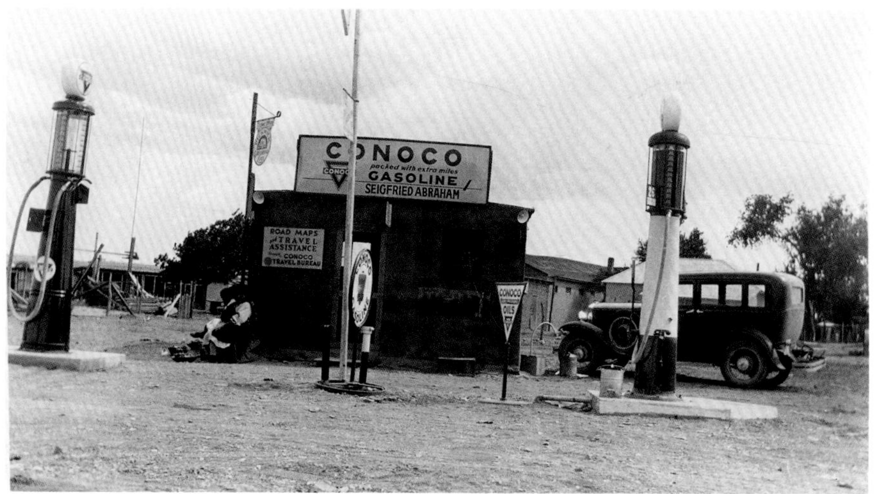

Close-up of Siegfried Abraham's gas station on rerouted U.S. 66, circa 1935. Note the Conoco station's two vintage gas pumps and the Nehi Cola sign. Gasoline was manually pumped up into the clear glass measuring containers near the top and then allowed to flow by gravity into the automobile's gas tank. Photographer unknown. Courtesy of Ron Fernandez.

down on their luck. They were proud, never asking for a handout but asking for work to buy food or gasoline. Sometimes there was no work, so local people would give them enough gas to get to Grants.

My grandpa Jack Stagner and uncle Grover Stagner built an auto campground with eleven cabins on the Marmon compound. We would rent them for $1.23 or $1.50 a night. Many of the people were destitute. Some were sick. One night we heard screams from the auto camp. A woman was having a baby and then it died. We buried it in the next yard where my grandfather was buried, and the family moved on.

The trading posts brought significant changes to the Laguna reservation, including the opportunity to trade locally produced agricultural products (wool, meat, vegetables, grains) and pottery for manufactured goods, fuel for heating and oil lamps, processed foods, and other products previously unavailable to the population.

The coming of the railroad initiated a series of changes in the way of life on the reservation. The new Route 66 increased the rate of change dramatically. Lagunas had new doors opened to them with regard to employment, as well as business opportunities on both an individual and tribal level. They were able to travel more easily to seek opportunities at greater distances from their homes. There was greater and easier access to goods and services from outside the reservation. Prior to the coming of the railroad

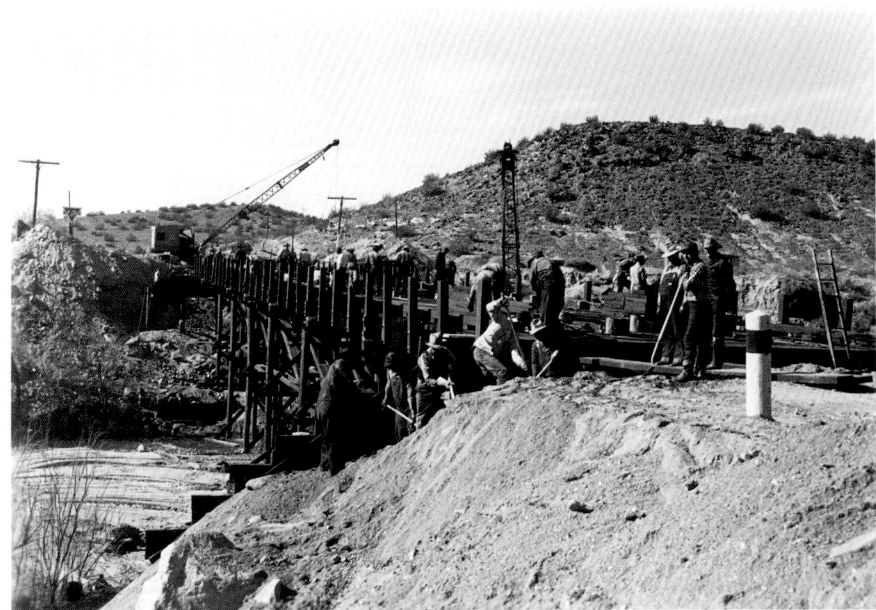

Rebuilding the wooden bridge over the Rio San José, circa 1934. The bridge was destroyed several times, either by fire following an accident or by a flooding Rio San José. Photographer unknown. Courtesy of Lee Marmon.

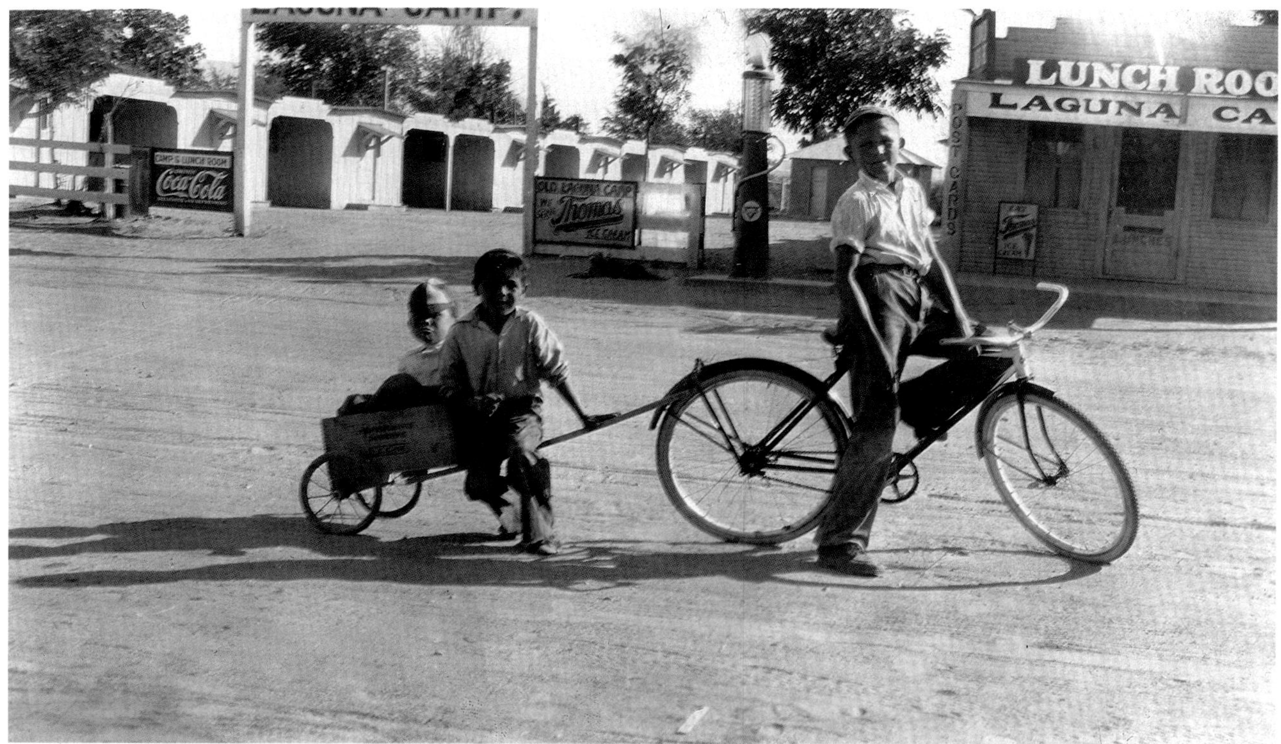

Laguna auto camp, circa 1931. The camp was constructed and run by the Stagner family in the old Baptist compound area. The little boy sitting in the cart is Lee Marmon. His brother, Polly, is next to him. Lee's cousin, T. K. Evans, is riding the bike. Photographer unknown. Courtesy of Lee Marmon.

and Route 66, agriculture had been the mainstay of the Laguna economy. But agriculture gradually declined as men began working for the railroad and other employers, and others began producing pottery and other goods for the tourist trade. Women progressively entered the economic workforce as demand increased for pottery and other artistic products and crafts.

In the 1960s, Route 66 was replaced by Interstate 40 as the major trade route. Constructed just south of and parallel to the old Route 66, the interstate brought even more changes to the Laguna economy, including a commercial center, the Dancing Eagle Casino at Casa Blanca, and the Route 66 Casino just west of the Rio Puerco. Unfortunately, many small "mom and pop" businesses that had catered to the tourist trade along Route 66 disappeared.

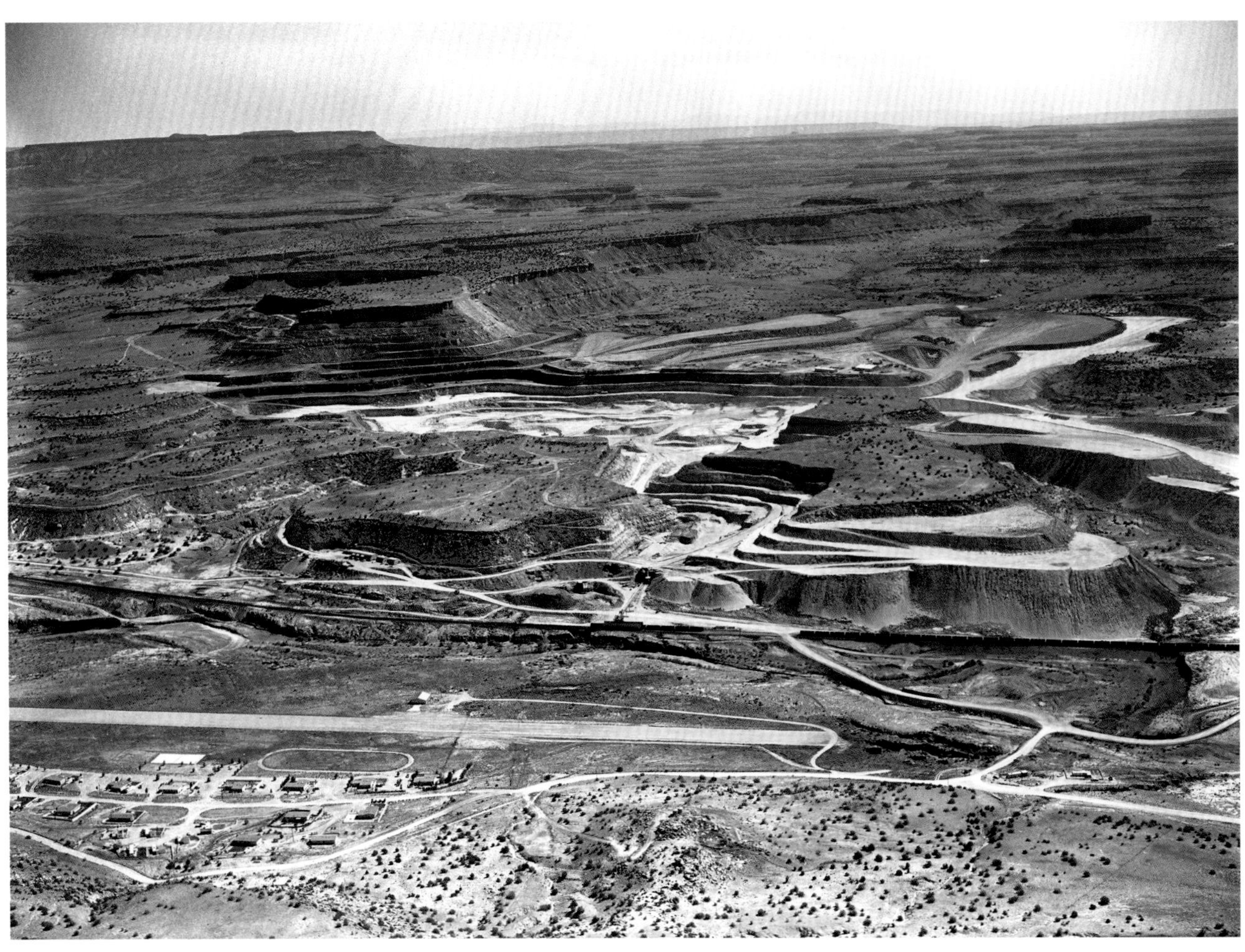

The Jackpile Mine Aerial View #1. Located adjacent to the village of Paguate, the Jackpile Mine was the world's largest open-pit uranium mine until it closed in 1982. Ore from this mine ranked among the most highly concentrated in all the mines on the Colorado Plateau. Photo by Lee Marmon (1958).

CHAPTER TEN

The Jackpile Mine

In the spring of 1950, uranium was discovered about fifteen miles west of Grants, New Mexico. Further exploration led to the discovery in 1951 of a large deposit of uranium ore near the village of Paguate on the Laguna reservation. This new site was discovered by an Anaconda Copper Company pilot using an airborne Geiger counter. The land team sent to investigate included a man named Jack, who, at the site, needed to relieve himself. The next day, as the story goes, the pilot was directed to return to the site; he told mining office employees he was going back to "Jack's pile"—hence the name Jackpile Mine.[1]

In 1952, an agreement was reached between the Pueblo of Laguna and the Anaconda Copper Company allowing Anaconda to mine the uranium on reservation land. The agreement required Anaconda to pay royalties to the pueblo, hire tribal members to work in the mine, and reclaim the site once mining operations ceased. The millions of dollars in royalties were used to build a tribal office building, support a tribal police force, and generate other activities greatly beneficial to the tribe. The jobs significantly increased the standard of living for those tribal members who worked in the mine.

Underground mining operations began in 1953 but later expanded to open-pit mining. In 1982, after twenty-nine years of operation, all mining ceased. Three open-pit mines and nine underground mines had been created; one of the underground mines tunneled directly under the village of Paguate. At its peak, the mine operated twenty-four hours a day, seven days a week. Blasting commenced two to three times a day, sometimes shaking and cracking the adobe buildings in Paguate.

Hundreds of Lagunas worked in the mines over the years. Many tribal members were employed as heavy-equipment operators, truck drivers, drillers, and crushers. Others worked in maintenance operations and as office personnel. They changed their livelihoods from farming and hunting and other customary vocations to jobs with regular hours and higher incomes. With regularly scheduled hours, many members of the community were no longer able to participate in customary tribal meetings, dances, and ceremonies.

What seemed like a windfall and something beneficial to the tribe was not without hidden risks, however. The occupational health risks for uranium miners and the environmental health risks surrounding uranium mines were not clearly understood or appreciated at the time; no significant regulations existed to protect miners—or families living near a mine. Years later, the tribe paid a price through the occupational and environmental diseases that followed.

The increase in personal income resulted in significant lifestyle changes. Riding in cars and pickup trucks replaced walking or running from one location to another. Sugary soft drinks, candy bars, and processed foods began to replace the traditional Native American diet of basic grains, range-fed animals, and game. TV replaced exertional recreation and other healthful activities. Obesity and diabetes and the complications inherent in these conditions began to appear in the tribe.

Large piles of tailings were produced during the mining process. These mountains of mining waste were situated adjacent to the mine, presenting an environmental hazard to the surrounding area—particularly the village of Paguate—through contamination of the air and groundwater. The reclamation services required in the contract were not provided in a timely manner, and years of negotiations between the Pueblo of Laguna and the Atlantic Richfield Company (who purchased the rights to the mine from Anaconda) ensued before reaching an agreement. Ultimately, the company gave the pueblo $45 million as a cash settlement. The pueblo created the Laguna Construction Company to reclaim the 2,700-acre site, providing jobs for many tribal members. Work on the restoration project extended from 1989 to 1994.

Once a significant source of employment and royalty income, the Jackpile Mine closed in 1982 because of decreased demand for uranium. Fear among tribal members was also mounting regarding environmental contamination and potential occupational and environmental disease related to the mine. The Laguna Tribal Council has declared a moratorium on uranium mining on the reservation, and efforts are underway to prevent new mines in areas adjacent to the reservation.

In 2012, renewed interest emerged in opening not only the Jackpile Mine but also other mines near the reservation boundaries. This increased

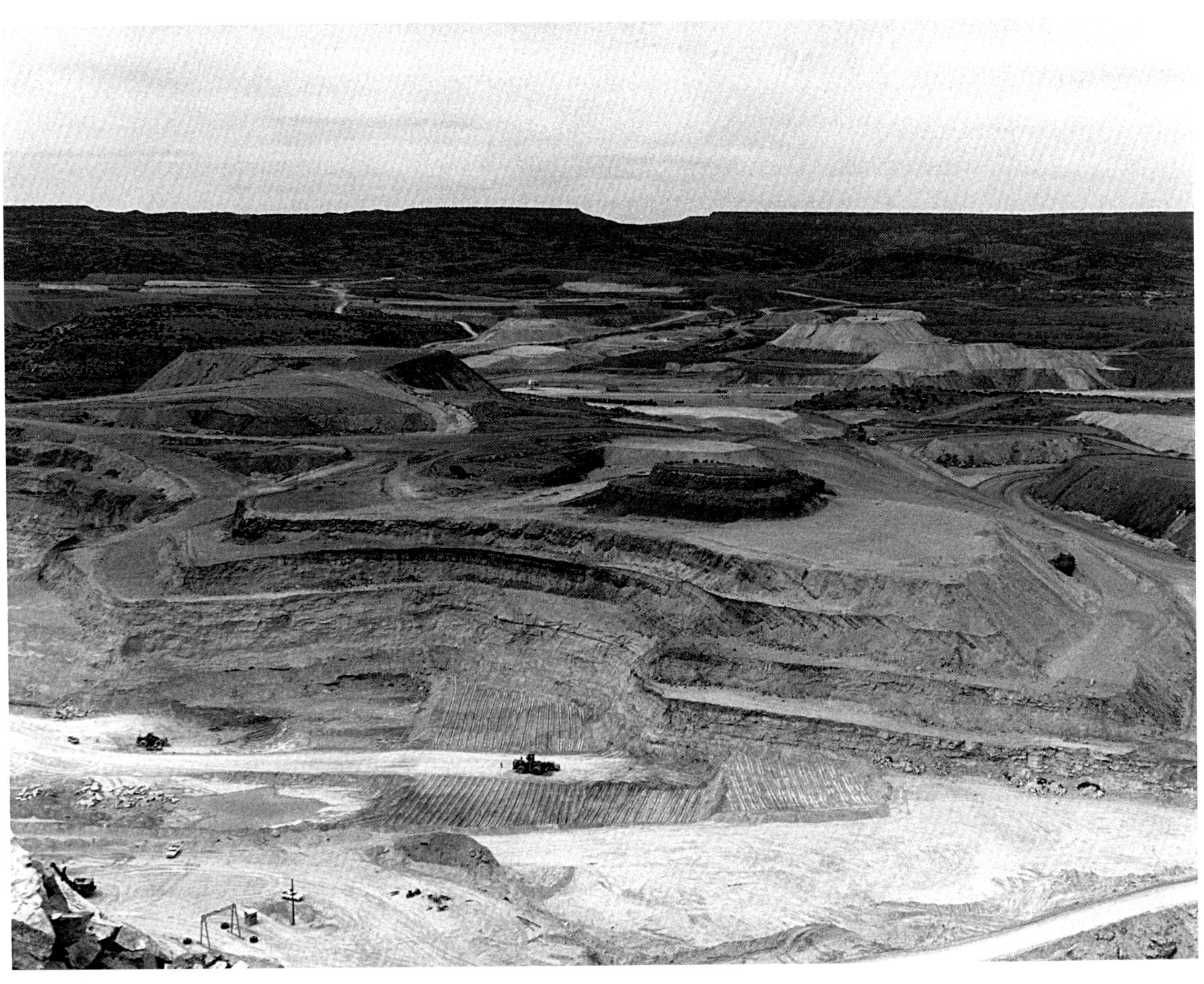

The Jackpile Mine Aerial View #2.
Photo by Lee Marmon (1958)

interest in opening the mines presents a difficult dilemma for the tribe. First and foremost, Mount Taylor and the surrounding area is considered sacred land, given to them by the Creator. Prior to the formation of the reservation, Lagunas roamed and hunted the area and performed religious and other ceremonies there. Laguna legends warn of defiling the sacred land and foretell disaster should these rules be violated. The tribe is adamant about preventing the opening of not only the Jackpile Mine on reservation land but also those mines on land once belonging to them. They worry about the pollution of their water and air, the potential for disease from uranium and other heavy-metal contamination, and other disasters as predicted in the legends.

CHAPTER ELEVEN

Customs and Culture

Material from this chapter was transcribed by Tom Corbett from recorded interviews with Lee Marmon.

I was fortunate to be able to document the changing culture of Laguna in photographs over the years. Some of the customs I observed and photographed are not practiced anymore. Others, like the dances and other religious activities, will continue unchanged. I hope these photographs will help to pass the old customs and activities on to future generations.

A few years ago I made a copy of an old family photograph of my aunt Edith and aunt Alice. It was taken in about 1912. The photographer took great pains to get them dressed up in buckskin with authentic headbands and to pose beside a mountain stream with tall trees in the background. It was wonderful for me to look at the photograph and realize that my aunts were once young and beautiful. I had only known them many years later after their youth had passed. That photograph brought back memories of the time I spent as a young boy listening to stories my aunt Alice remembered hearing about the Civil War from her father, Walter G. Marmon, who first came to New Mexico in 1868 to survey for the government. I am telling the stories about these photographs now to show how photography can reach across time to bring back images of long ago and how it can change a person's feelings about some long-forgotten person, event, or place.

Other changes have occurred that I cannot document in photographs. As I walk through the village, I notice people speaking to each other less in Keresan and more in English. The Laguna Constitution provides for one member of the tribal council to be an interpreter. This position was necessary in the past because the meetings were held in Keresan. Some of the tribal officials did not speak English in the old days, but now just about everybody does. Sadly, many of the young people today do not speak Keresan. The old stories and legends, the basis for the Laguna culture, used to be passed down by word of mouth in Keresan, from older generations to younger generations, and now some of the details and meanings of the stories are lost in translation. The trend appears to be reversing, however. The Laguna language is being taught in the Head Start program, and classes in Keresan are now offered at the Laguna-Acoma High School.

Another thing I notice is that the people today are more prosperous than they were in earlier years. They have modern appliances and use cell phones. Not many families had cars when I was growing up in Laguna, and they did not travel very much. When someone did get a car, it usually was an older vehicle, not in good shape. Today almost every family has a car, and most of them are new or relatively new, and people travel a lot.

Health care has improved markedly. Public health programs over the years have provided indoor plumbing and sanitation facilities for homes. A new program is underway to jointly replace the older deteriorating plumbing facilities and bring in high-speed Internet to each home.

It is sad to see some of the changes that have occurred, but the increases in the standard of living, health care, and public health have been remarkable and good for the people.

Laguna Tribal Dress (Circa 1880)

Laguna tribal dress. Photo by Ben Wittick (circa 1880). Courtesy of the Palace of the Governors Photographic Archives (NMHM/DCA), #15985.

Western-style clothing has largely replaced the traditional Laguna apparel. Traditional dress is now worn only at ceremonial times and for dances.

This photograph, taken by early western photographer George Benjamin "Ben" Wittick (1845–1903), demonstrates the traditional Laguna clothing worn by men and women at that time.

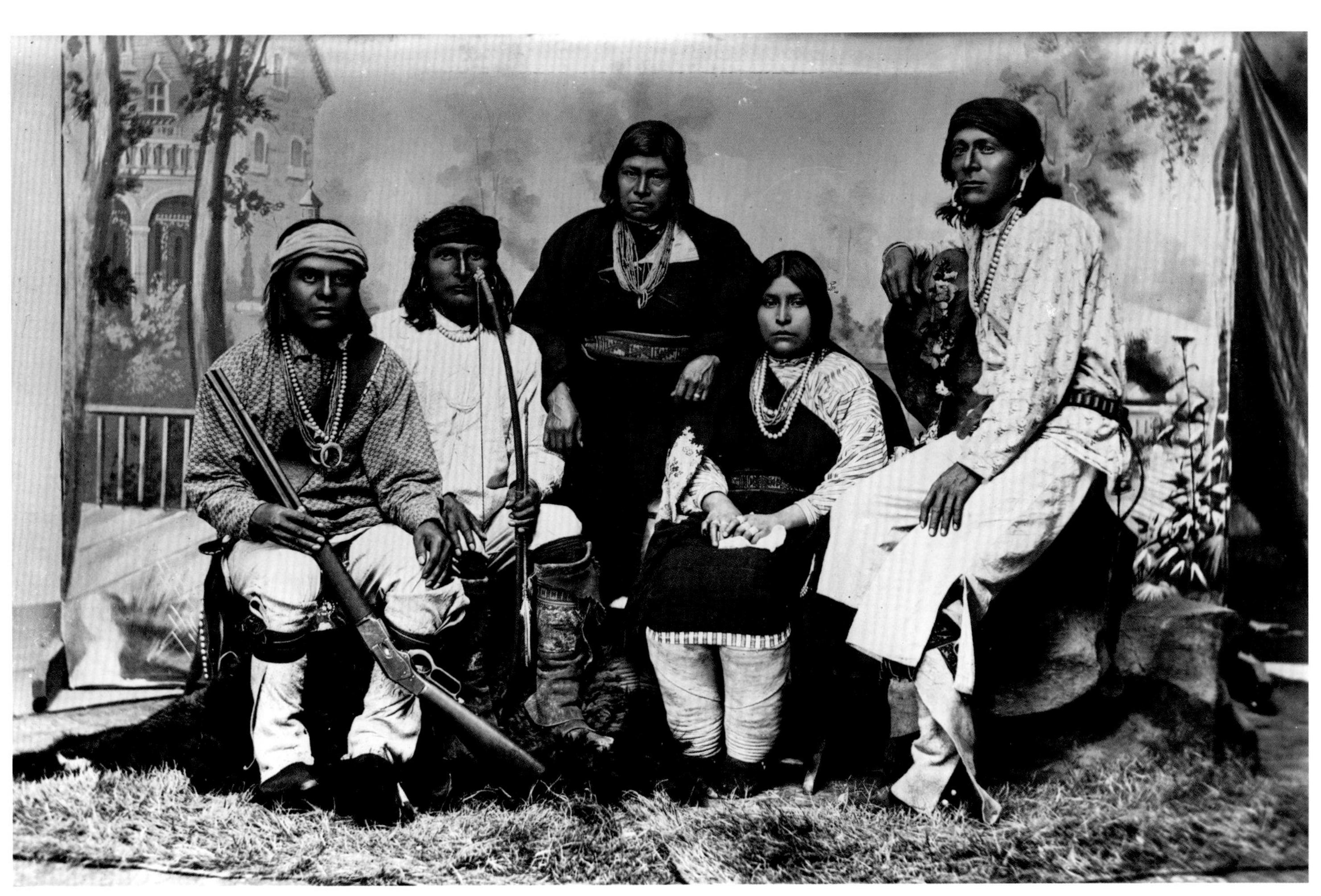

Old Laguna (1955)

Old Laguna. Photo by Lee Marmon (1955).

The village of Old Laguna has changed markedly over the past century. The people lived in typical pueblo-style homes—one- and two-story structures composed of stacked stones or adobe covered with plaster. Houses had no running water or plumbing until the 1960s. Outhouses were located at the lower edge of the village near the Rio San José.

As newer homes with more modern facilities were constructed in other areas of the reservation, people left the main village and abandoned many of the traditional homes. Many of these original pueblo-architecture homes have been torn down; only a fraction remain.

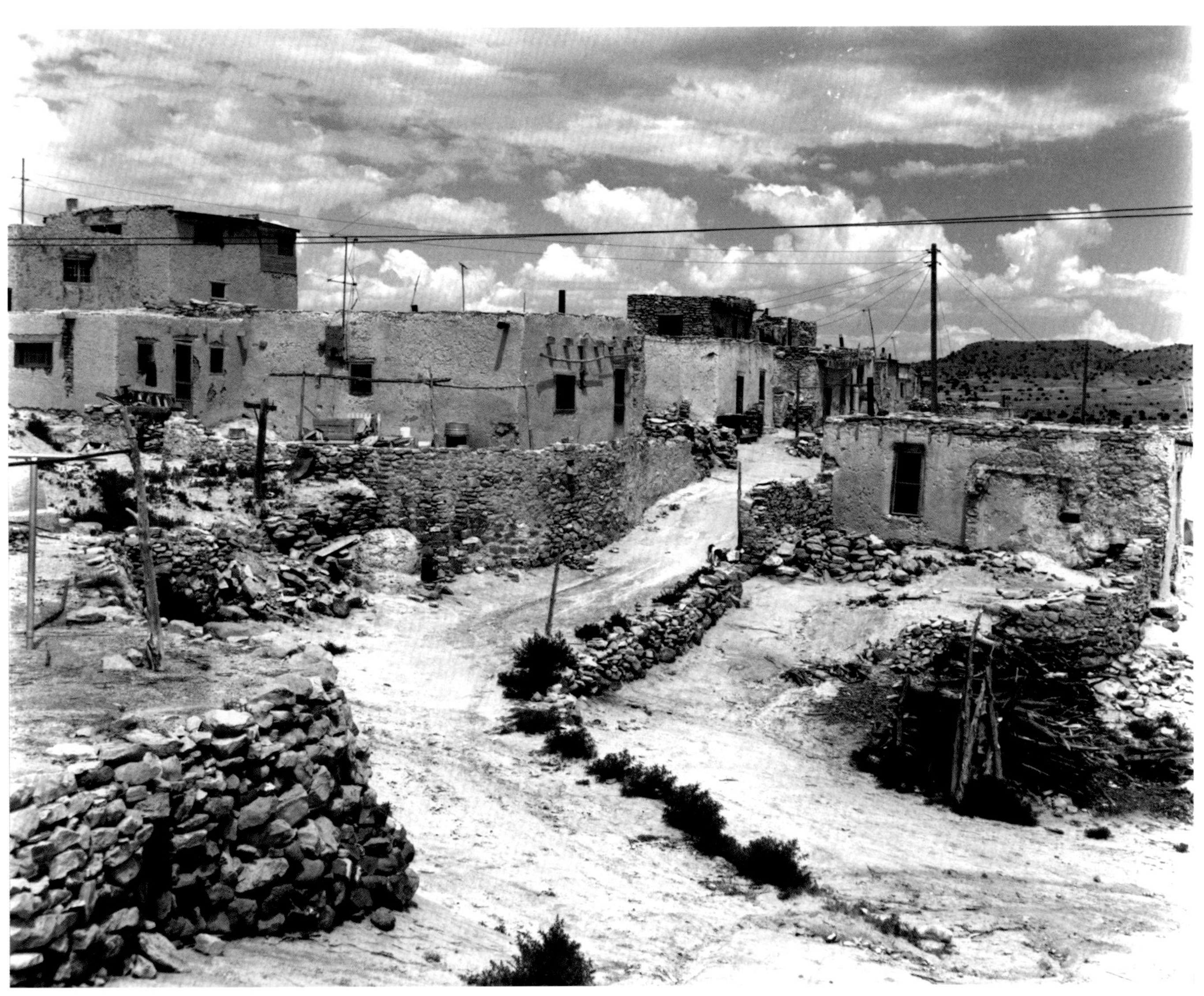

Last Wagons at Laguna (1949, 1953)

St. Joseph's Feast Day here in Laguna used to be one of the largest, if not *the* largest, native celebrations in the state. It was originally celebrated on March 19, but the date was changed to September 19 to take advantage of the harvest, and it became a big day in the fall for trading. On the 19th, church members would take the statue of St. Joseph out of the church and parade through the pueblo. They would then set the statue up in the plaza. There was feasting and dancing. Visitors from all over brought goods to trade.

During the busiest St. Joseph days, in 1937, 1938, and 1939, hundreds of covered wagons arrived from all over New Mexico and parts of Arizona. The Navajos were the most colorful. In wagons with white canvas covers, entire families would come a few days ahead of time and stay a few more days after the fiesta. They would set up camp in and around the village. At night you could see hundreds of campfires. When the morning came the first rays of the sun would strike the top of the Laguna Mission and slowly filter down to the covered wagons lined up along the top of the village and surrounding hills. It was a beautiful sight, and I can remember it very clearly. If I had a camera and had been able to record some of the sights, it would have been a wonderful record of days gone by.

The Navajo rugs, shirts, skirts, and colorful decorations of the horses would have made wonderful images; even photos in black and white would have made quite a record. The people who came to the fiesta were all dressed in their "fiesta best," and what an assortment of people they were! Jewelry and rugs were everywhere, and melons, corn, and chili were sold or traded. Pictures everywhere! The picture of the "last wagons" with my youngest daughter sitting on the fence is one of the few fiesta photographs I have from those days.

St. Joseph's Feast Day at Laguna. In the late 1930s and 1940s, hundreds of Navajo wagons camped in the fields around Laguna. Photo by Lee Marmon (1949).

The colorful sights of the fiesta along with the smell of campfires cooking mutton, chili stew, fry bread; the smell of boiling coffee in the old-style enamel

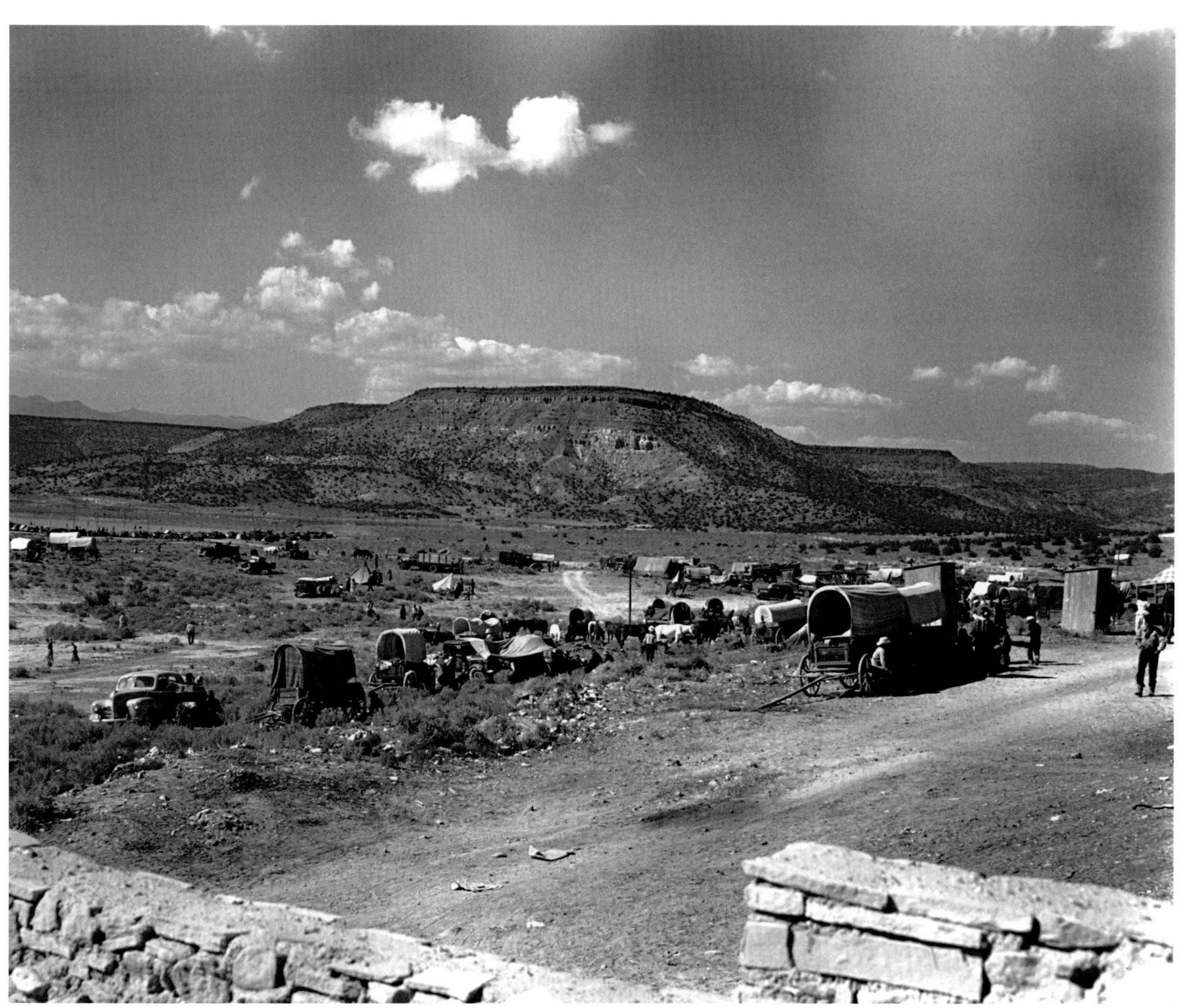

Last Wagons at Laguna. The last of the Navajo wagons passes the Marmon home as they leave Laguna. Photo by Lee Marmon (1953).

pot with a few chips gone; and the dust combined to make an aroma that couldn't be described except as "fiesta at Laguna." It has been over fifty years since the old-style fiesta I remember, and the smell is still as strong as yesterday.

Equally vivid is the sound of the drums and singing from the squaw dance the Navajos used to perform in front of the mission. They would start about midnight and sing and dance until the sun started peeking over the mesas to the east. Sometimes late at night, I can still hear the sounds that put me to sleep on September 19 over fifty years ago.

I think these memories had something to do with getting interested in preserving something that would someday be gone. Even with all this, I didn't realize how soon some of the old ways would disappear. World War II was the end of a lot of the old ways. Men went off to war and parts of the world they never dreamed they would see and probably had never heard of—and many never came back.

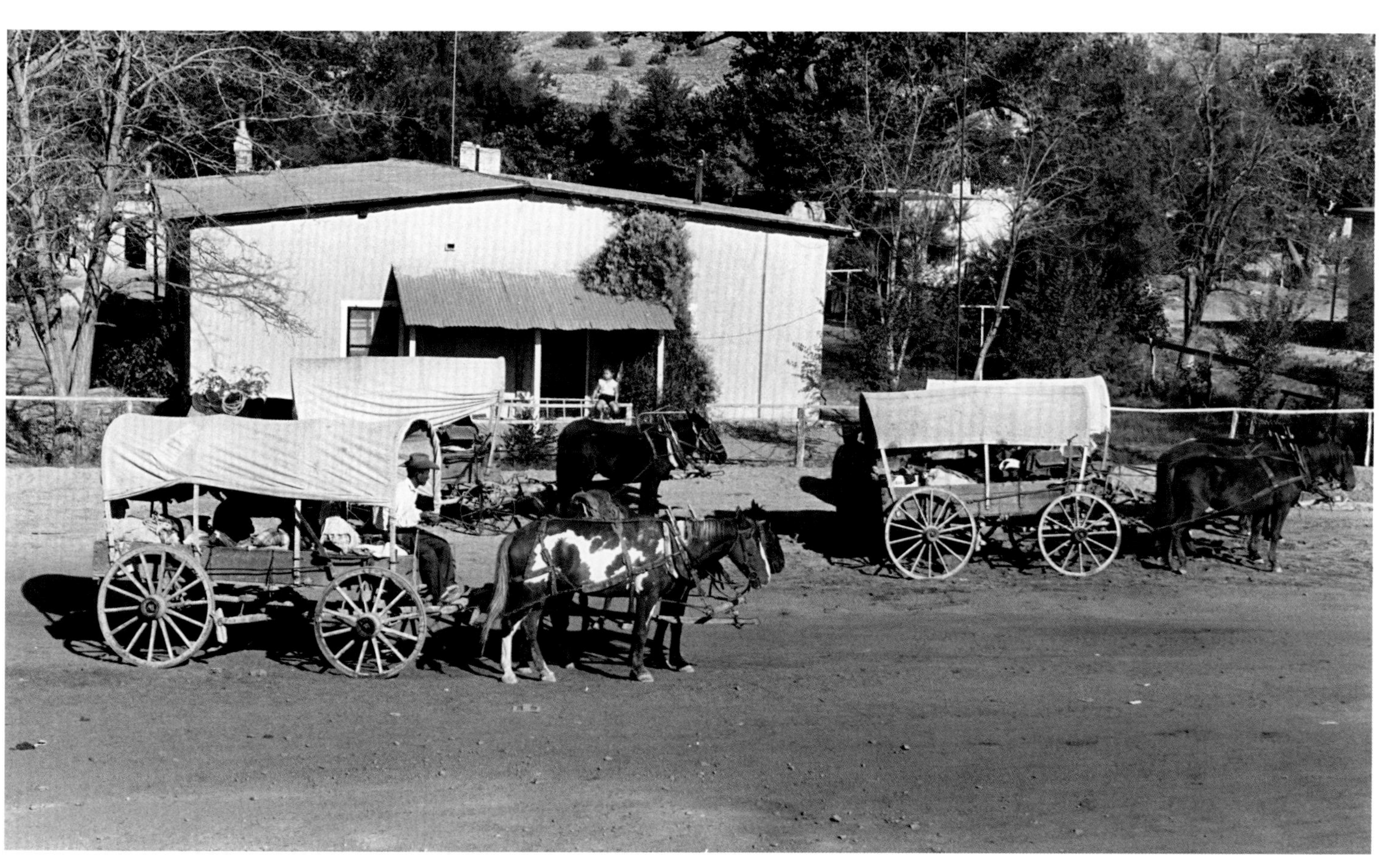

Cattle Drive (1955)

This photograph features a cattle drive from the L-Bar Ranch across Laguna land. The cattle men used to drive the cattle across the reservation.

We don't have as many cattle men and sheep men as we used to. Laguna had a lot of ranchers quit to work for the railroad. That was a more dependable income, so a lot of them liked to work and travel for the railroad. They got a free pass, and a lot of people moved to Winslow, Arizona, and Barstow and Richmond, California.

The drought during the 1930s drove a lot of the remaining ranchers out of business. Only a few of them came back. Then when the uranium mine opened, we lost more of the ranchers and sheepherders to salaried jobs. They became heavy-equipment operators and truck drivers and occupations like that.

There were a few families that hung on, and strangely enough, they are now better off than those who left to work in the uranium mine. The guys who worked in the mine made a lot of money, but they spent most of it. The cattle people just rode along steadily, and they have everything paid for and are doing quite well.

Cattle Drive. Photo by Lee Marmon (1955).

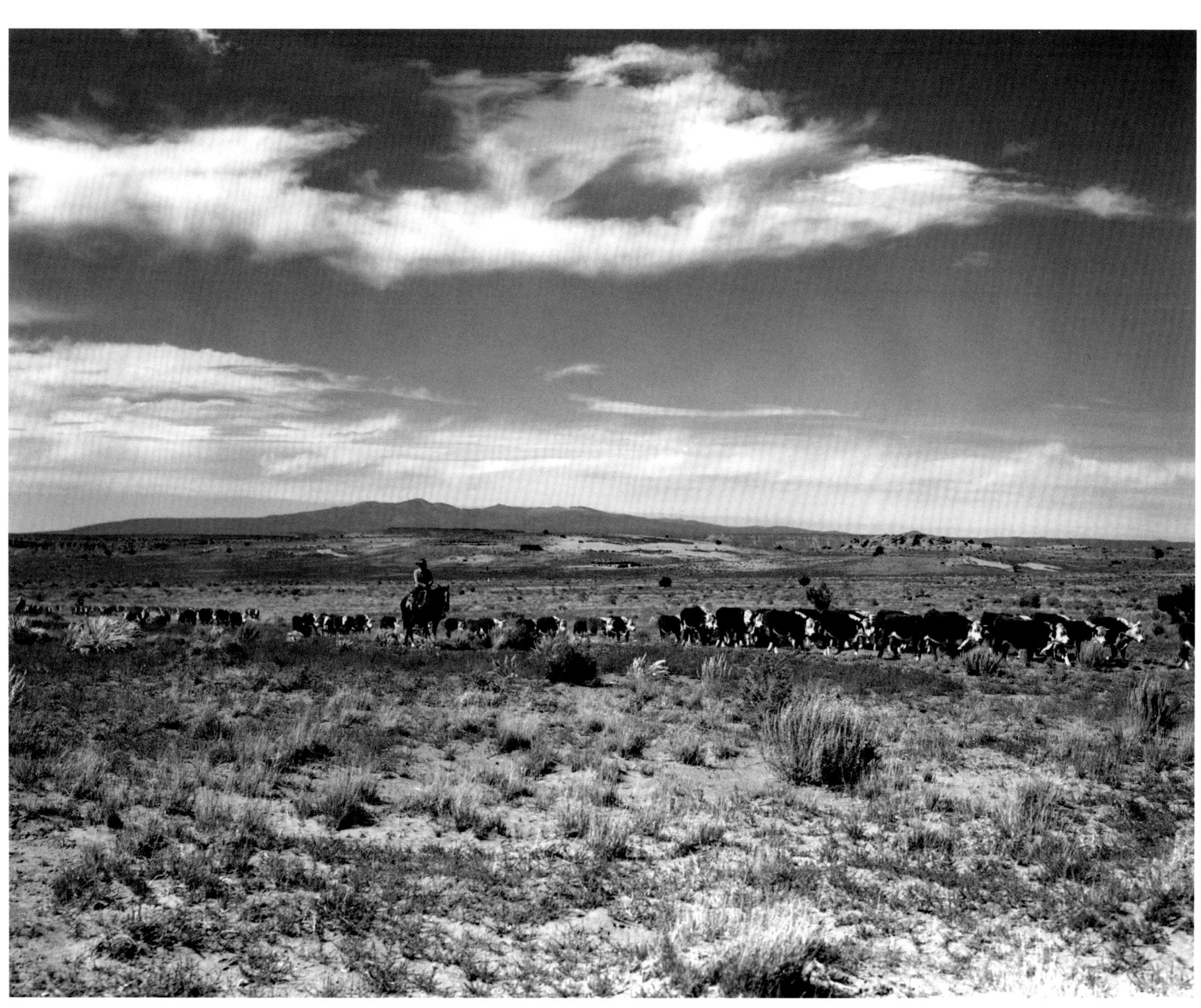

Bennie at Sheep Camp (1984)

Bennie at Sheep Camp. Photo by Lee Marmon (1984).

One of my favorite photographs is the one I call *Bennie at Sheep Camp.* One day in the summer of 1984, my son, Chris, and I went south on the road to Acoma, out to the sheep camp. Bennie was there on his horse, herding the sheep. We spent a little time there that day, taking pictures of Bennie. I took this great shot of him with his horse and the sheep and goats in the background—some of them cooling themselves in the sides of the sandstone cliffs.

Sheepherding has been a way of life for the Lagunas for centuries. It used to be a main source of income for the tribe. It began to decline with the coming of the railroad as many men switched from farming and ranching activities to salaried jobs.

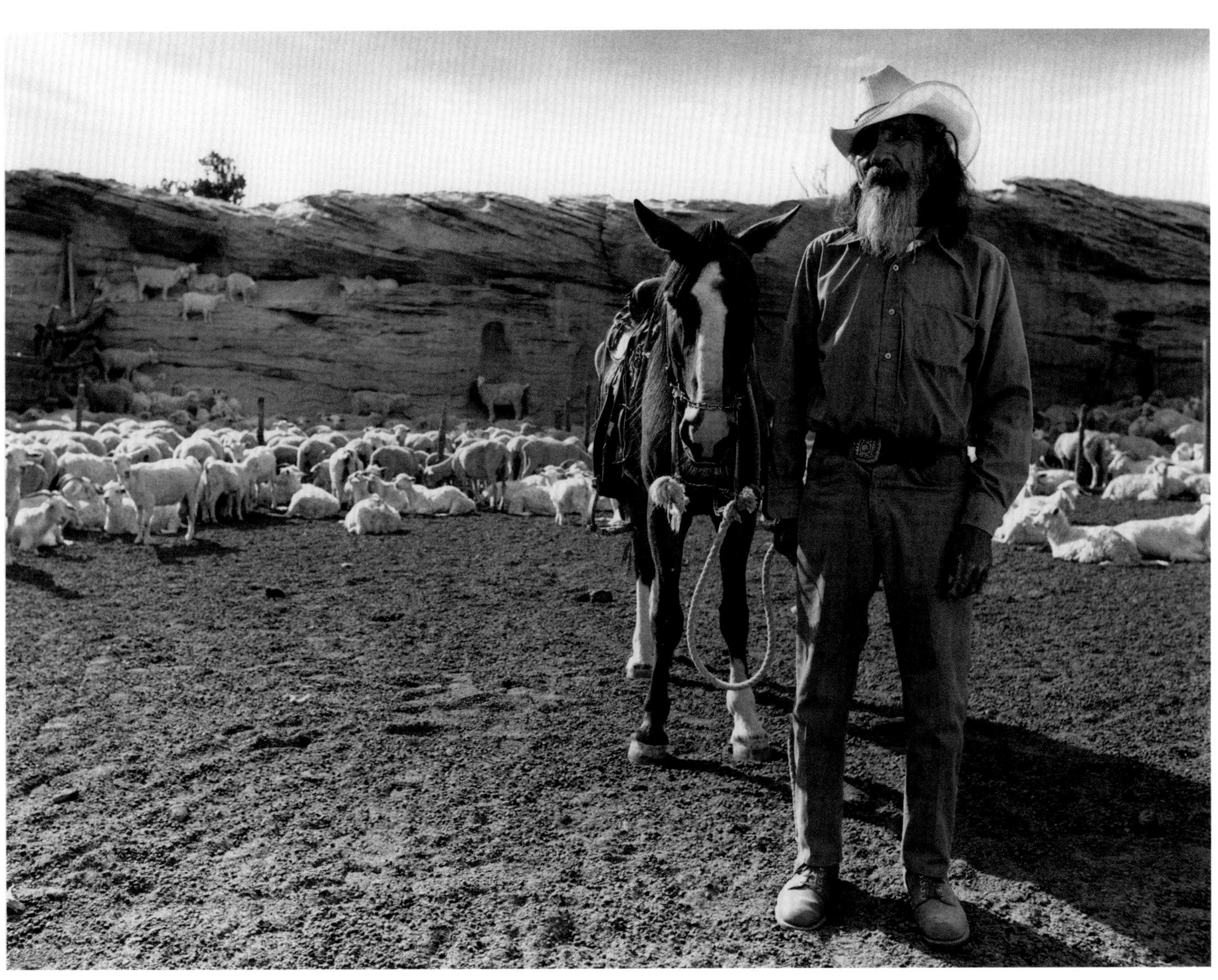

Blue Corn (1949)

I call this picture *Blue Corn*. I came across this older couple sitting on the step, with their little granddaughter, shucking blue corn—the kind they use to make blue cornmeal. The Laguna people don't raise as much corn now as they used to.

Agriculture used to be a major source of income for Laguna. But like the ranchers, many of the farmers preferred salaried jobs with dependable incomes and went to work for the railroad. Even more left farming when the Jackpile Mine opened.

People used to have farmland along the banks of the Rio San José. The farms had irrigation ditches and there was plenty of water. But when the Bluewater Dam was built in 1925, the amount of water flowing in the river was greatly reduced and there was no longer enough water to irrigate the crops.

Blue Corn. Photo by Lee Marmon (1949).

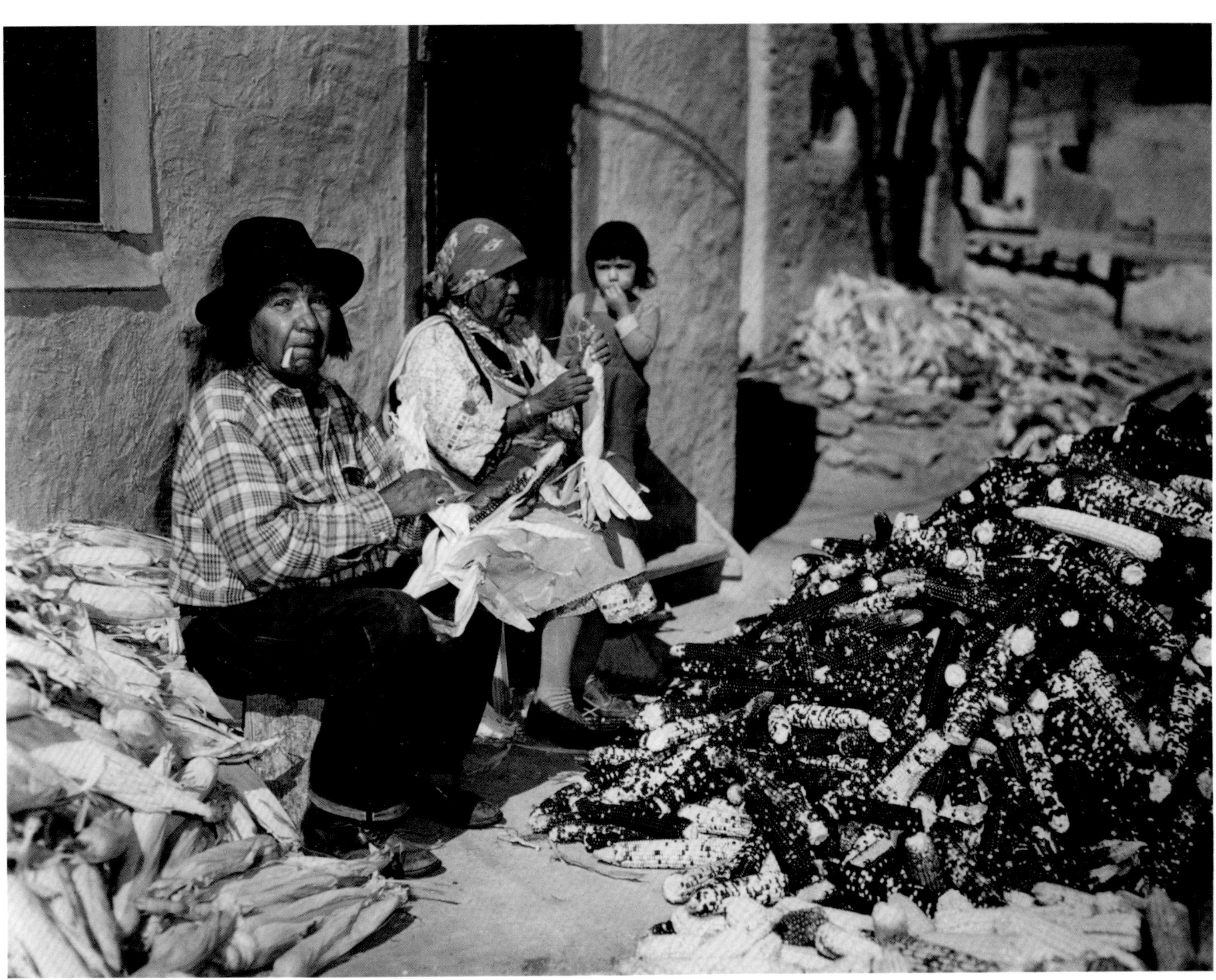

Women Grinding Plaster (1955)

While I drove around in the pickup delivering groceries, if I saw anything interesting going on, I would stop and get the camera out.

On one such afternoon, I passed a group of women who were grinding up plaster, getting it ready to plaster a house, so I stopped and took a picture of them. They put the white plaster, white clay they dug up west of the village, either in a pile or a tub to soak it down overnight to soften. But it still had lumps, so they had to use stones to grind it down in order to make a fine, smooth plaster. Then they mixed it with straw.

Most of the plastering was done by the women. They don't do that anymore, so this is a historical picture. Workers in this craft no longer take time to soak the plaster and grind it. Now everybody uses concrete plaster or regular plaster they buy in bags at the big-box or hardware stores.

Women Grinding Plaster. Photo by Lee Marmon (1955).

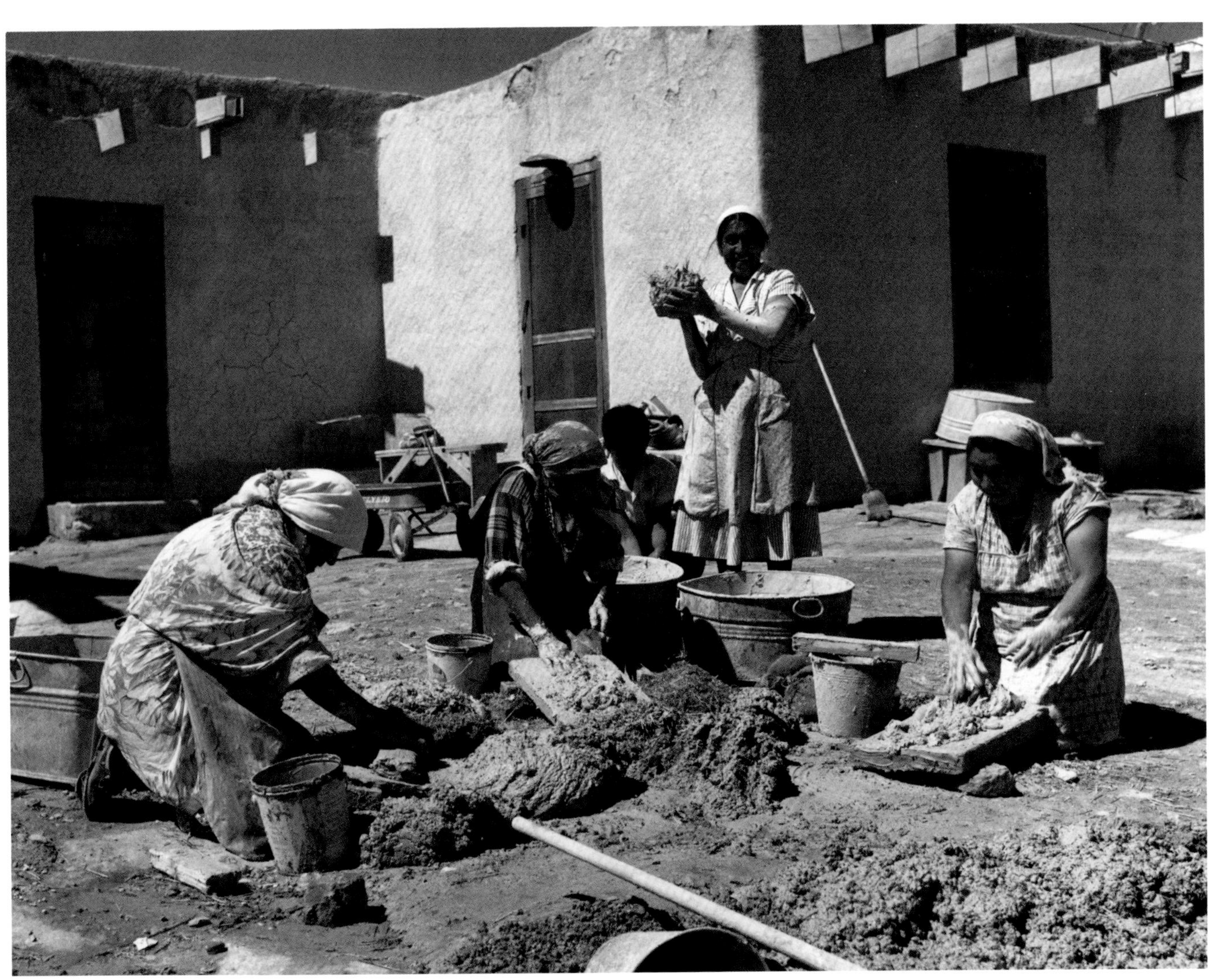

The Dances

Dancing is an integral part of Laguna culture. Some dances are social while others are deeply spiritual. Dances may celebrate particular events—historical or recent. Some are held publicly while those with deep religious significance are held in private settings, and photographs are strictly forbidden.

One particular dance commemorates the migration from White House to Laguna. All the people of the pueblo are invited to participate. As with all tribal dances, the rhythm and chanting or singing is provided by a group of drummers. The dancers—often hundreds of people—step rhythmically to the drums, counterclockwise around the periphery of the plaza. The dancers, dressed in traditional Laguna apparel, paint their hands white in honor of White Hands, the legendary leader who led the migration.

Other dances celebrate the hunt. Yet another celebrates victory in battle. Some, such as the Eagle Dance, employ ornate, complex costumes. The Deer Dance celebrates the hunt and the sacrifice made by this greatly prized animal to feed the pueblo.

I have captured images of dancers throughout my career. Presented here are images of Eagle Dancers, Buffalo Dancers, Deer Dancers, and others. Laguna Eagle Dancers are well known for their beautiful and graceful representation of this magnificent raptor.

Eagle Dancers #1. Photo by Lee Marmon (1962).

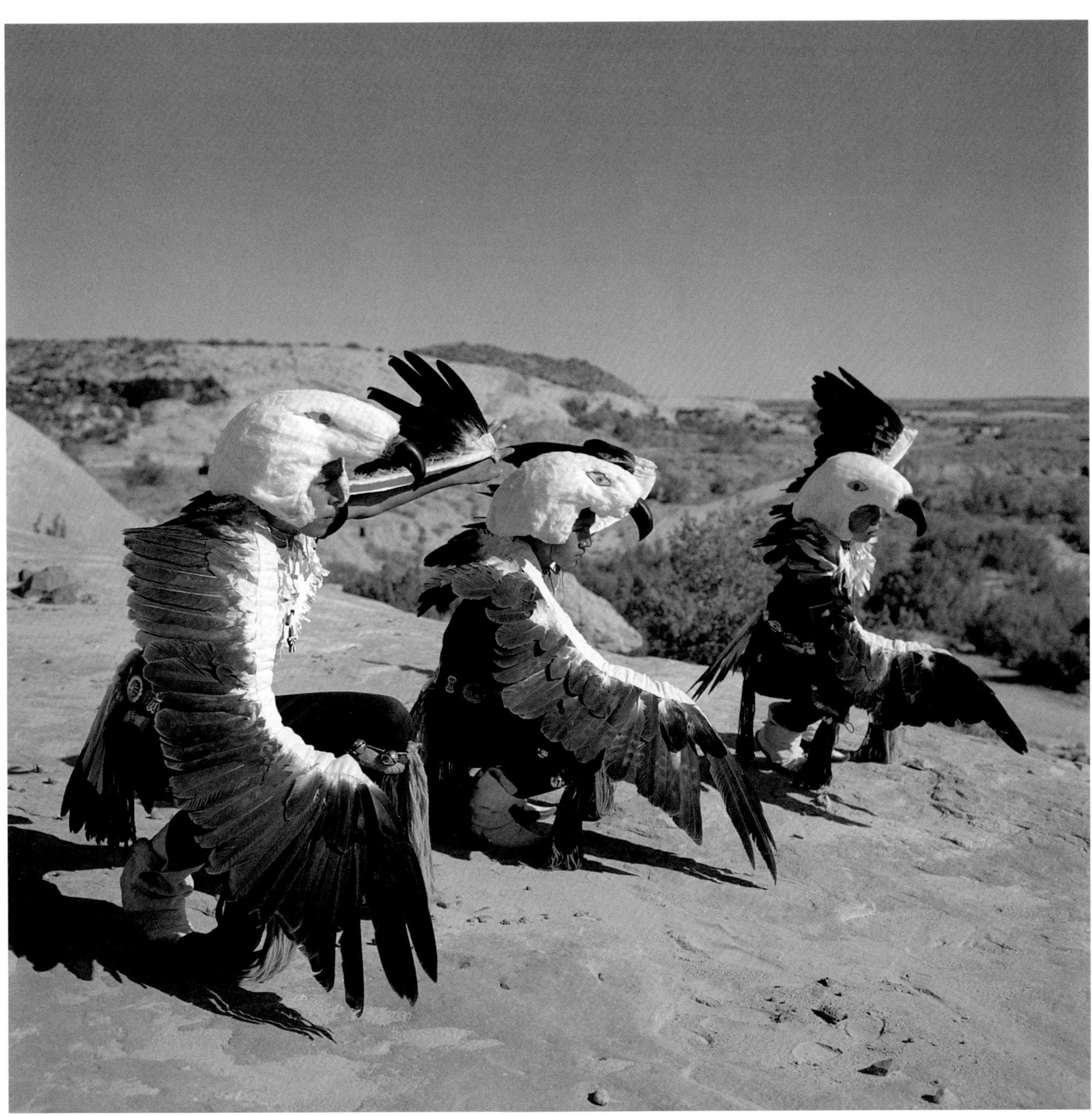

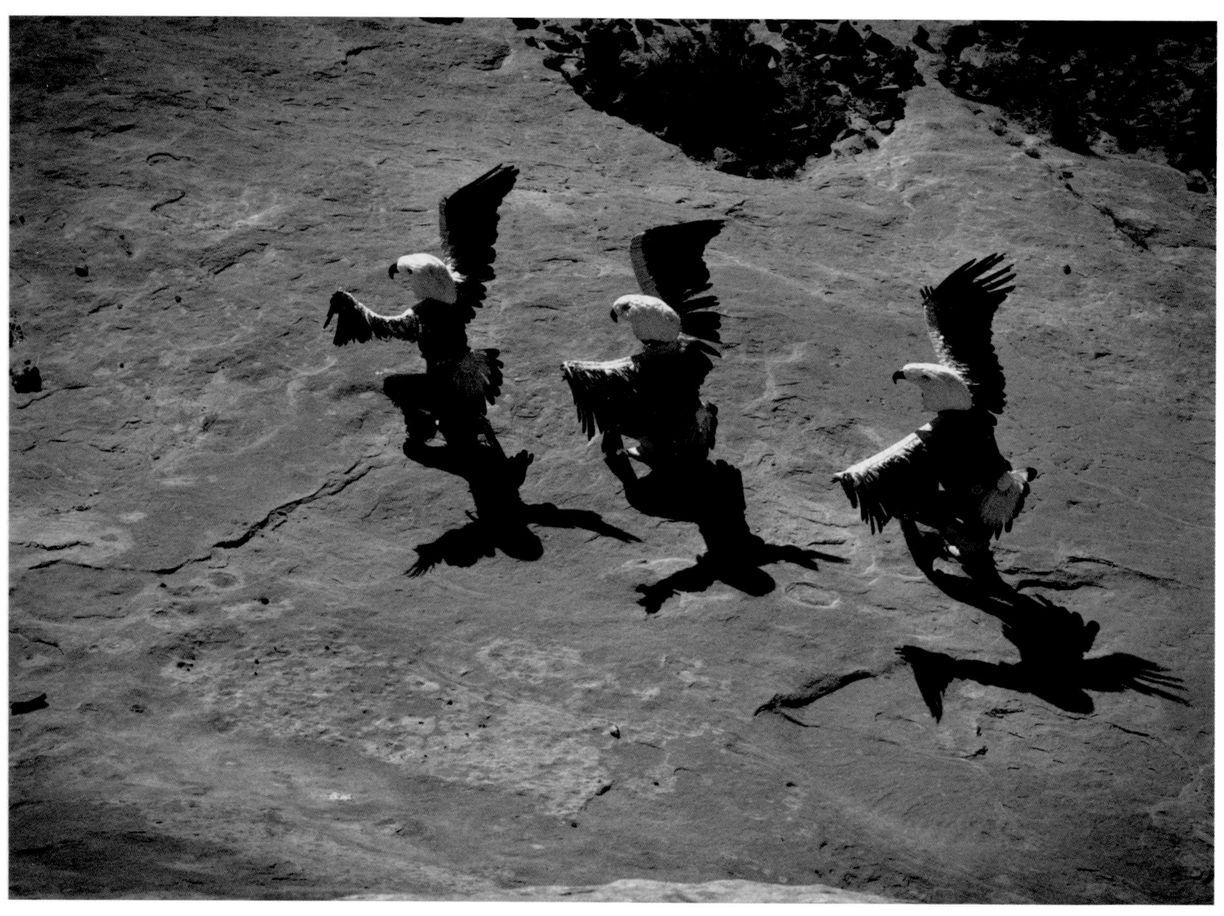

Eagle Dancers #2. Photo by
Lee Marmon (1962).

(*opposite*) *Buffalo Dancer #1*. Photo
by Lee Marmon (1962).

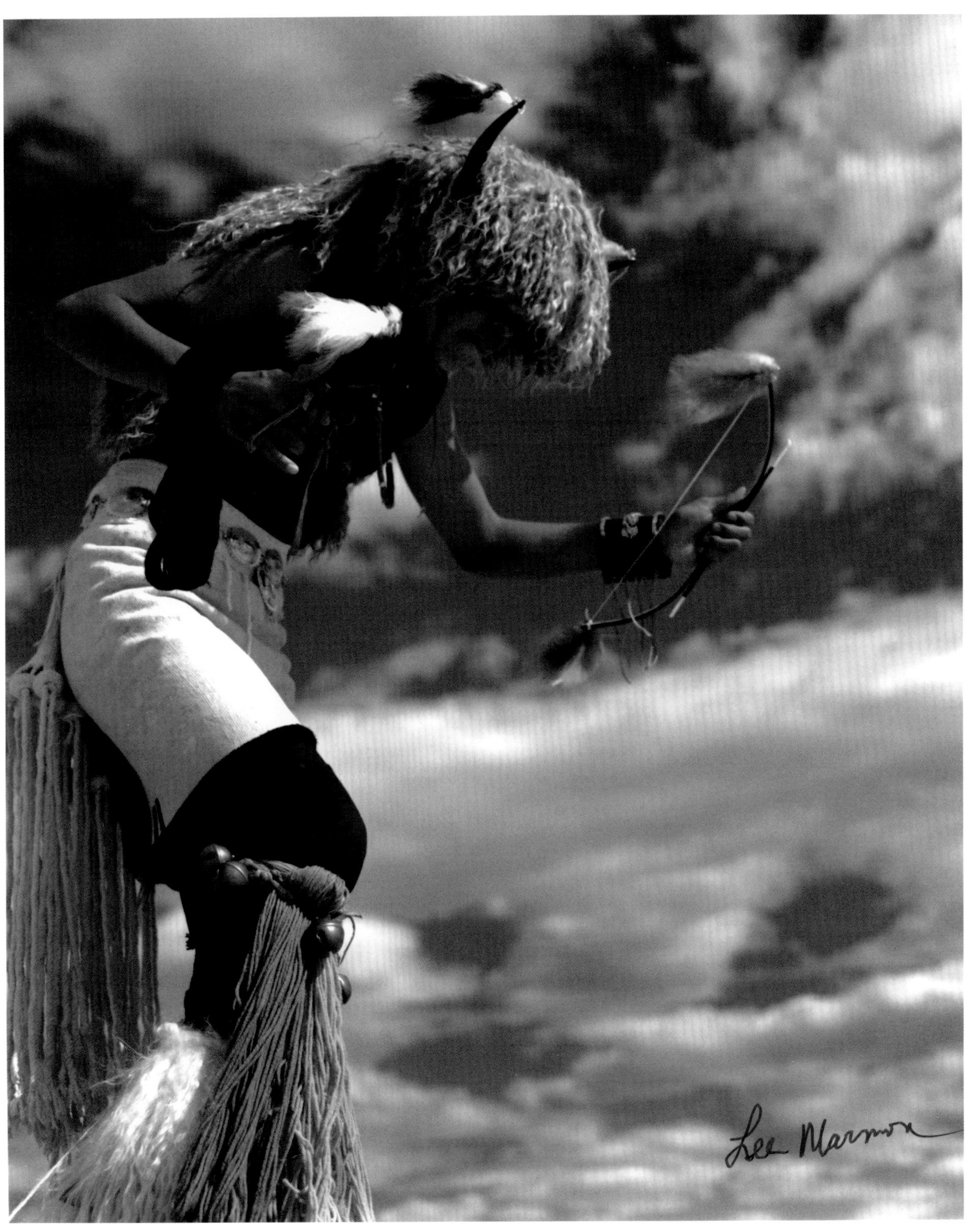
Lee Marmon

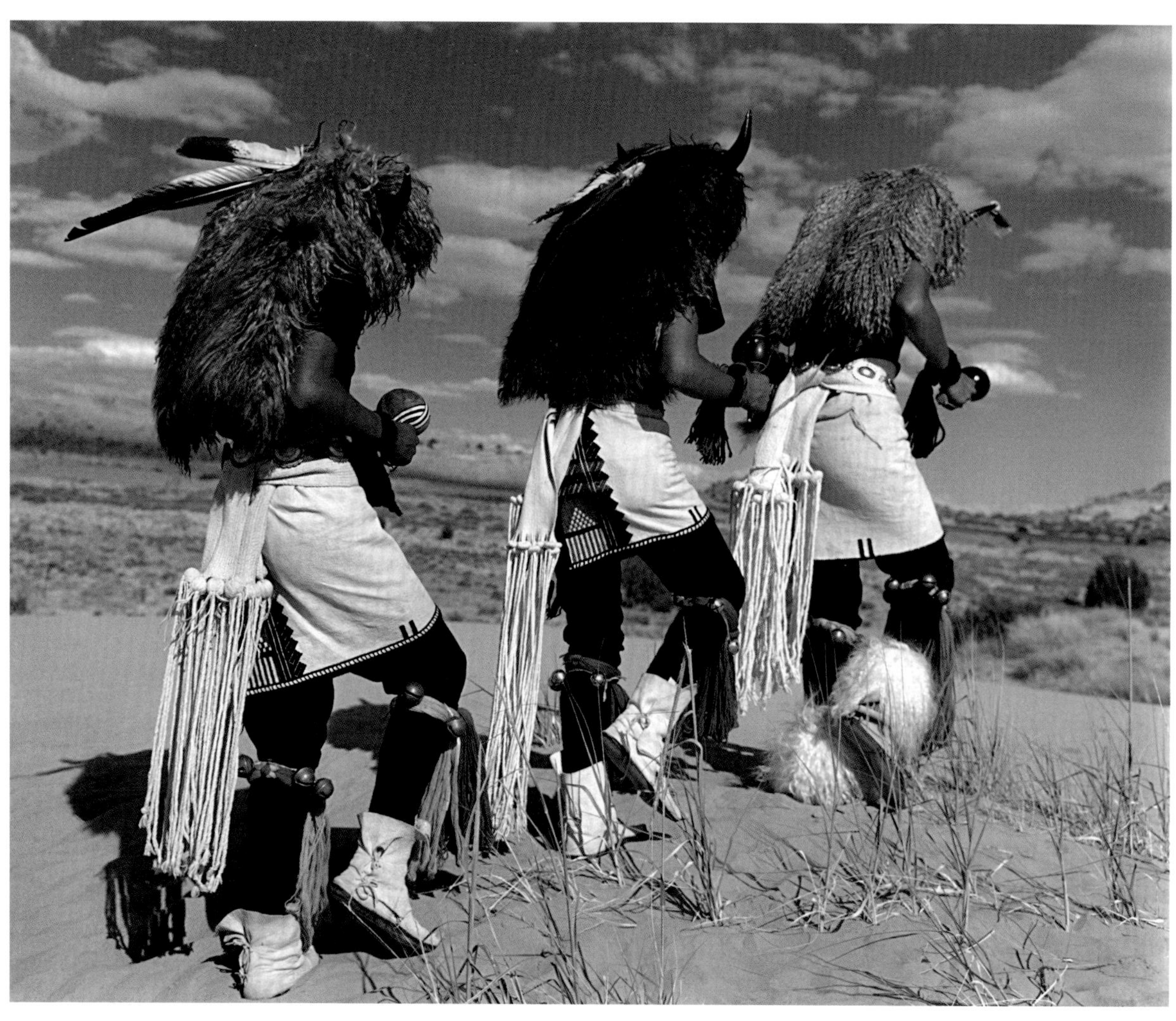

Buffalo Dancers #1. Photo by Lee Marmon (1962).

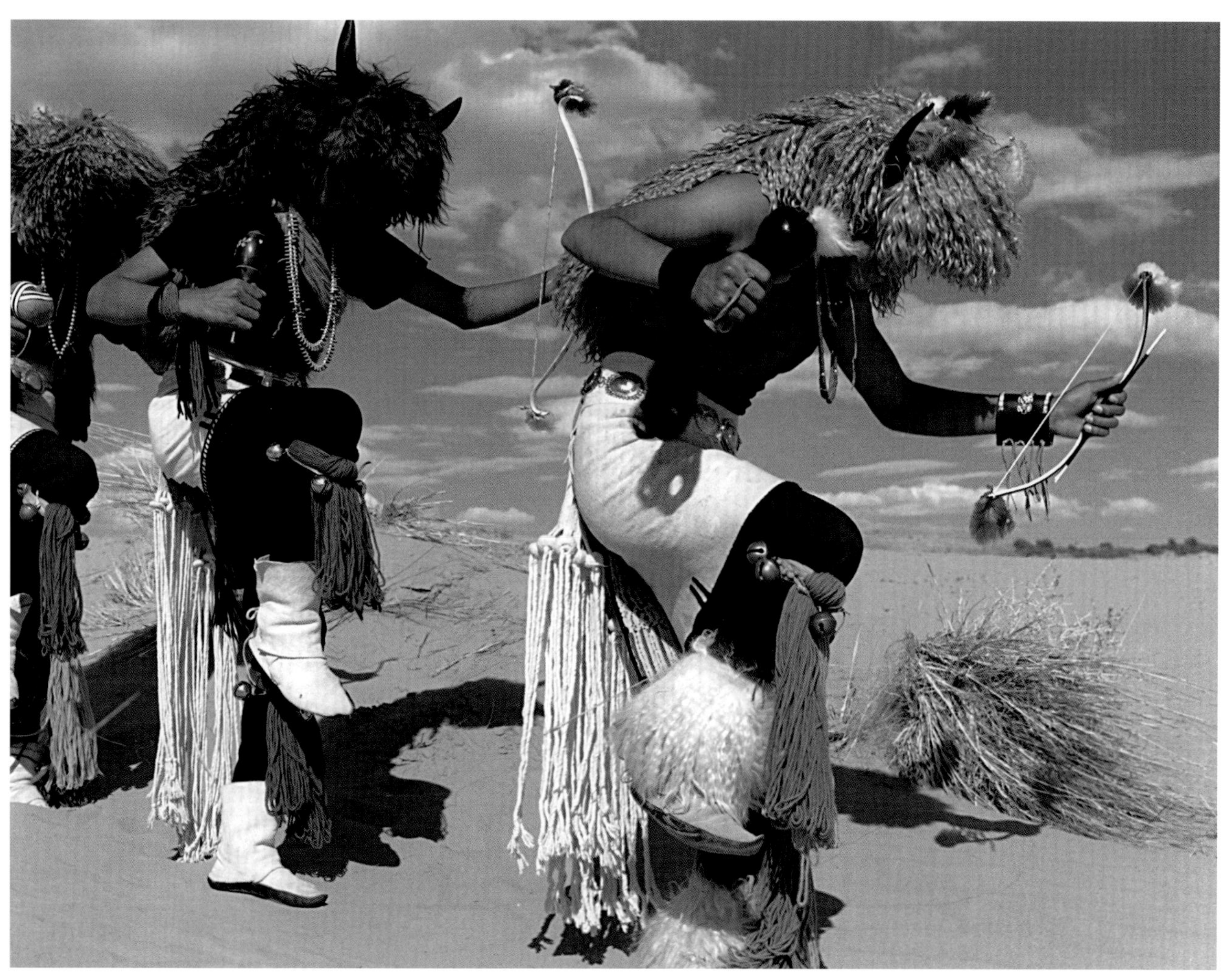

Buffalo Dancers #2. Photo by Lee Marmon (1962).

Dancers on a Sandhill. Photo by
Lee Marmon (1962).

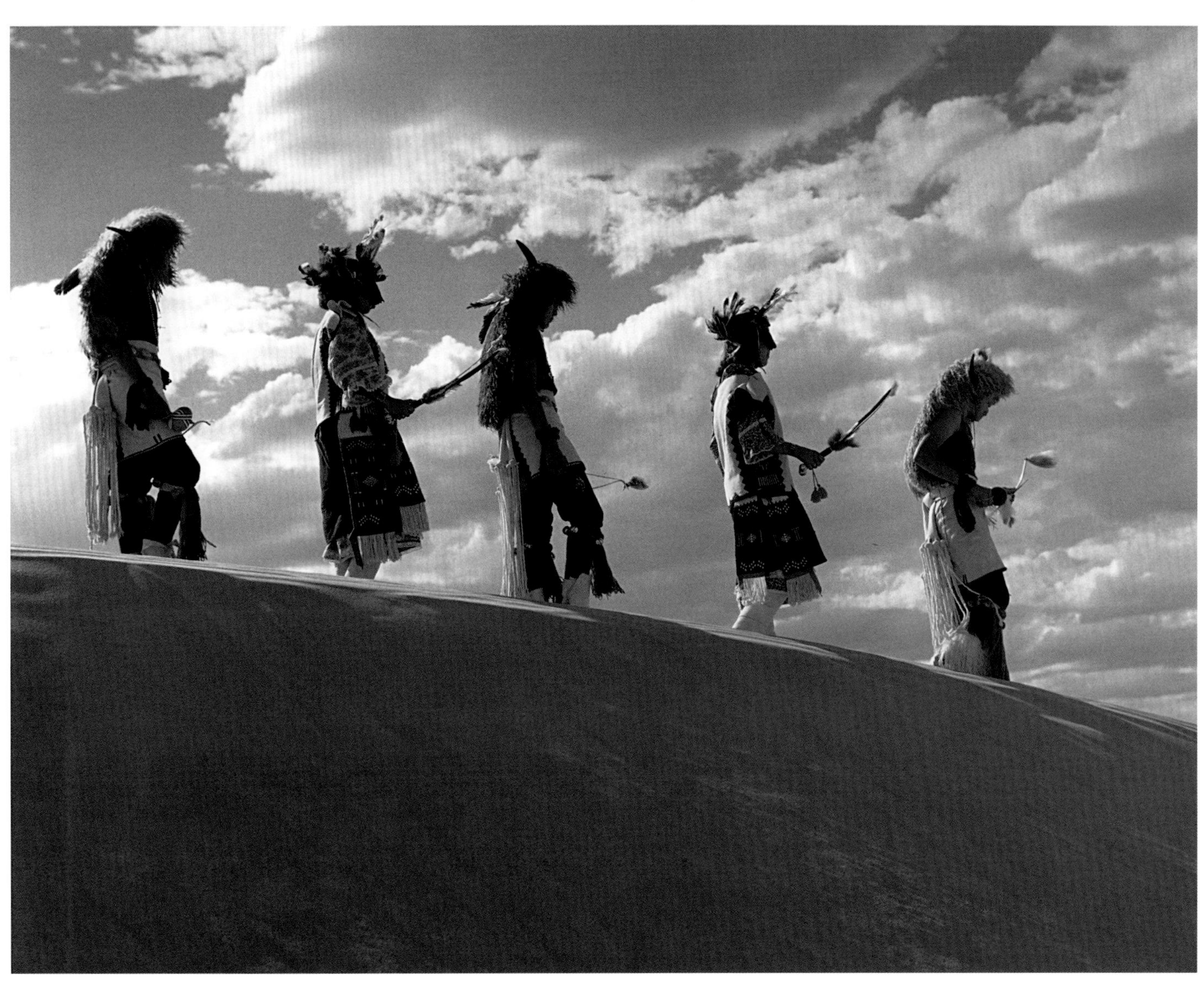

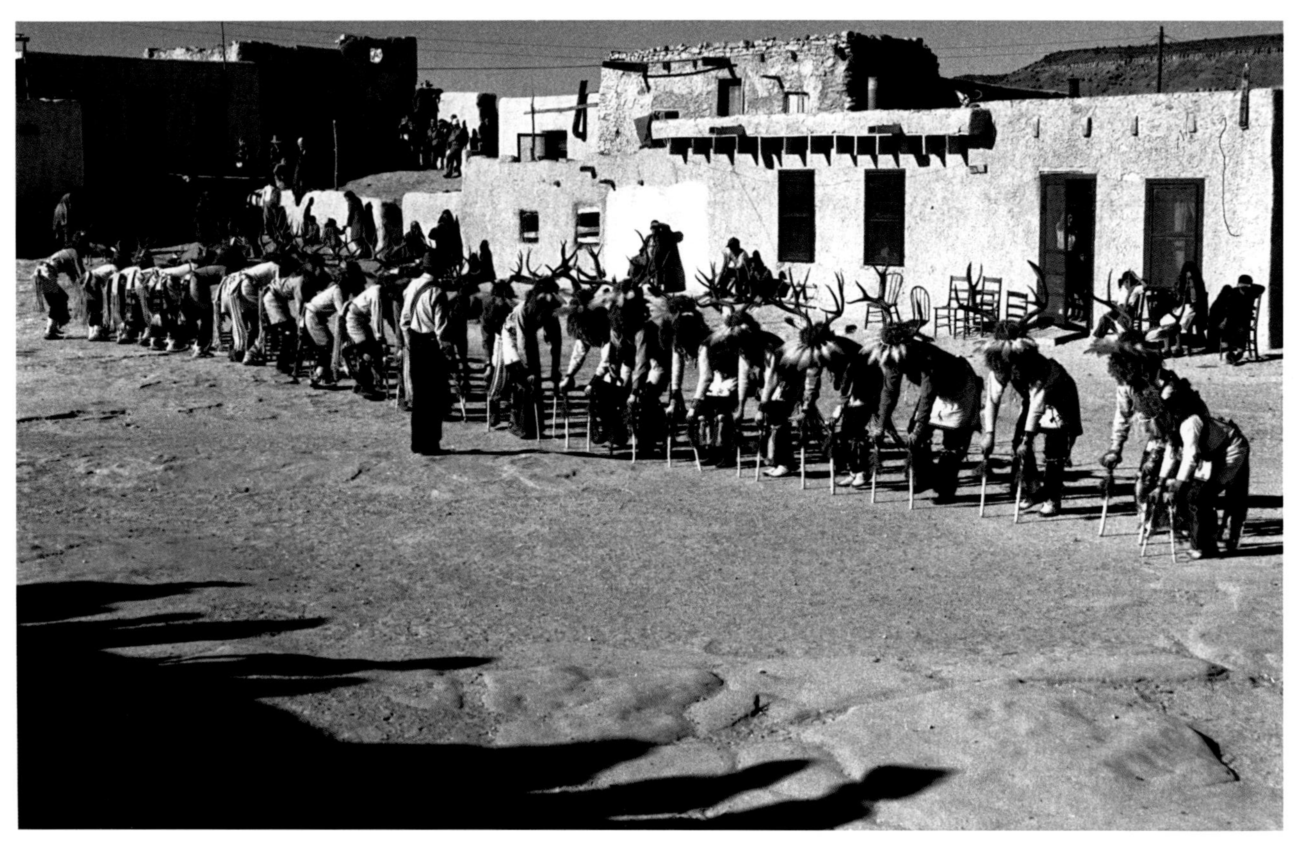

Deer Dancers #1. Photo by
Lee Marmon (1947).

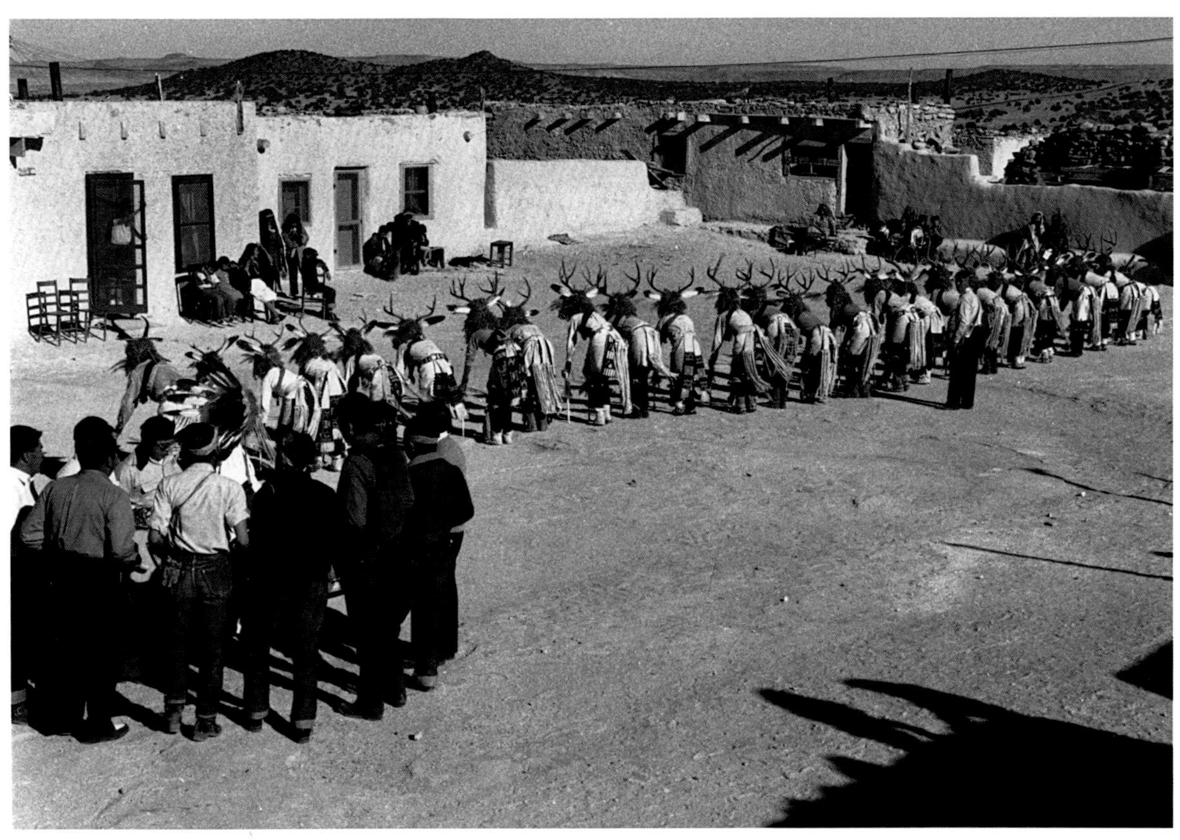

Deer Dancers #2. Photo by
Lee Marmon (1947).

Group Dancers on the Plaza. Photo by Lee Marmon (1962).

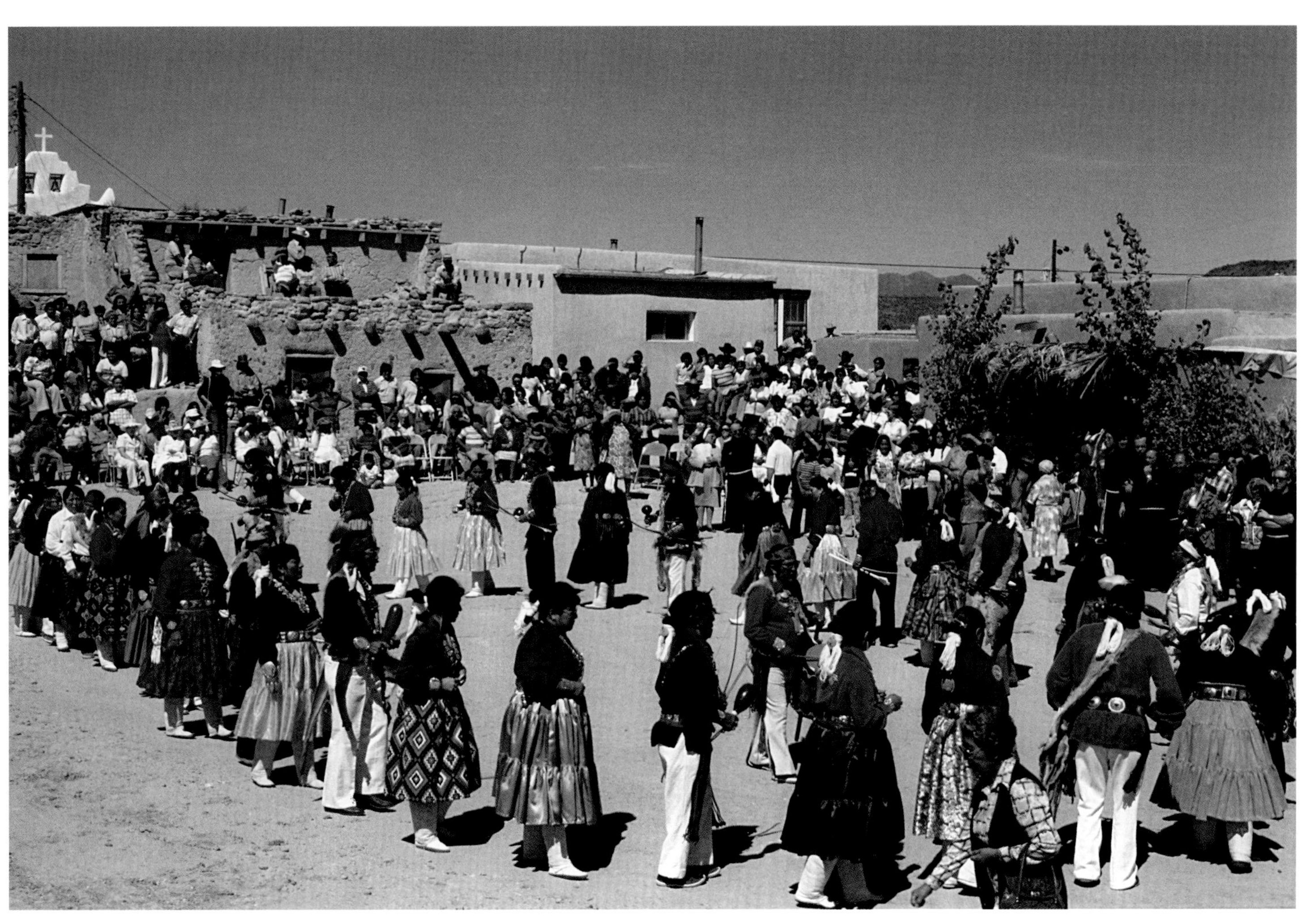

CHAPTER TWELVE

Portraits

Material from this chapter was transcribed by Tom Corbett from recorded interviews with Lee Marmon.

Photography appeals to people for different reasons. I can't really remember what attracted me to taking pictures in the first place.

I guess one experience I had when I was about ten or eleven was a big influence. I had taken some photos of a truck wreck near Laguna with an old Kodak postcard camera my dad let me use and then sold several of my postcard-sized prints to the trucking company. I received two dollars for the pictures and was very happy to have made so much money for only a few minutes' work. That was back about 1936 or 1937, and one of my biggest regrets is that I did not take photography seriously from that time on. That came later, after World War II.

For a time, I worked with my father in the trading post. During those years I spent a lot of time at night in the darkroom trying to perfect my photography. I had been taking some pictures, but I had not really decided to do a lot of them until one evening when my dad and I were standing around the old potbelly stove there in the trading post.

It was just about dark. Snow was coming down lightly, and here this old fella rode up on horseback. My dad recognized him right away and was telling me he had come all the way from Paguate, about ten miles north of Laguna. The man was around eighty-five—a magnificent-looking old guy. My dad said, "You should get his picture because as a boy he saved a herd of horses from the Apaches. He drove them by himself up into a box canyon and hid the horses from the Apaches."

So I started negotiating with him and his family. One weekend he couldn't make it and the next weekend I couldn't make it, and before you know it he caught pneumonia and died. So I missed what would have been one of my most important pictures. After that I became more aware of the old folks and tried to document them with more portraits.

From that time on, while delivering groceries in and around the villages on the Laguna reservation, I took along a camera in the truck with me. When I'd see one of the old people outside I would stop and ask if I could take their picture. Usually they said yes, but a lot of times they said no. At first I was pretty shy about asking some of the people I didn't know very well, but later on I got better at getting their permission to pose for me. Most of the time I would take the picture as they were. Then there were a few who wanted to get dressed up to have their picture taken. Many people who wanted to wait until they got dressed up never did, and I never got their photographs. I regret missing so many of the old people that I knew so well. It is so nice to have the ones that I do have—to look at the photos and remember the people from the early days.

I wanted to preserve a small part of the Pueblo people as they were in the 1940s, '50s, and '60s. I hope presenting them here has helped document history a little bit by showing the images I recorded of the people living then, people working so hard to make a better place for their children and grandchildren to live. They were beautiful people and should be remembered for all the good qualities they had and for the hardships they had to overcome to survive. Their faces should not fade from our memories.

White Man's Moccasins (1954)

White Man's Moccasins. Photo by Lee Marmon (1954).

One of my most famous pictures is that of Old Man Jeff. It's the one I call *White Man's Moccasins.* I took this in the late summer of 1954. I was delivering groceries up in the pueblo and happened to have my camera in the pickup. I was carrying a box of groceries across the plaza when I noticed that Old Man Jeff was sitting out there in the sun as he frequently did, visiting with the tourists and telling them tall tales about his gold mine and about a root he would chew to keep the women happy.

So I stopped momentarily and asked, "How about a picture today?" And he replied, "No picture today!" So I kind of argued with him and said, "Well, I took your picture when you were with your daughter about a month ago, but you were wearing dark glasses."

He said, "No picture!"

So I went on my way and finished delivering the groceries, and then I came back and talked to him some more and finally offered him that cigar he is holding in the photo. He said, "Okay, you can take a picture or two." So I went and got the camera and took three or four pictures of him. Since he was wearing tennis shoes, I called it *White Man's Moccasins.*

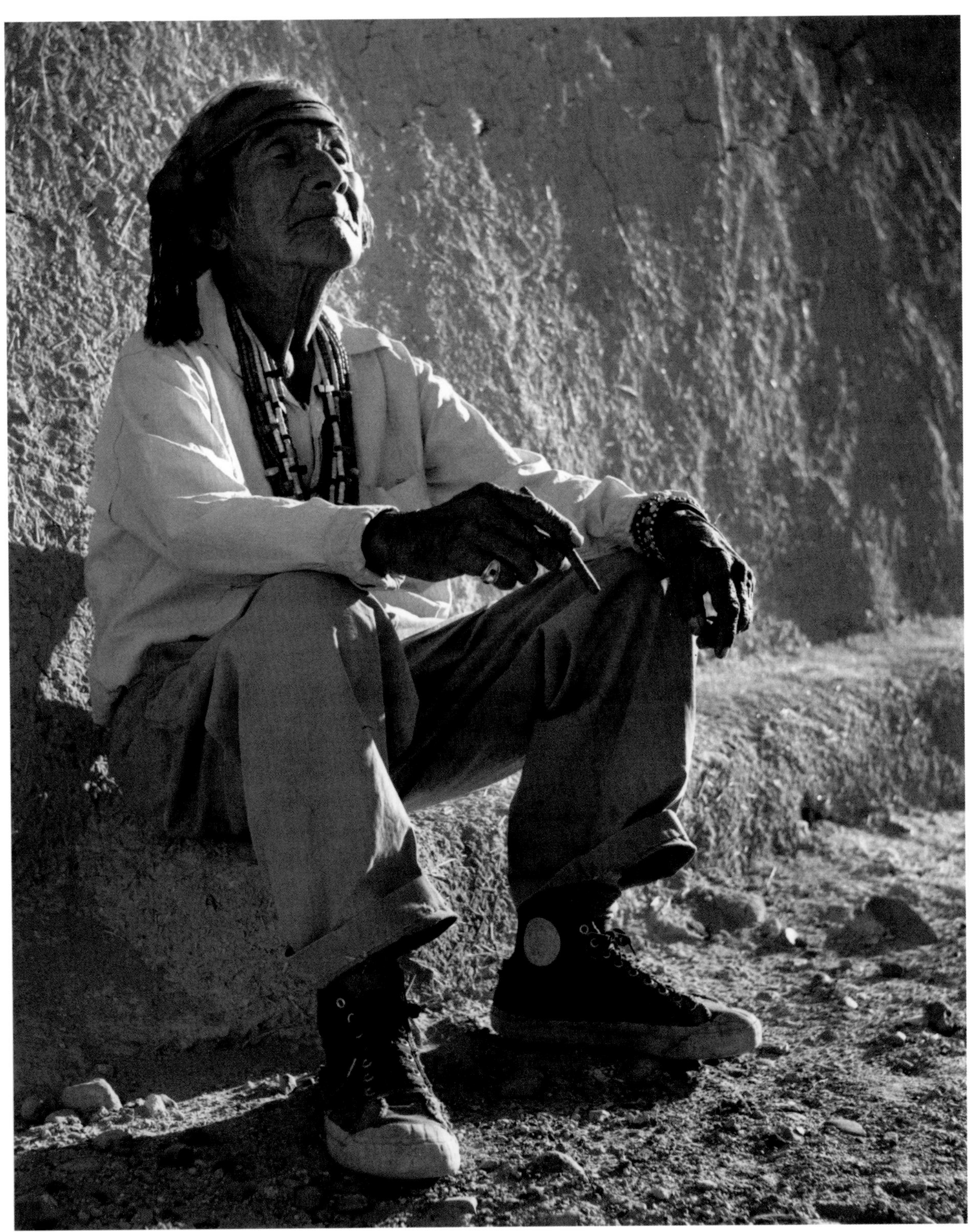

Juanita Quicero (1961)

Juanita Quicero (1858–1965) was one of Laguna's most skilled potters, and, like many other Laguna women back then, she took her pots down to the old railroad station to sell to tourists on the Santa Fe trains that stopped to take on water and coal.

Juanita married Henry José Quicero, a Laguna shepherd, and they had ten children. They lived most of the time at his sheep camp, about five miles east of Laguna.

When Juanita was in her eighties she was still very active, walking to Laguna to buy groceries that she would carry back to the sheep camp in a sack slung over her shoulder. My memory of her is that she was real bent over, carrying a heavy sack on her back, walking east, going to the sheep camp.

It would take her all day to go the four or five miles to Laguna, she was so old. And then she'd stay overnight, and the next day you'd see her walking back to the sheep camp with her sack of groceries. That's how I remember her.

I went to school in the eighth grade with one of her daughters. And later on the daughters asked me to take Juanita's picture. She got herself fixed up, and so I took her picture late one afternoon. Her portrait has been one of my most popular photographs.

Juanita Quicero. Photo by Lee Marmon (1961).

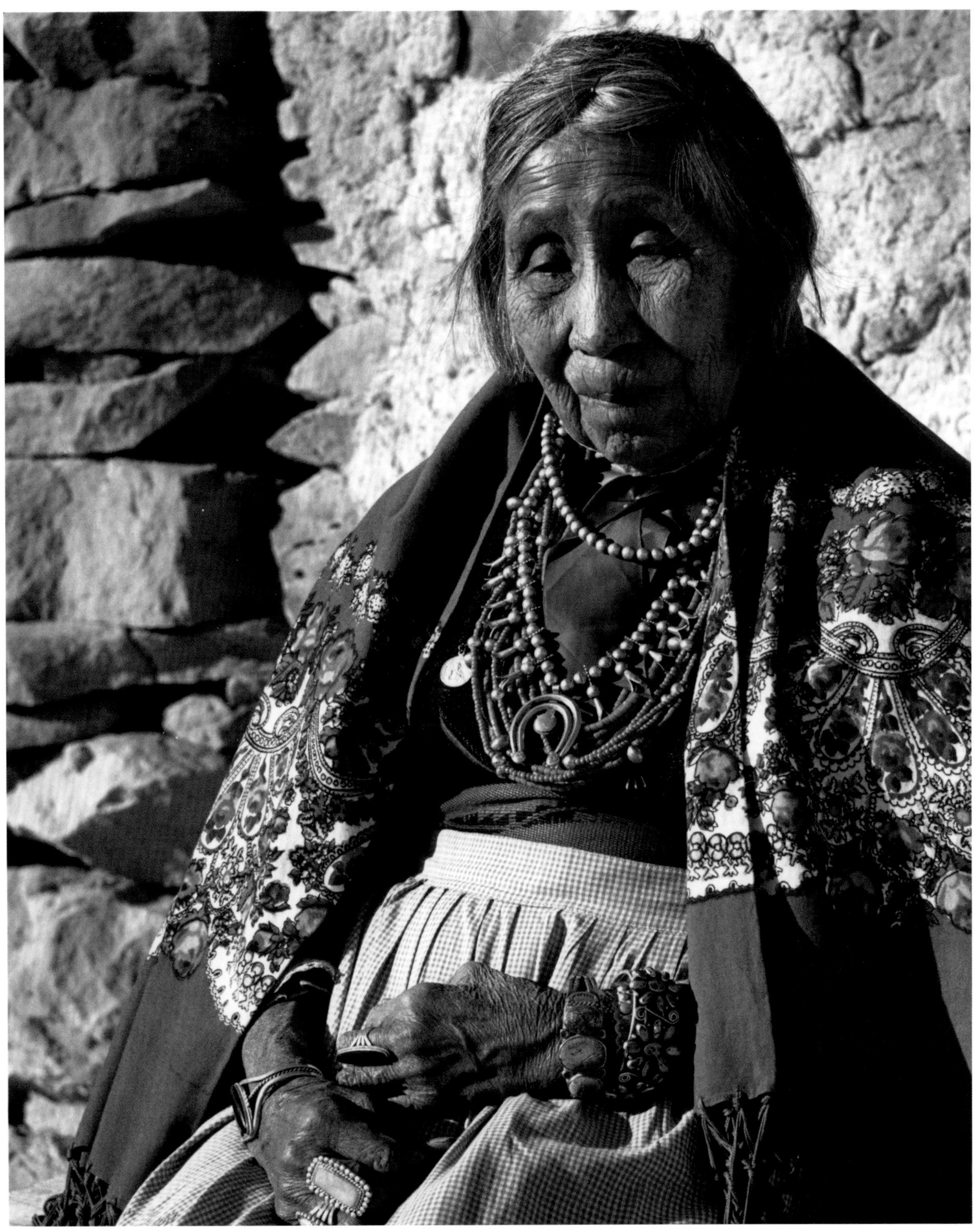

Bennie Pacheco. Photo by Lee Marmon (1984).

Bennie Pacheco (1984)

I took this great shot of Bennie the sheepherder (see also *Bennie at Sheep Camp* on page 81) after he got off his horse.

Not too long after I took this picture, Bennie was found shot. I never learned the details of his death.

Bennie's full name was Bennie Pacheco. His older brother, Mariano Pacheco, was the first Laguna killed in World War II. He's buried at the Laguna Mission.

Many Laguna men served in the army, navy, and marines during the World War II. Just about every able-bodied guy joined the military, including me (and my brother and everybody else). Many of those who returned had severe adjustment problems.

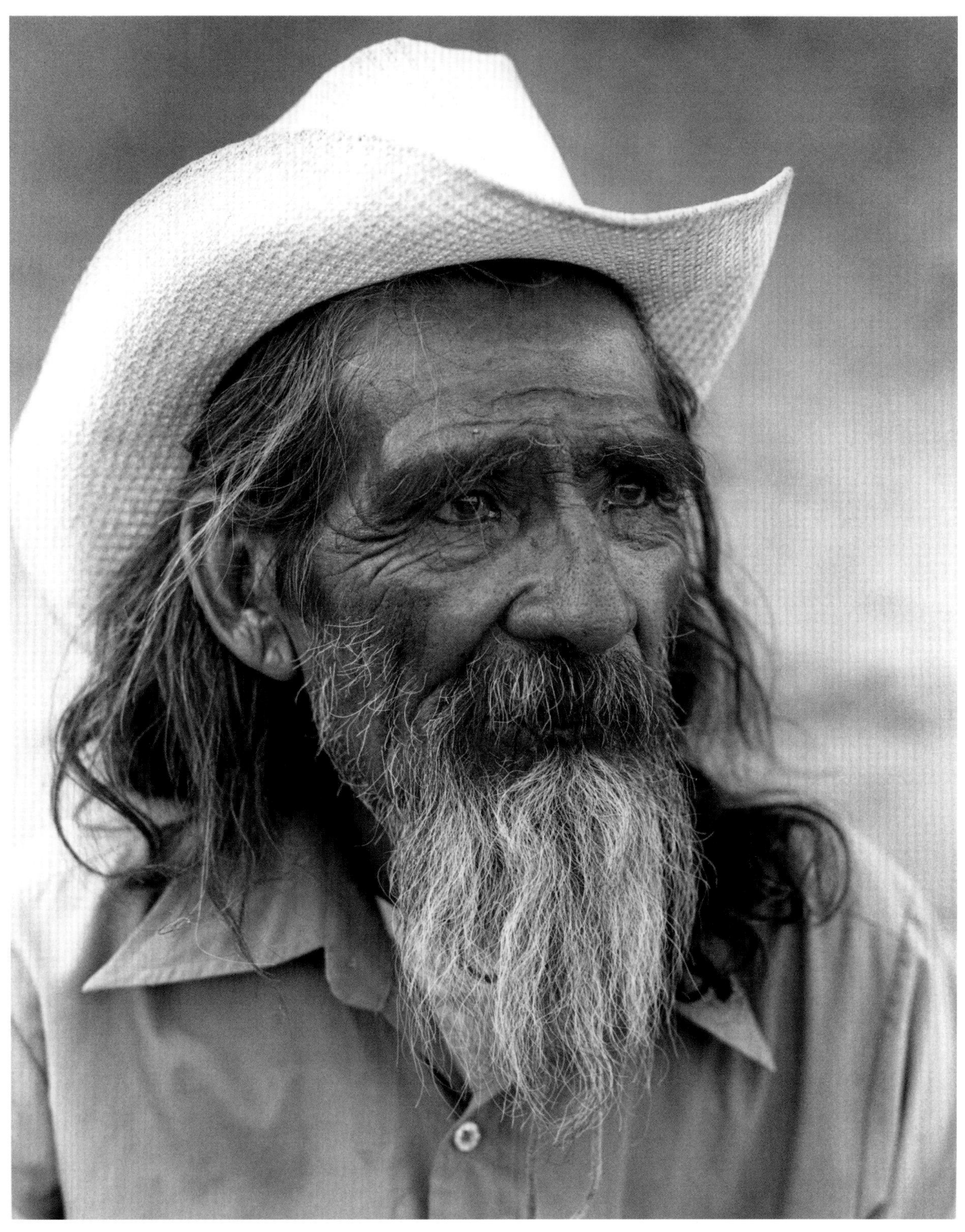

José Teofilo (1961)

José Teofilo (1875–1963) was born and raised in Laguna Pueblo and was a farmer for most of his life. He was regarded as an excellent hunter and was still hunting deer when he was in his mideighties.

One of Jose's earliest memories was the railroad coming to Laguna in the 1880s when he was five years old. He and a friend were lying on the top of a mesa watching the first train go by, when suddenly the engine blew its whistle. The foreign sound frightened the children enough to make them run all the way home.

José Teofilo was eighty-five years old when I took this photograph. He was very active, and while I was taking his picture, his granddaughters came out and said he had just come back from deer hunting. He went out with a group, and while they had gone, he stayed back at camp. A deer came back through camp and he killed it.

He has earrings in both ears, and my daughter used him as a character in one of her short stories in the book *The Man to Send Rainclouds.*

José Teofilo. Photo by Lee Marmon (1961).

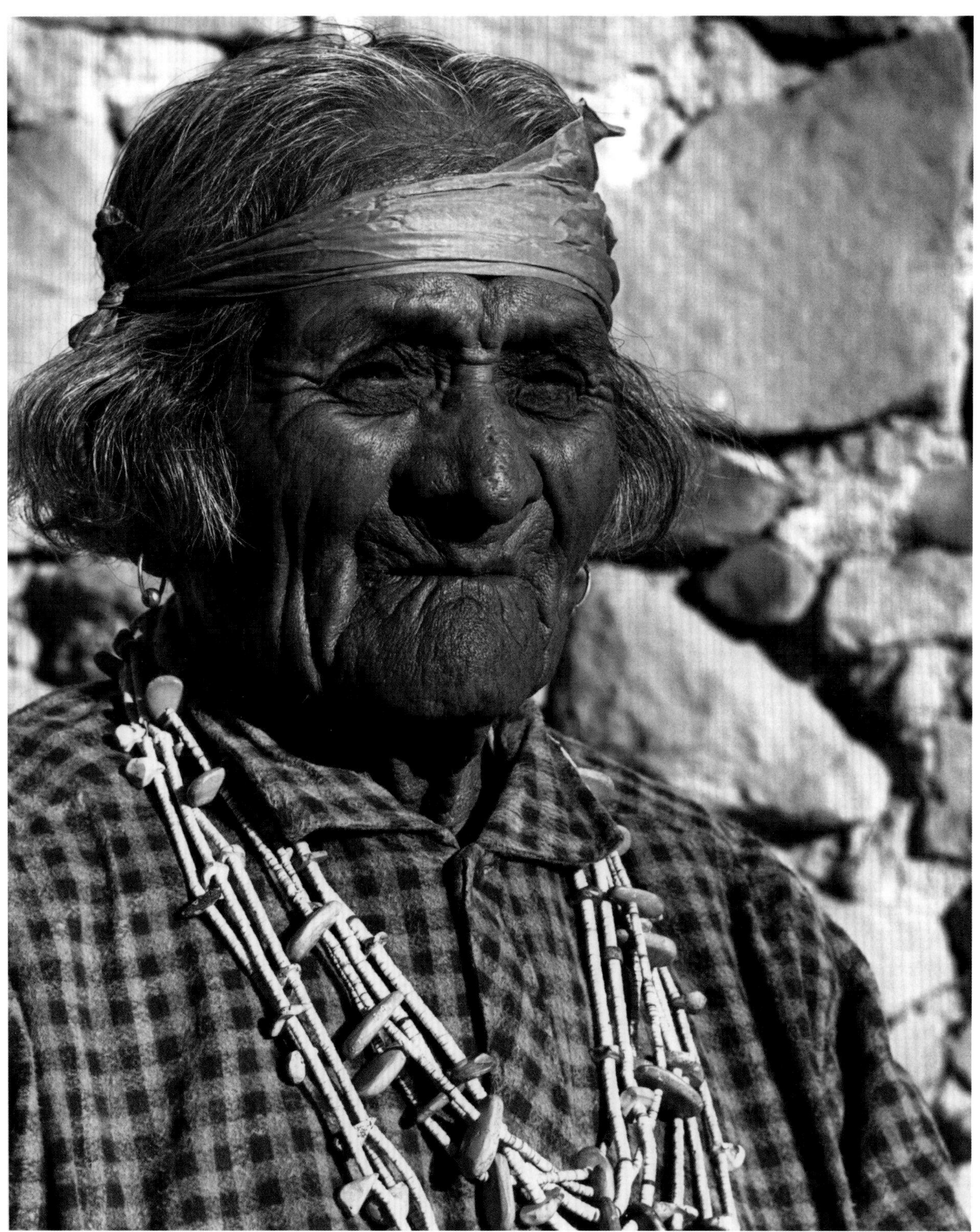

Old Man Platero (1958)

I had just gotten a new Hasselblad camera, and we went down to Cañoncito to take some pictures of the Navajos. They came to Laguna to celebrate our feast days and to trade with us. I hadn't taken any pictures of the old-timers down there, so my daughter Leslie and I went down one Sunday morning in 1958. A fellow we knew down there set it up.

We went to Old Man Platero's place. He was living inside a little building the government built, not a hogan (the traditional dwelling of the Navajos). He was asleep when we got there, but he got up and tried to brush his hair back. He didn't have any teeth. He said in Navajo, "When you get old, you're just like a baby. You don't have any hair and you don't have any teeth, and somebody has to take care of you."

Anyway, he came out and sat down, and we talked for a while. His biggest story was about the time a horse bit his finger off. He kept showing us his finger.

It was an interesting shoot, and when he learned that my last name is Marmon, he remembered that my grandfather had done some survey work for him many years ago. He then asked what I would be doing next.

I said, "Well, I think I'll be going deer hunting."

So we talked about the ranch where I was going to go deer hunting; he said he used to hunt deer there when he was young. I said, "If we get a deer, we'll bring you some deer meat."

Sure enough, I went hunting that year and killed two deer, so when we got home, I took him half a deer. He danced around and laughed and rubbed his hands—he was so happy to get that venison!

It was a great experience. He was a nice old man and had a good memory for names. My grandfather had passed away in the early 1930s, and he remembered him.

Old Man Platero. Photo by Lee Marmon (1958).

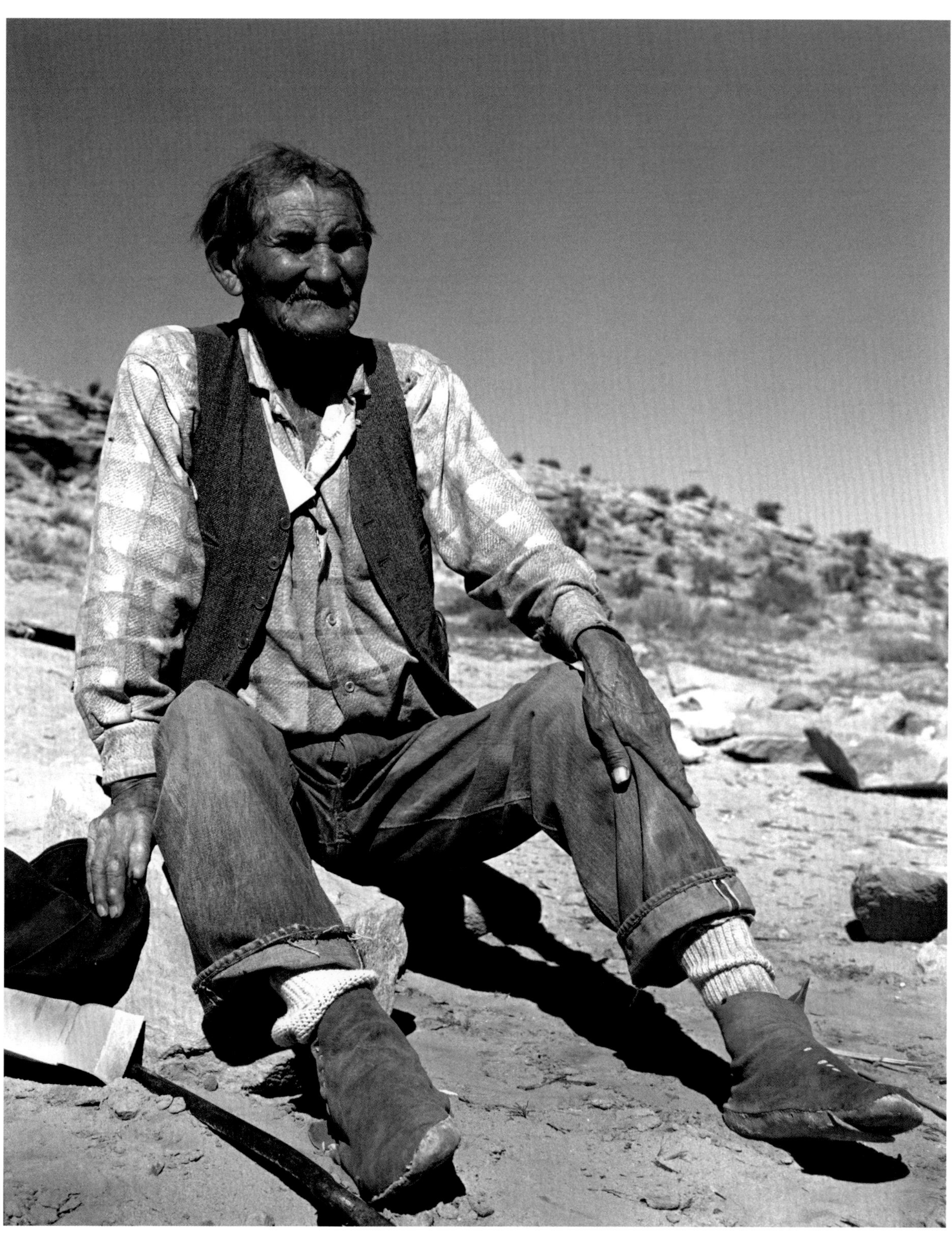

Juana Marie Pino (1959)

Juana Marie Pino (1871–1969) was born in Paguate village on the Laguna reservation and lived in the area known as Chinatown. She used to make Hopi paper bread from corn she and other women from the village used to grind. Juana had a number of grinding stones (metates) used by the other women when they came to her house, and together they would grind and sing the corn-grinding songs.

One of the highlights of Juana's life was her trip to California to surprise her grandson, stationed at El Torro marine base, on his birthday. Wearing her traditional clothing, Juana traveled in the back of a van with her grandson's stepsons and her granddaughter, Blondie, as interpreter. Somehow, Walt Disney heard of her visit and invited her and her family for the day at Disneyland. He greeted them personally and gave them free passes for the day. The *Los Angeles Examiner* publicized this event and on its front page carried a photo of Juana, clearly enjoying the Flying Dumbo ride.

Juana Marie Pino. Photo by Lee Marmon (1959).

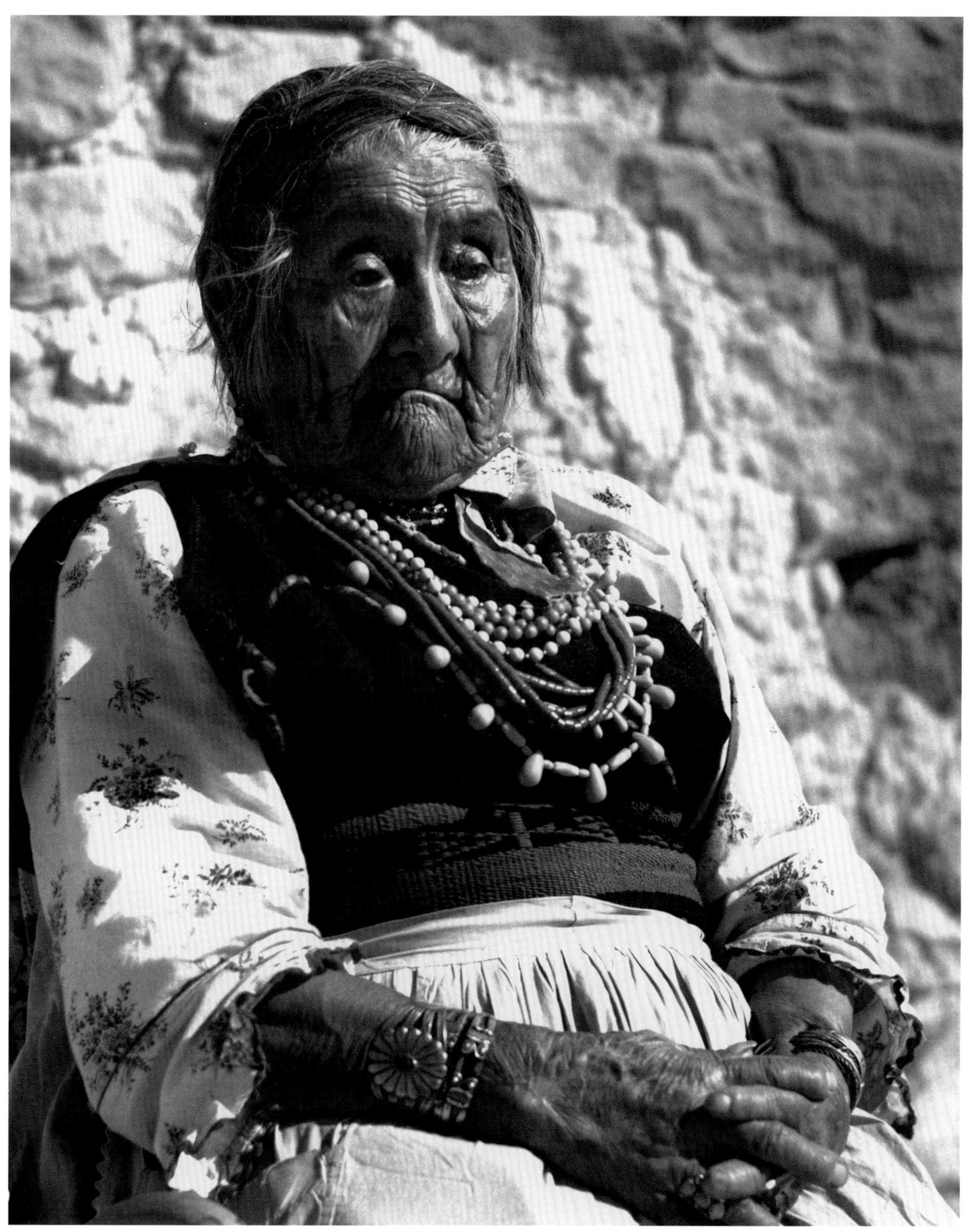

Santiago Thomas (1962)

Santiago Thomas (1895–1997) was born and raised in Laguna. He had little formal education, but during his life he was seldom without work. In 1919, he worked for the Santa Fe Railroad in the roundhouse in Winslow, Arizona, and then in 1933, he worked for the railroad operating a steam crane fueled by coal, building bridges throughout the western division. When he wasn't working for the railroad, Santiago was a farmer and rancher.

Santiago Thomas lived in the village of Laguna his entire life. He was one of the dancers, and I photographed him during rehearsals on several occasions. I have photographs of him in costume for the Shield Dance. He danced most of the Pueblo dances, including the Eagle Dance and the Buffalo Dance.

Santiago was a very entertaining individual.

Santiago Thomas #1. Photo by Lee Marmon (1962).

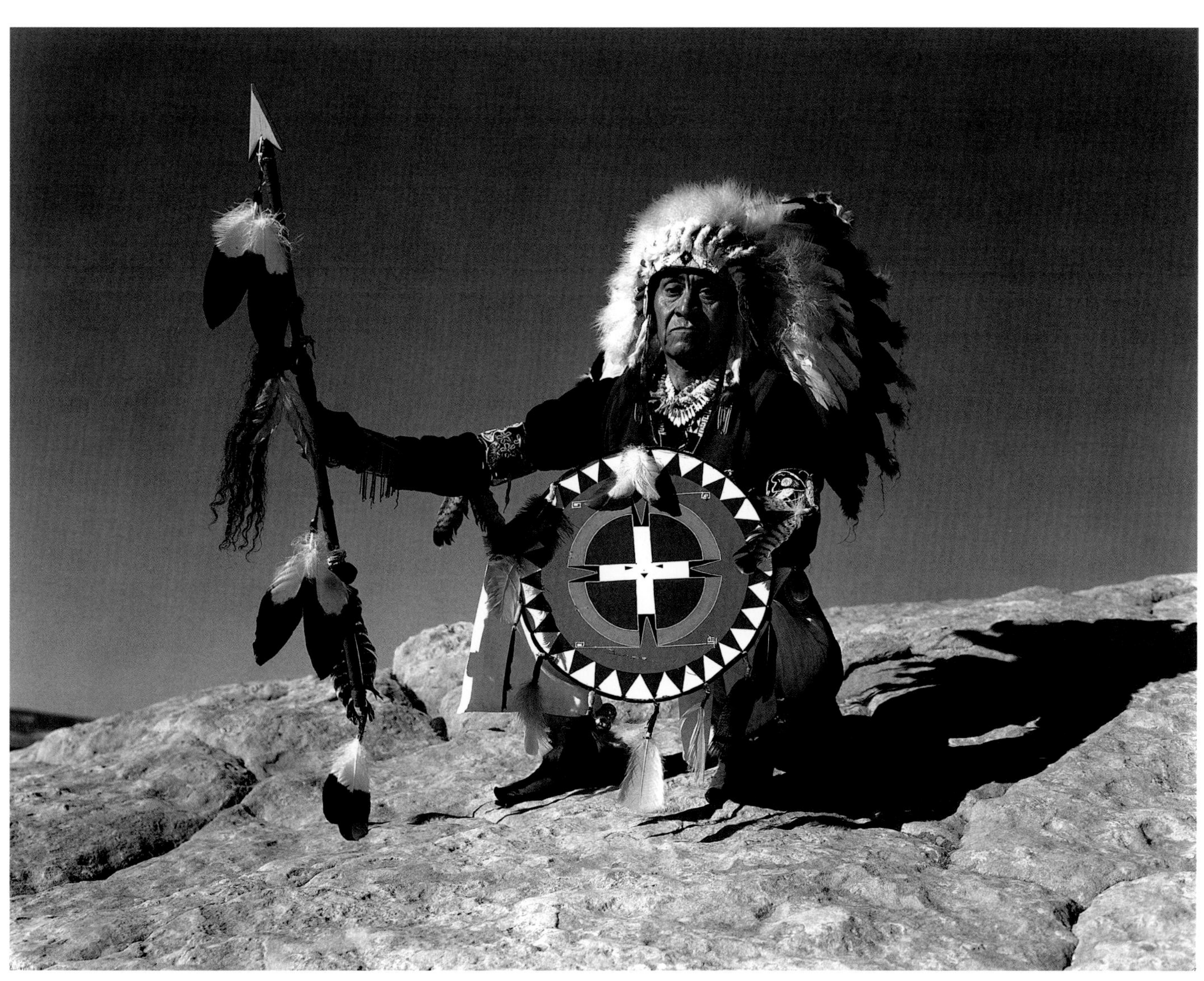

Santiago Thomas #2. Photo by Lee Marmon (1962).

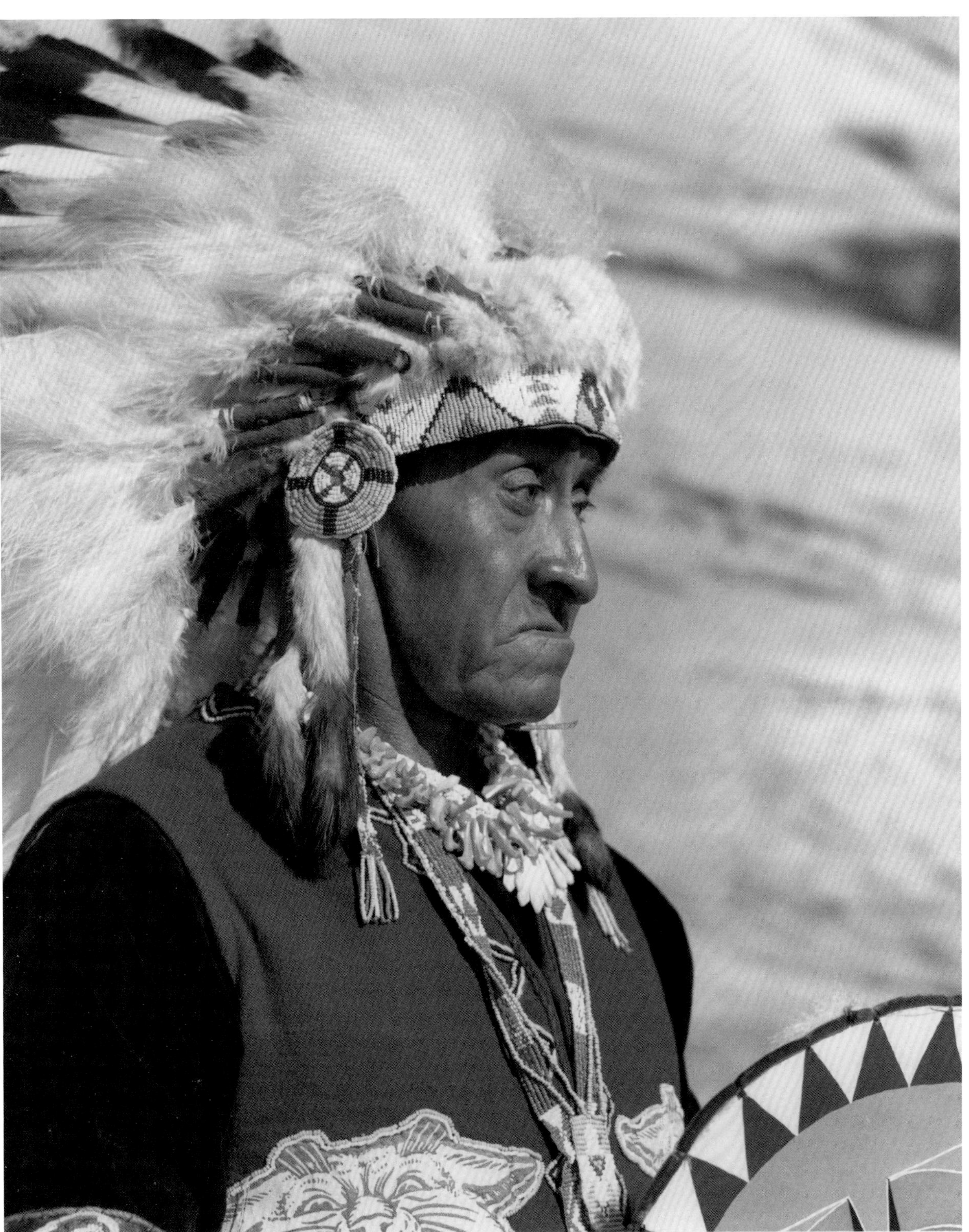

Bill Pradt (1949)

Bill Pradt was my neighbor. His father, Major George H. Pradt, was a Civil War veteran who knew my grandfather and later joined the Marmon brothers in Laguna. He also was a surveyor and served as a militia officer with the Laguna Battalion.

Bill Pradt lived right behind our darkroom and house in the old Baptist Mission, a complex my grandfather and his father bought from the early Baptists. Major Pradt, my grandfather, and my granduncle Walter were all surveyors, so they made a compound together when they bought the old Baptist Mission.

Bill served in the navy during World War I. When he returned, he went to work for the Forest Service up in Flagstaff as a firewatcher, and I think that's what he did for the rest of his life—forty years or more. He had to go up a steep hill to get to the firewatcher's tower. In order to get a stove up there, each year he had to disassemble the stove and take it up piece by piece; there was no road, so he had to take it up by horseback.

He was an interesting old fellow, a typical bachelor. He loved to ride horses. He would ride his horse from Laguna to Flagstaff in the spring and stay all summer at the firewatch. Then in the fall, he'd ride his horse back to Laguna, almost three hundred miles.

He really liked guns—pistols and rifles. Bill was always trading pistols and rifles. Sometimes he would trade back to get the same one he just traded away. He used to come over to our house and have coffee, and I'd give him magazines and other items. Bill was a good guy and a good neighbor.

Bill Pradt. Photo by Lee Marmon (1949).

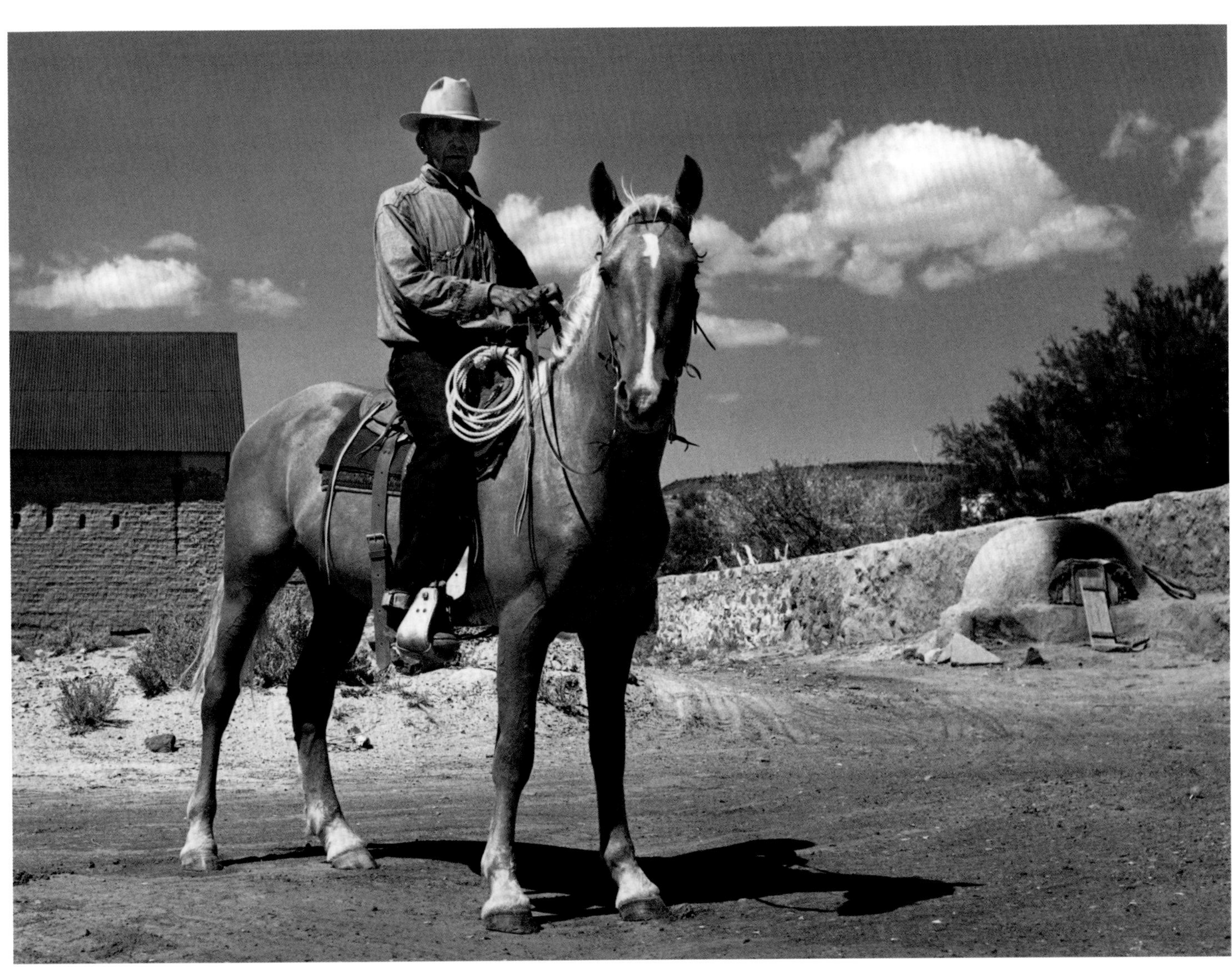

Henry Ward Beecher and Wife (1948)

One of the great leaders of Laguna Pueblo was a man named Henry Ward Beecher. He was quite a big fellow and a great orator. He was governor of Laguna several times.

I was able to get a picture of him and his wife. I would like to have gotten a close-up of him, but I was always a little afraid of him. He was a big, gruff old guy.

Henry Ward Beecher was a member of the Marmon Battalion, which chased Geronimo back in the old days. When my grandfather took over the outfit, he had to make out the payroll. My grandfather tried to spell the Indian names phonetically. Some were so difficult that he just gave those guys new names. Some were the names of famous people. We had Henry Ward Beecher, and we had Abraham Lincoln and George Washington—and that's how we got so many Rileys at Laguna.

It was the same with the railroad. That's where we got a few Smiths and Joneses and a few more Rileys.

Henry Ward Beecher and Wife. Photo by Lee Marmon (1948).

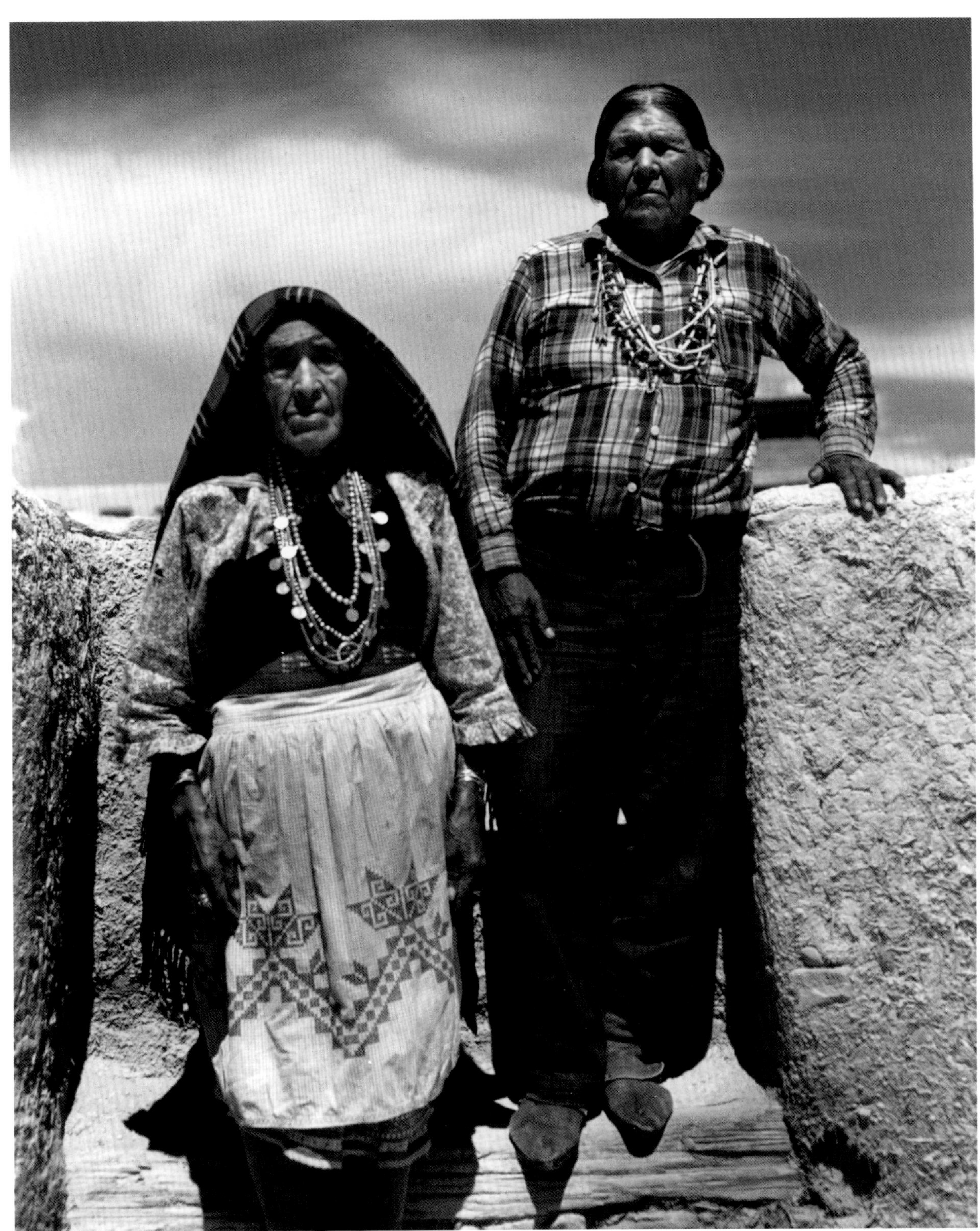

Lee Antonio #1. Photo by Lee Marmon (1992).

Lee Antonio (1992)

Lee Antonio served his country in World War II. He fought all through the African campaign and in the Battle of the Bulge. He was in the army for quite a number of years.

Following his discharge from the military, he moved back to Laguna. But while he was gone, fighting for his country, his marriage failed. And like many of the Laguna men who fought in World War II, Lee Antonio had a difficult time adjusting after he returned.

He chose to live alone out at a sheep camp about six to eight miles from Laguna. Once in a while he would ride to the village on his motorbike to get groceries and visit with people and then ride alone back to the camp.

I went out there to get his picture one day. He was just a veteran out there all by himself at the sheep camp. When I got there, he was reading the Bible. He was a deeply religious man and frequently quoted the Scriptures.

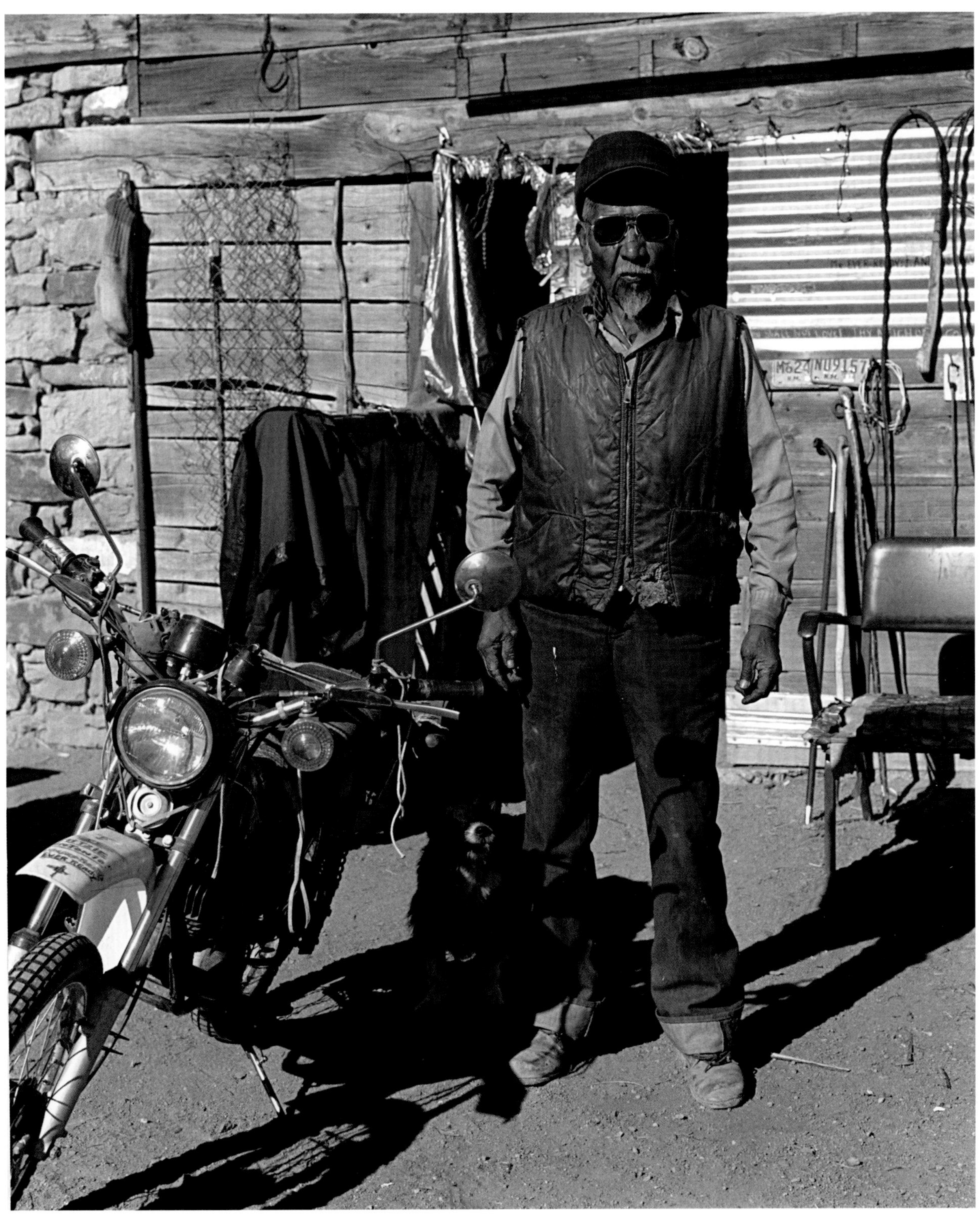
M624
NU9157

Lee Antonio #2. Photo by
Lee Marmon (1992).

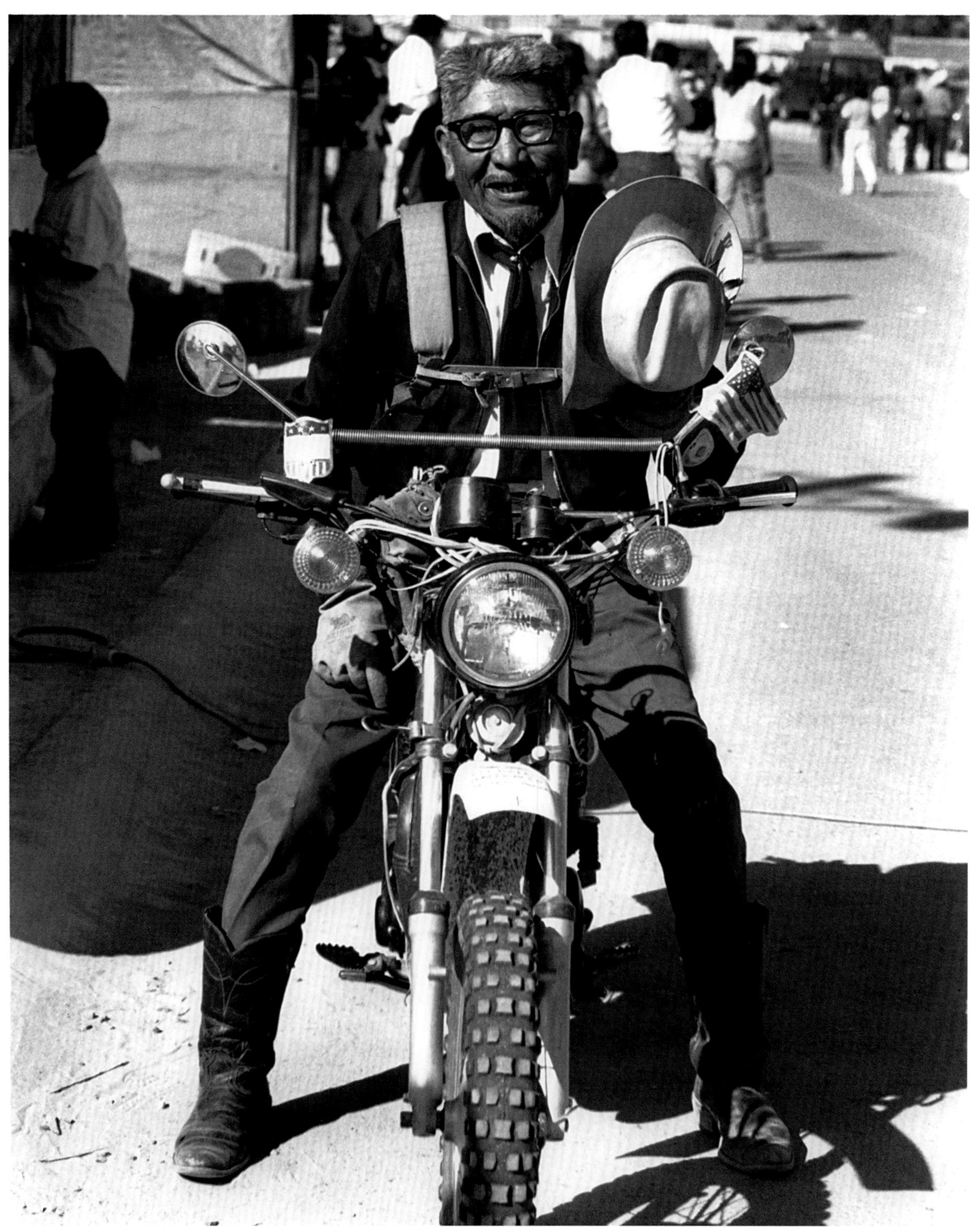

Kashana (Medicine Woman) (1950)

Kashana was a medicine woman. She delivered babies, fixed broken bones, and gave massages. She had certain treatments for the flu and colds, and those worked quite well. She was one of the last medicine women. She died shortly after I took this photograph.

She spoke only a little English. She understood and agreed when I asked her to let me get her picture. She sat down; I clicked the camera once, and she got up and left, which is kind of funny. I had taken a picture of her maybe ten years earlier when I was a real beginner. So I wanted to get another good shot of her.

Before government medical programs, people like Kashana were all that was available. There were also medicine men, but they worked primarily in the religious aspects. The women were more involved with delivering babies and setting bones, trying to diagnose ailments and prescribing different remedies using herbal medicines.

Kashana (Medicine Woman). Photo by Lee Marmon (1950).

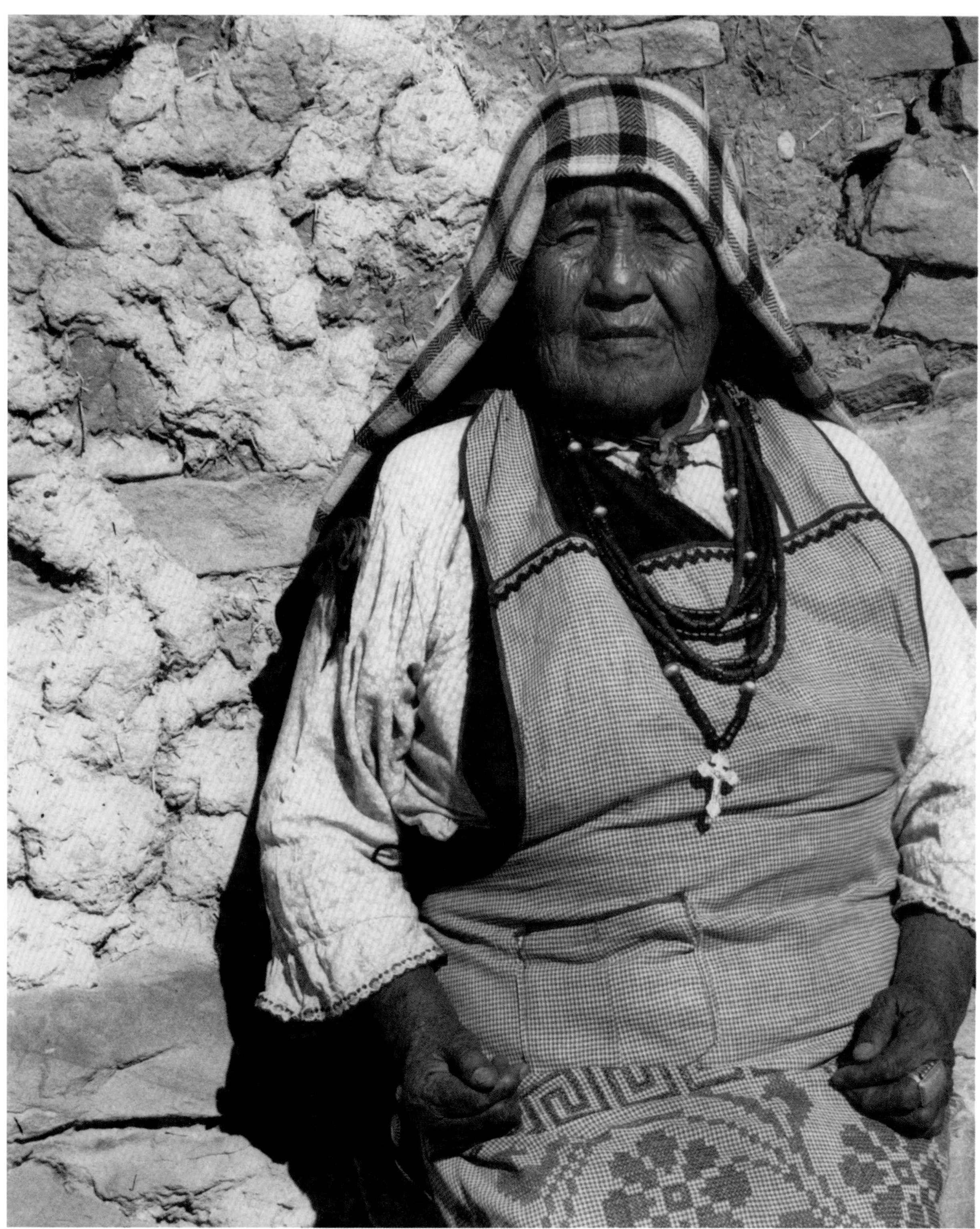

Bruce Riley (1965)

Born in 1905 and raised in Laguna village, Bruce Riley was educated at St. Catherine's Indian School in Santa Fe. After the eighth grade, he came home for fiesta and never returned to school.

During his lifetime, Bruce worked at many occupations, including raising sheep on a Kansas farm and working for the federal government on the Mescalero Apache reservation. A summer job on the section gang for the Santa Fe Railroad led to a full-time job, and Bruce ended up in Winslow, Arizona, for five years, working on the railroad and playing in the Santa Fe Indian Band. His last job was with the Anaconda Copper Company at the Jackpile Mine, the main source of income for the Lagunas for many years.

At the time of this portrait, Bruce was a war chief of Laguna tribe. In the old days, the war chiefs were in charge of protecting the village—fending off raiding Navajos and Apaches, for instance—but now they oversee various community duties and religious rituals.

Bruce Riley. Photo by Lee Marmon (1965).

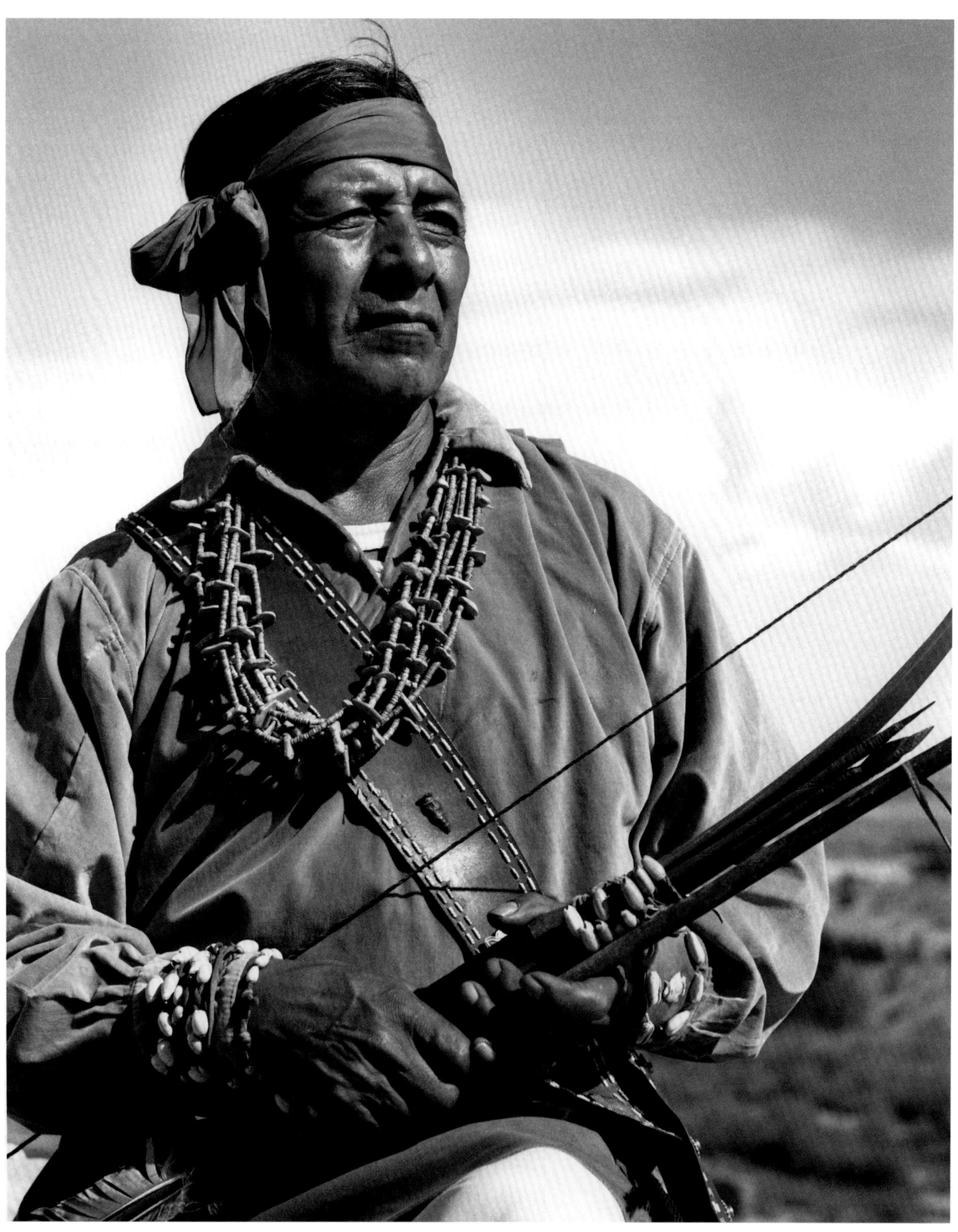

Lupe Garcia Siow. Photo by Lee Marmon (1960).

Lupe Garcia Siow (1960)

Born and raised in Laguna village, Lupe Garcia Siow (1890–1977) survived the smallpox epidemic during her youth (in the late 1890s) that killed many Laguna people. If you look closely at the photograph, you can see the residual pockmarks from the disease on Lupe's face. That epidemic, along with earlier epidemics of smallpox, measles, and diphtheria, devastated the Laguna population.

Although she attended school for a few years at the old meeting hall, Lupe was more interested in her pottery. She became an excellent potter and sold her wares to passengers on the Santa Fe trains that stopped at Laguna. I attended school with one of Lupe's six children, Louise, and I came to know Lupe, as did other villagers, as a very good storyteller and cook.

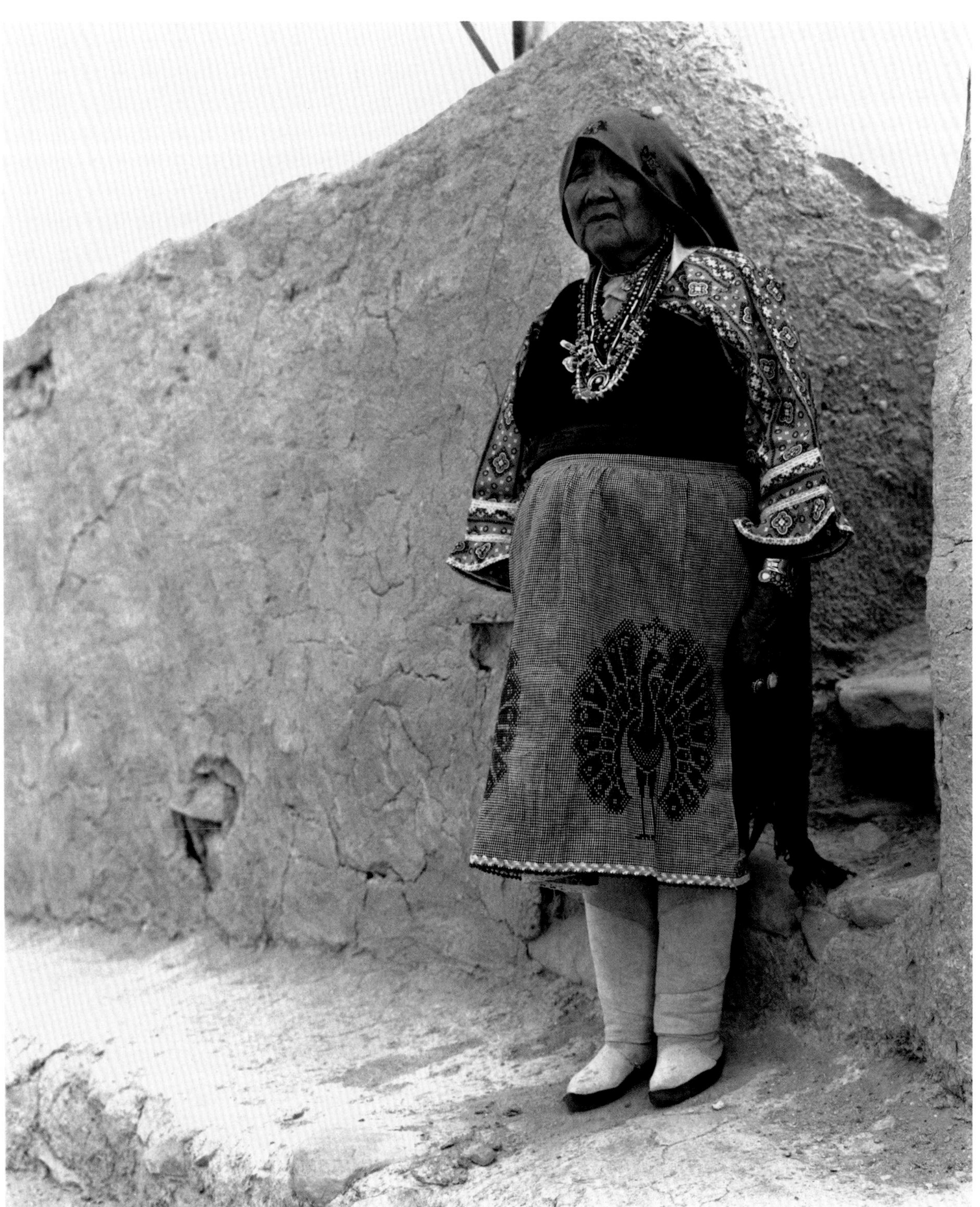

Eulojia Martin Johnson (1970)

Born in the village of Paguate on the Laguna reservation, Eulojia (1877–1982) grew up in the Paguate watchtower, a stone structure built in three levels and photographed by Edward Curtis in the late 1890s. The lower level was used for storing corn and wheat; the middle level was used for grinding the grains; and the upper level, accessible only by ladder, was used as a lookout and for protection of women and children during the Apache and Navajo raids. It was also used at times as a shelter for men and women who had journeyed for the day from the village of Laguna to farm the Paguate valley. Ultimately, the watchtower became the home of the Johnson family.

Eulojia married Paul Johnson, a rancher and farmer prominent in tribal politics. He was involved in religious societies and served as governor numerous times. Eulojia and Paul had eight children, four of whom are still living. Eulojia herself lived to be 105. She was 93 when the photo was taken.

Eulojia was my aunt Susie's half sister. One day my mother was helping Eulojia cross the backyard to Aunt Susie's place. "You ought to get her picture," my mom said. I told her the sun was not right. But my mom insisted. She went in and got a kitchen chair and put it in the middle of the yard. I took two or three close-ups.

Eulojia Martin Johnson. Photo by Lee Marmon (1970).

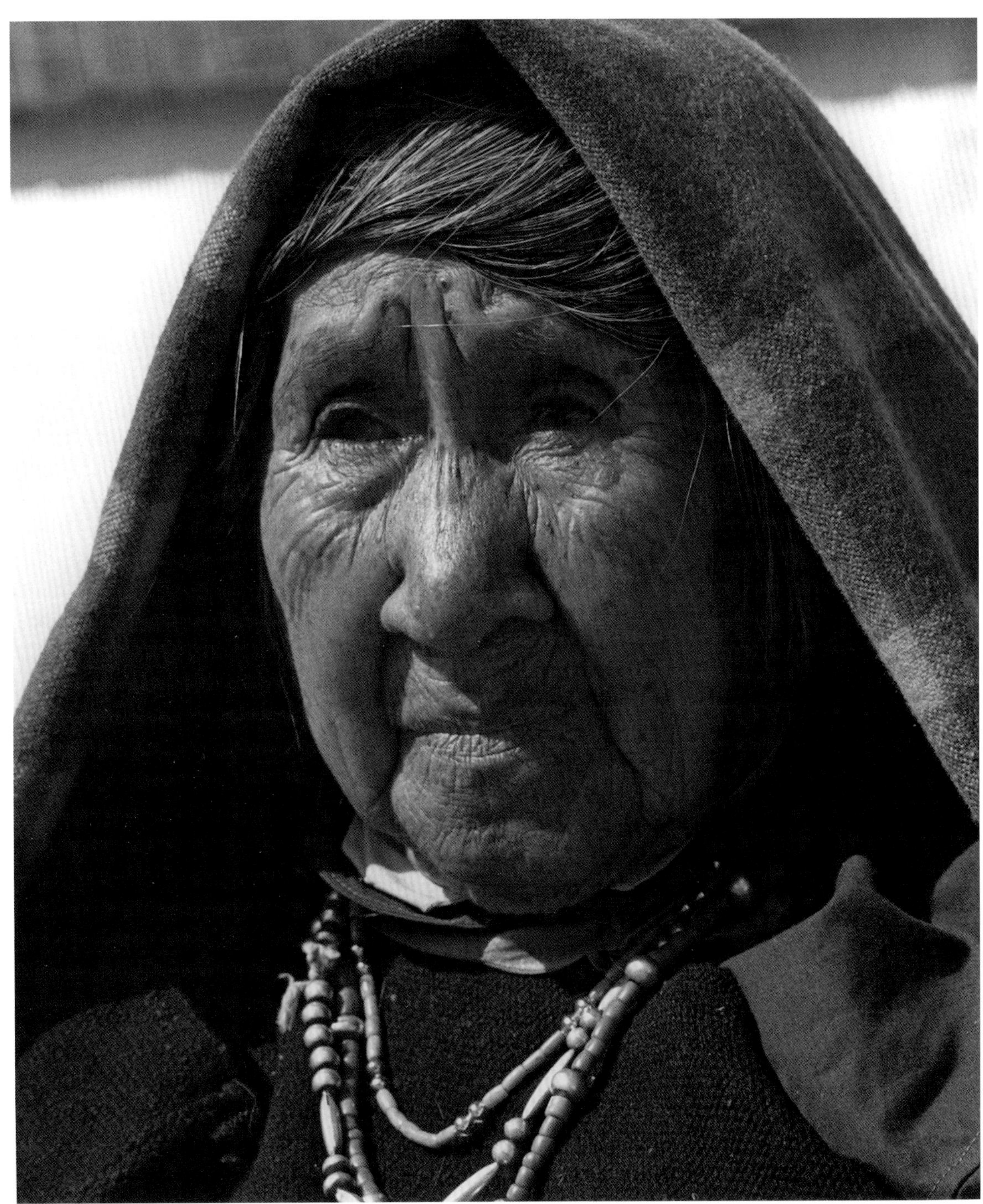

José Sanchu (1963)

José Sanchu (1879–1968) was born in Mesita, a village on the Laguna reservation. Some of his first memories were of the Santa Fe trains that first came to Laguna in the 1880s.

José married a woman named Raphelita and they farmed in Mesita. They were close friends of Henry Marmon, my father, who at the time was running the family trading post in Laguna. It was while I was delivering groceries for my father that I was able to take Jose's picture.

I remember José and Raphelita as a very friendly, intelligent couple. José was a war chief and served many times as a village officer. He also took on the responsibility of driving tribal council members in his wagon to their day-long meetings in Laguna. When my daughter Leslie was seven or eight years old, she used to like to ride in Jose's wagon. So on meeting day, which was every Monday, she would go down to the river and wait for him to come by. She would wave him down and he would put her in the wagon to ride up to the meeting hall with him. Many times I would leave Leslie in Mesita with the Sanchus, and she would often return to Laguna with them in that same wagon.

José Sanchu. Photo by Lee Marmon (1963).

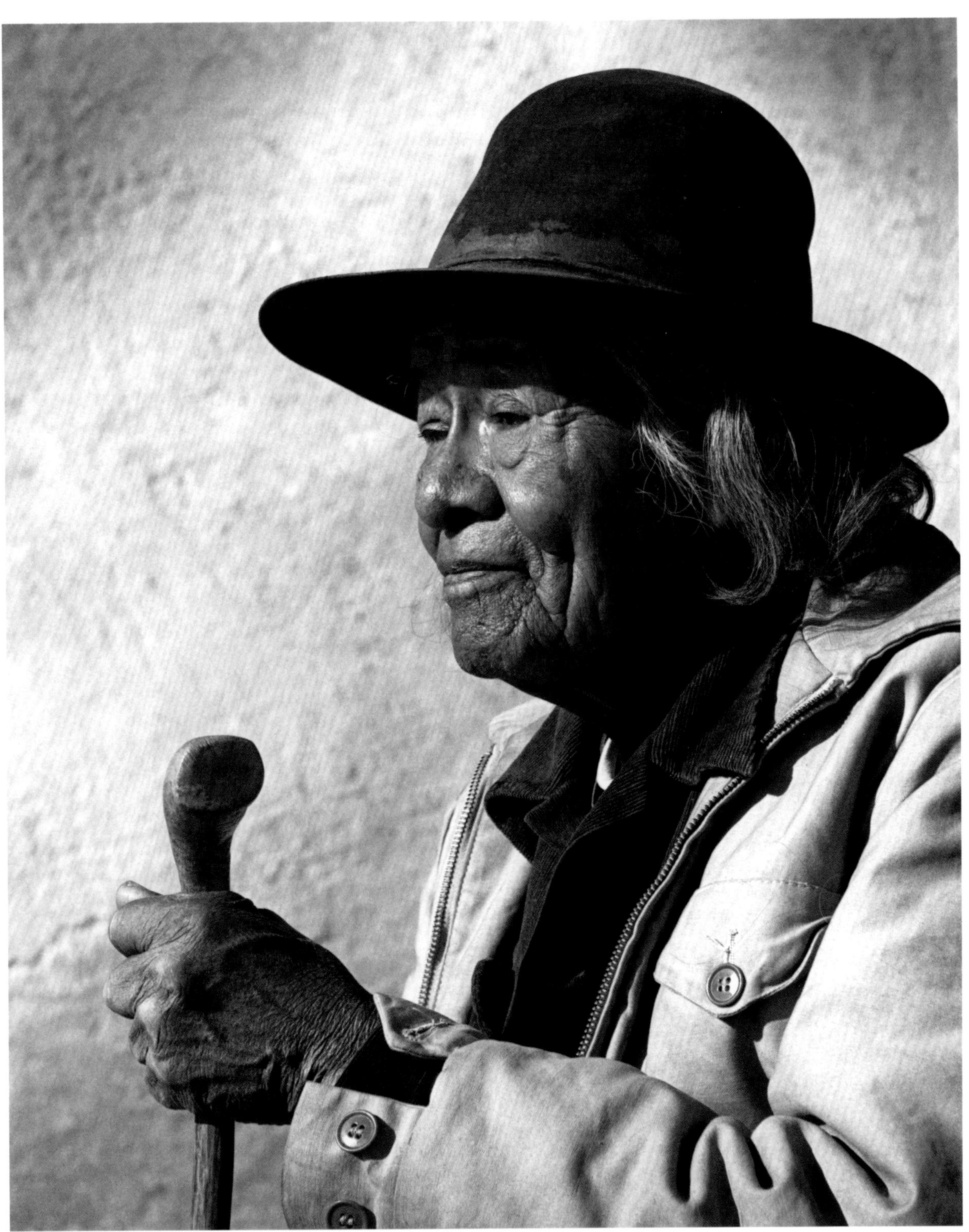

Susie Rayos Marmon (Aunt Susie) (1987)

Aunt Susie (1877–1988) was born the only child of Laguna parents in Paguate village in 1877. Her birth name was Dawa-Go-Mai-Tsa (pronounced Daiwa-gomatsi). She was given the name Susie when she was sent to the Albuquerque Presbyterian Mission, now the Menaul School. She also went to school in Carlisle, Pennsylvania, in the 1880s. Aunt Susie stayed out east to attend Bloomsburg State Teachers College in Pennsylvania, eventually returning to the reservation. She married Walter K. Marmon, the oldest son of my grandfather, Robert G. Marmon.

Aunt Susie is recognized as the first Laguna college graduate, having received a degree in education from Bloomsburg State Teachers College in 1906.

She was fluent in both her native Keresan and English and became Laguna Pueblo's matriarch educator. She devoted much of her life to her people by advocating higher education.

The North American Indian Women's Association, at its 1972 convention, honored Aunt Susie as the outstanding woman in the field of education for her fifty years as a teacher at both Laguna and Isleta Pueblos.

She was honored by Governor Garry Carruthers on April 15, 1987, which he proclaimed "Susie Rayos Marmon Day." Similar acknowledgments were received at the time from President Ronald Reagan, Senator Jeff Bingaman, and Senator Pete Domenici. She was given an American flag that had flown over the U.S. Capitol that day. In addition, the nineteen New Mexico pueblo governors, through the All Indian Pueblo Council, honored her "for her untiring efforts on behalf of all Indian people."

Aunt Susie lived to be 110 years old, passing away just eleven days short of her 111th birthday. I took this picture on her 110th birthday. She lived right behind our house with my uncle Walter.

Aunt Susie. Photo by Lee Marmon (1987).

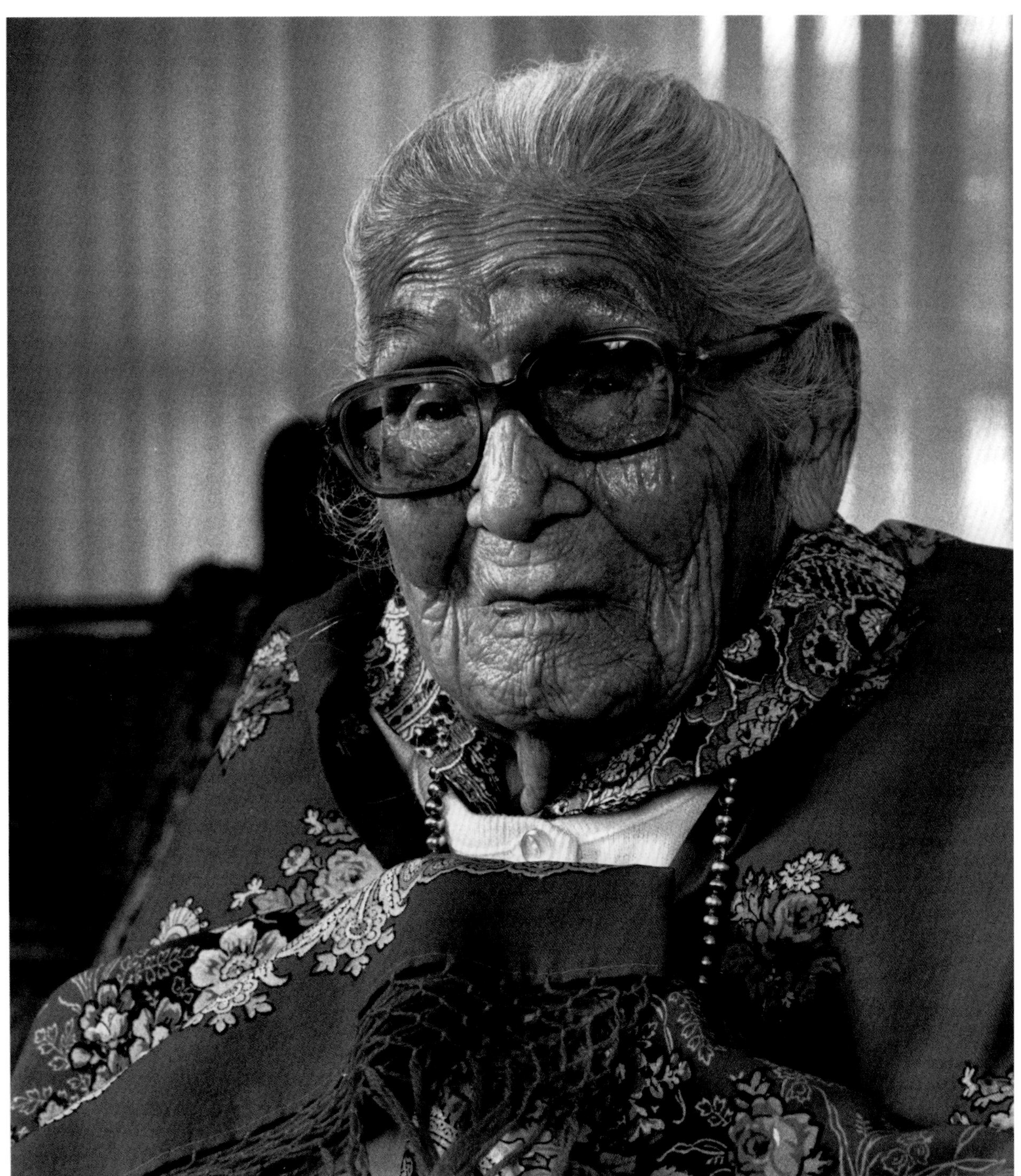

Rosita Johnson (1958)

Rosita Johnson (1876–1976) was born and raised in Laguna village. She married Frank Johnson from Paguate and had four sons—Valentine, Larry, Pete, and Frank. She was an expert potter. Customers from as far away as California came to New Mexico just to buy her pottery. She also sold her pottery to passengers on the Santa Fe trains that stopped at the Laguna station.

In addition to her artistic skills, Rosita was a very good adobe plasterer. She often hand-plastered houses in the village. While she was working one day, I asked her to pose for me. She agreed and changed into her traditional fiesta clothes.

Rosita Johnson. Photo by Lee Marmon (1958).

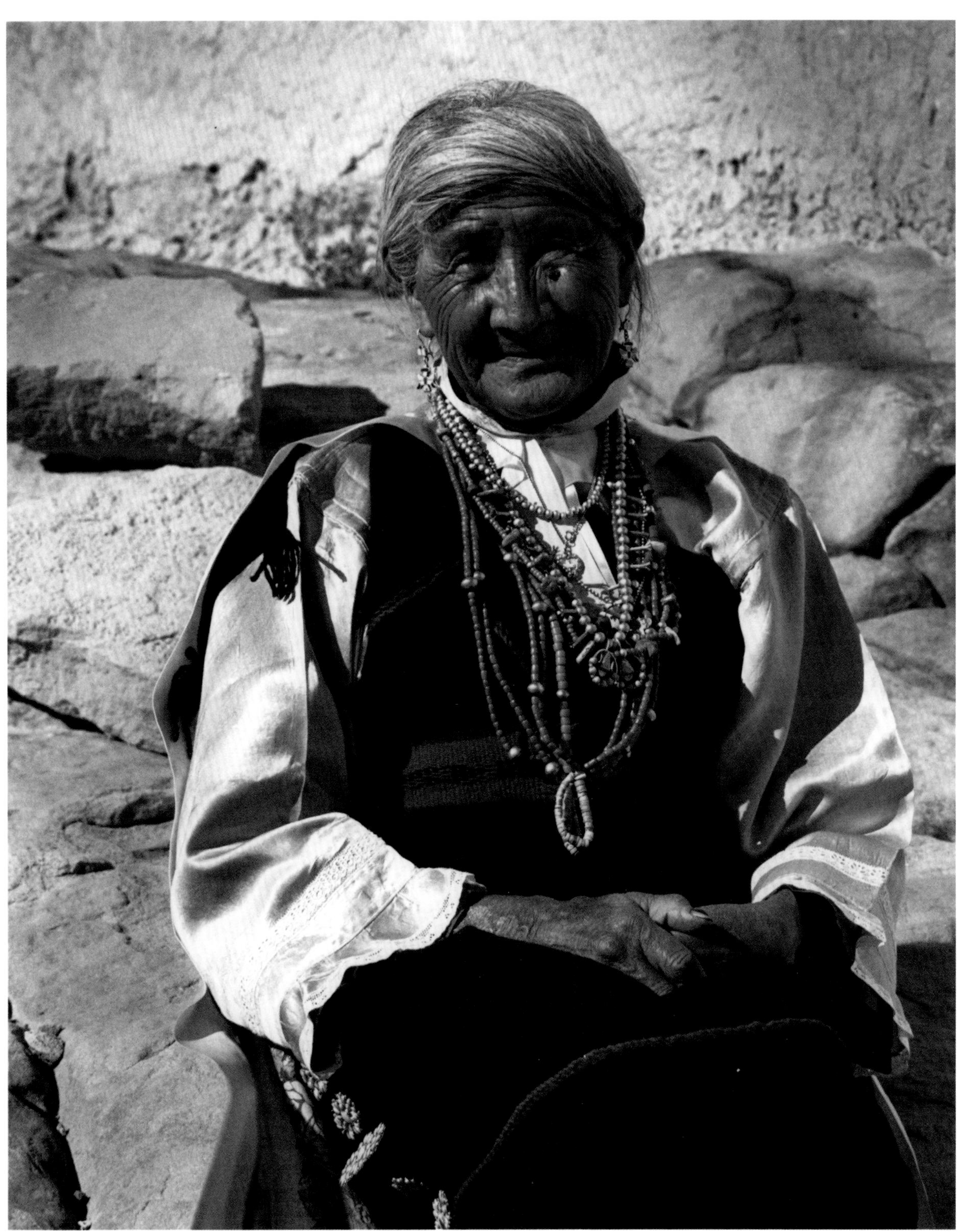

Etta Kycero (1955)

Etta Kycero. Photo by Lee Marmon (1955).

Etta Kycero was one of my neighbors. She made and sold pottery to the tourists. Her other expertise was making Indian bread—the best bread in the pueblo. She used to bring us a loaf about once a week. That was many years ago, and I sure miss that bread!

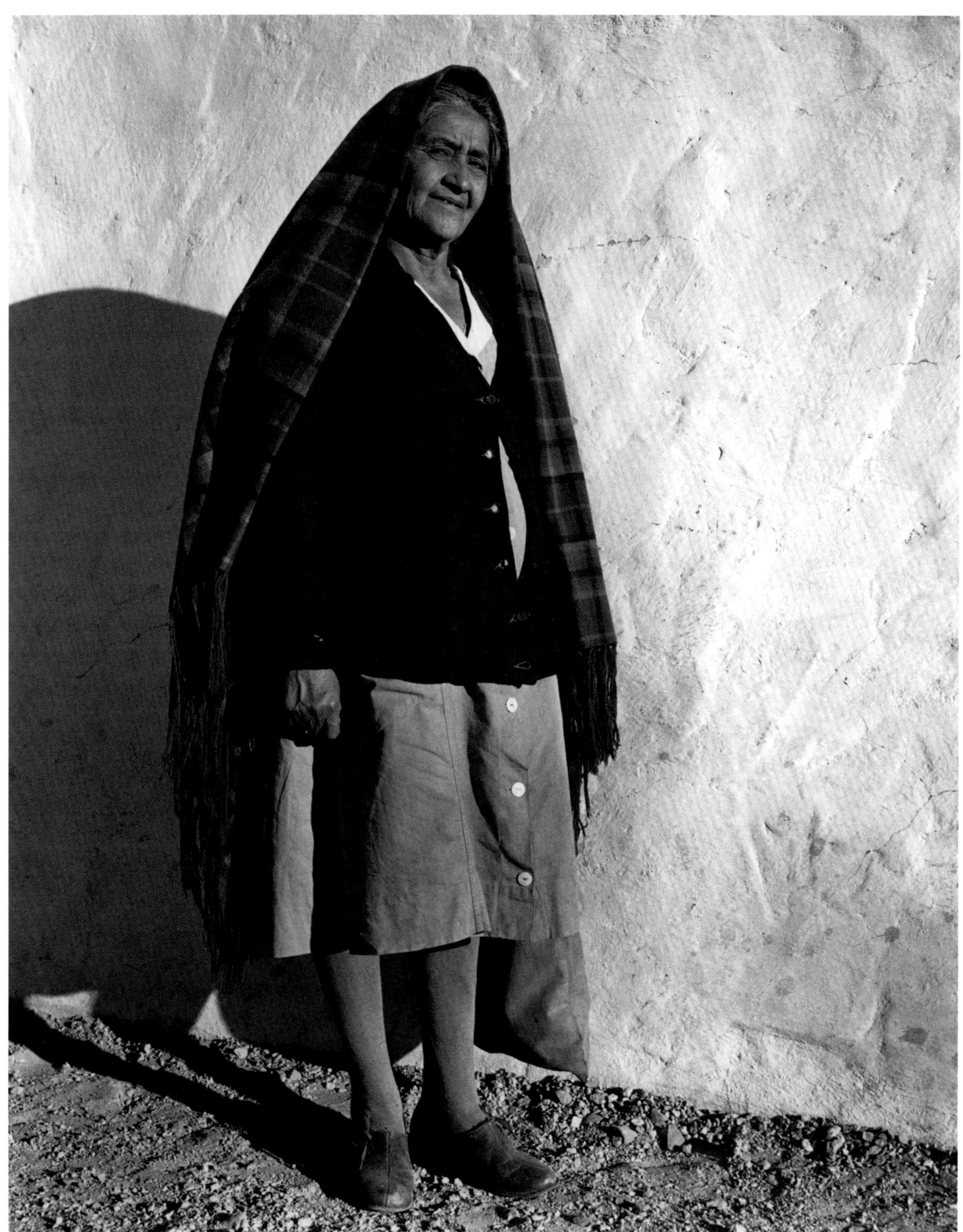

Romero Fernando (1963)

Romero Fernando was a successful sheepherder and cattleman from the village of Mesita.

He was getting very old and was losing his eyesight. When I crossed paths with him at a roundup, I asked about a picture, and he said, "Sure. Come on, take my picture." I took two or three pictures of him.

His two sisters took care of the sheep on the ranch where they lived east of Mesita. They're the ones I played a trick on one time. Somebody had left two stray dogs at the trading post. They were not puppies and weren't very cute. I knew no one would take them. I wondered what we were going to do with them.

Romero's two sisters came by the trading post one day, not long after the dogs arrived. They asked, "What kind of dogs are those?" Knowing they had sheep, I said, "They are very rare sheepdogs. Very expensive. From Australia. People left them here because they couldn't take them any farther into California. They're worth a lot of money, and I was going to sell them for a hundred dollars apiece, but I don't have time to find an owner. Would you be interested in taking them? They're really good with sheep!"

"They're really sheepdogs?" they repeated.

I said, "Yeah, and they're expensive."

"Oh! Okay, we'll take them," they said. So they took those two dogs.

About six months later, I went down to their sheep camp to deliver a refrigerator. It was a hot summer day. One of the girls came out of the house.

"You big liar!" she said. "These aren't sheepdogs! They're lazy and they just lie in the shade! They're not even good watchdogs!"

But at least I got rid of those dogs, and they had a home for a few years!

Romero Fernando. Photo by Lee Marmon (1963).

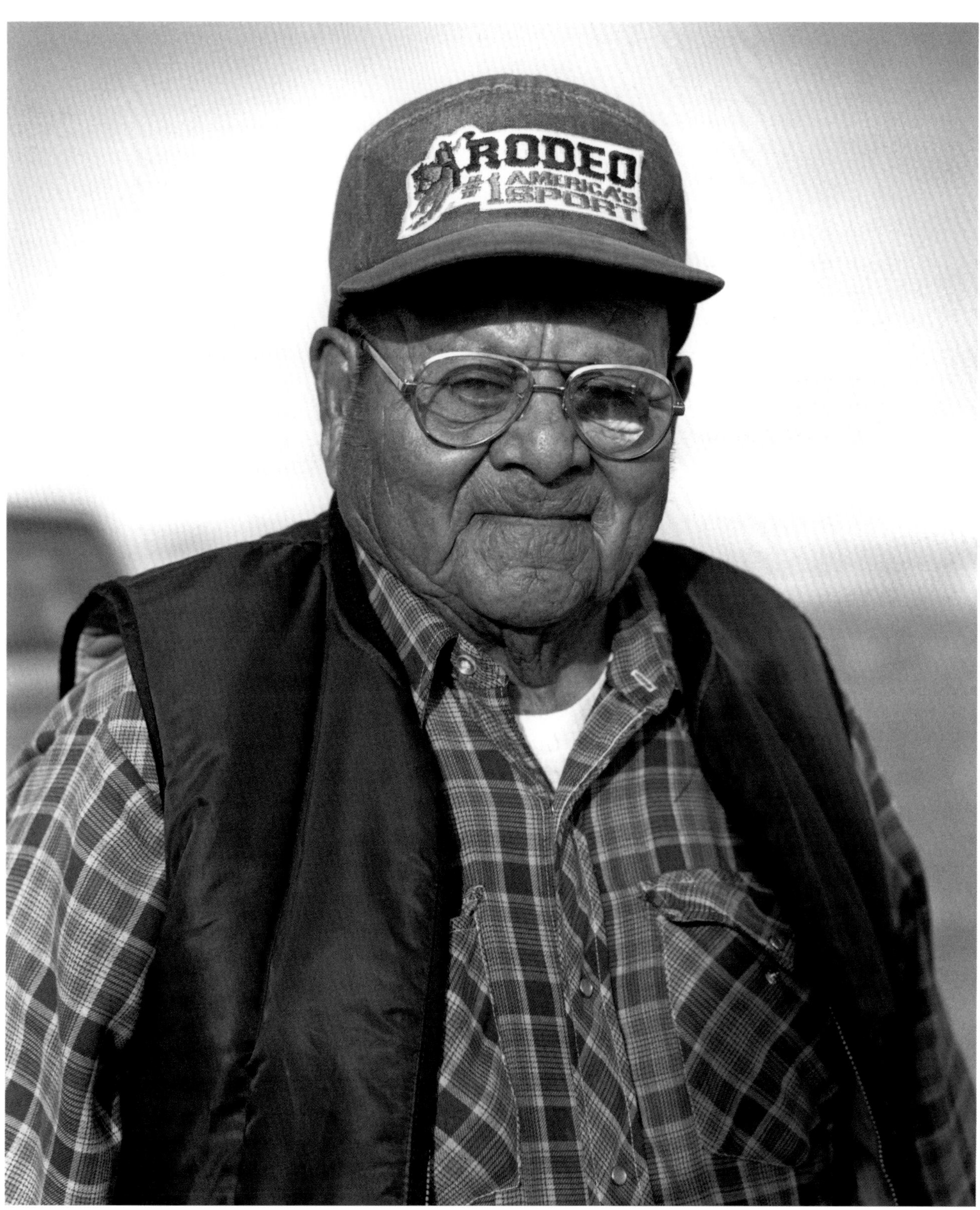
RODEO
#1 AMERICA'S SPORT

Lola Steele (1982)

Lola Steele. Photo by Lee Marmon (1982).

Lola Steele lived in Mesita village, east of Laguna. I used to visit her when I was out delivering groceries. After I left to go to California, I'd come back every so often. One time my mother wrote and told me Lola was looking for me—she wanted to talk to me about something. I told my mom that next time I returned, I'd visit Lola and see what she wanted.

When I got back from California, I went to Mesita village and knocked on her door. I didn't hear anything. I knocked again and then just walked in. She was lying there on her bed. She wasn't feeling very well, so I visited awhile with her and then said, "My mom said you were looking for me. What do you need?"

"I've been waiting for you," she said. "I want you to measure a window glass for me. You're the only one who measures them right!"

I measured the window for her and got the glass and put it in, and she was satisfied. She had waited almost a whole year for me to come and fix that window.

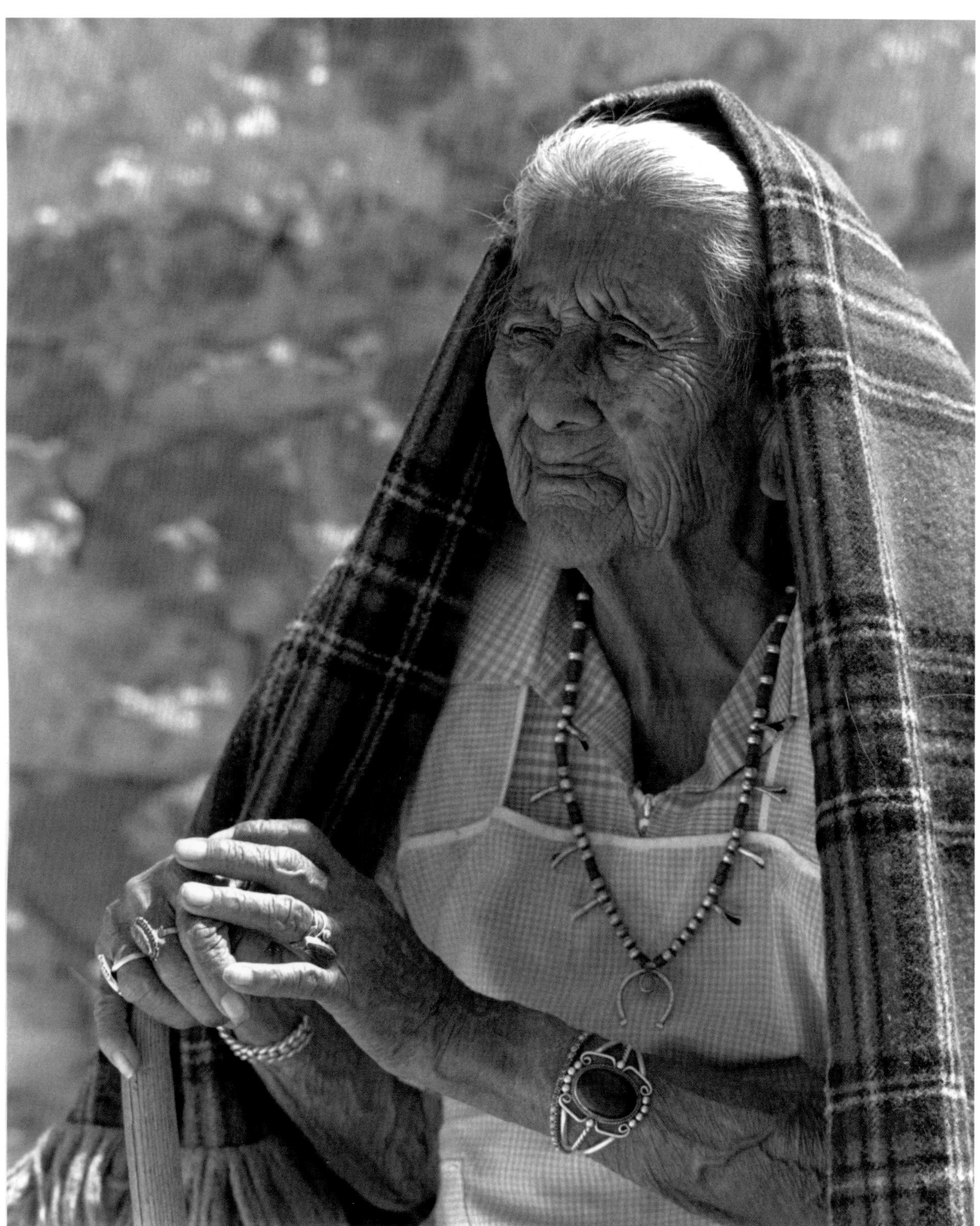

Santiago Fernando (1949)

Irvin W. Shiosee, Laguna oral historian and grandson of Santiago Fernando (1874–1972), provided this account of his grandfather's life.

Santiago Fernando learned the lessons of hard work and family responsibility at an early age. Raised by his grandmother, he had to earn money to help pay for food for his grandmother, younger brother, and himself.

In 1887, when Santiago was in his early teens, he looked for good-paying jobs that would allow him to continue supporting his family. One day, he approached a railroad foreman while his crew was working on the tracks near Mesita village and asked him for a job. The foreman told him he was too young to hire; railroad rules stated that teenagers could not be hired to do the manual labor required.

As Santiago looked around, he noticed one of the workers drinking water at the station, quite a distance from where the man had been working. Santiago then asked the foreman if any rules had been made against hiring a water boy and suggested that it would save a lot of time for the workers if they did not have to walk back to the station to drink water. He could take the water in a bucket or cup to the workers instead. So Santiago was hired.

Several years later, the railroad gave him a job as a track inspector. He drove a handcar (pump trolley) up and down the tracks to look for damage from rain, flooding, or other causes. If he found damage, he would put up a flag to let the train engineer know to stop. Then he would return to Mesita to let the workers know they needed to repair the track. A construction crew, along with a team of horses, would be dispatched to repair the damage.

Later, Santiago decided to travel with the railroad crew to California. There, he worked hard and saved enough money to return to Mesita. With his savings, he purchased livestock—cattle, sheep, and horses—and farm equipment. He planted fruit trees of different kinds and raised vegetables. He also planted hay and grain for the livestock and for human consumption.

Because of his accomplishments on his farm, many fathers in the village asked him to marry their daughters. Santiago eventually accepted one of the proposals, married, and had eight children. Following in their father's footsteps, his four sons all worked for the railroad.

Santiago Fernando passed away in 1972. He left his livestock and fields to his children.

Santiago Fernando. Photo by Lee Marmon (1949).

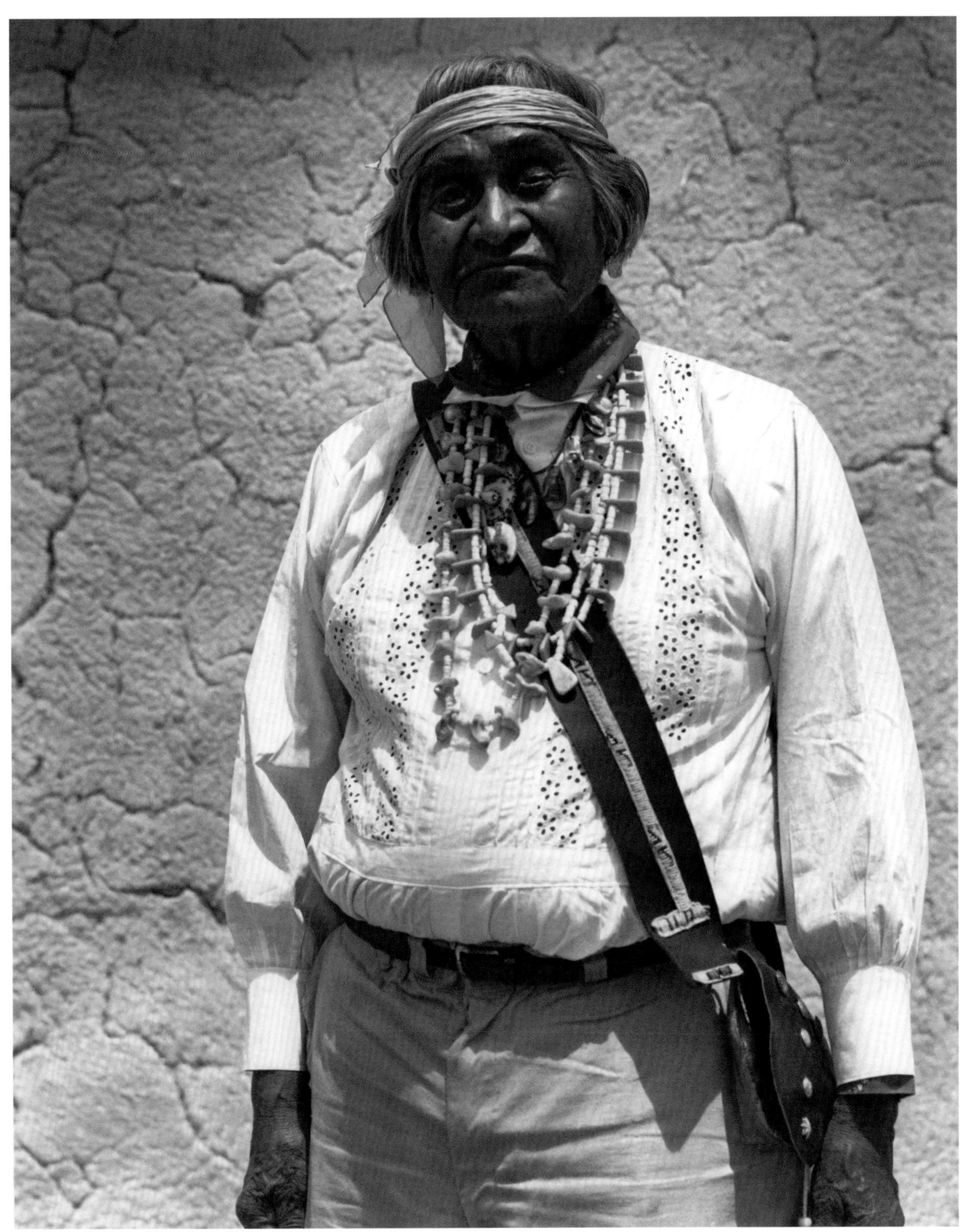

John Riley (1950)

This is one of my favorite pictures.

In 1950, I had just purchased a new four-by-five-speed graphic and was walking around the village with the camera. I came upon John Riley sitting there beating the drum. His grandchildren were dancing. And of course the real shot would have been all of them together, but for some reason, when I moved in and took a picture of him alone beating the drum, the children stopped dancing.

John Riley. Photo by Lee Marmon (1950).

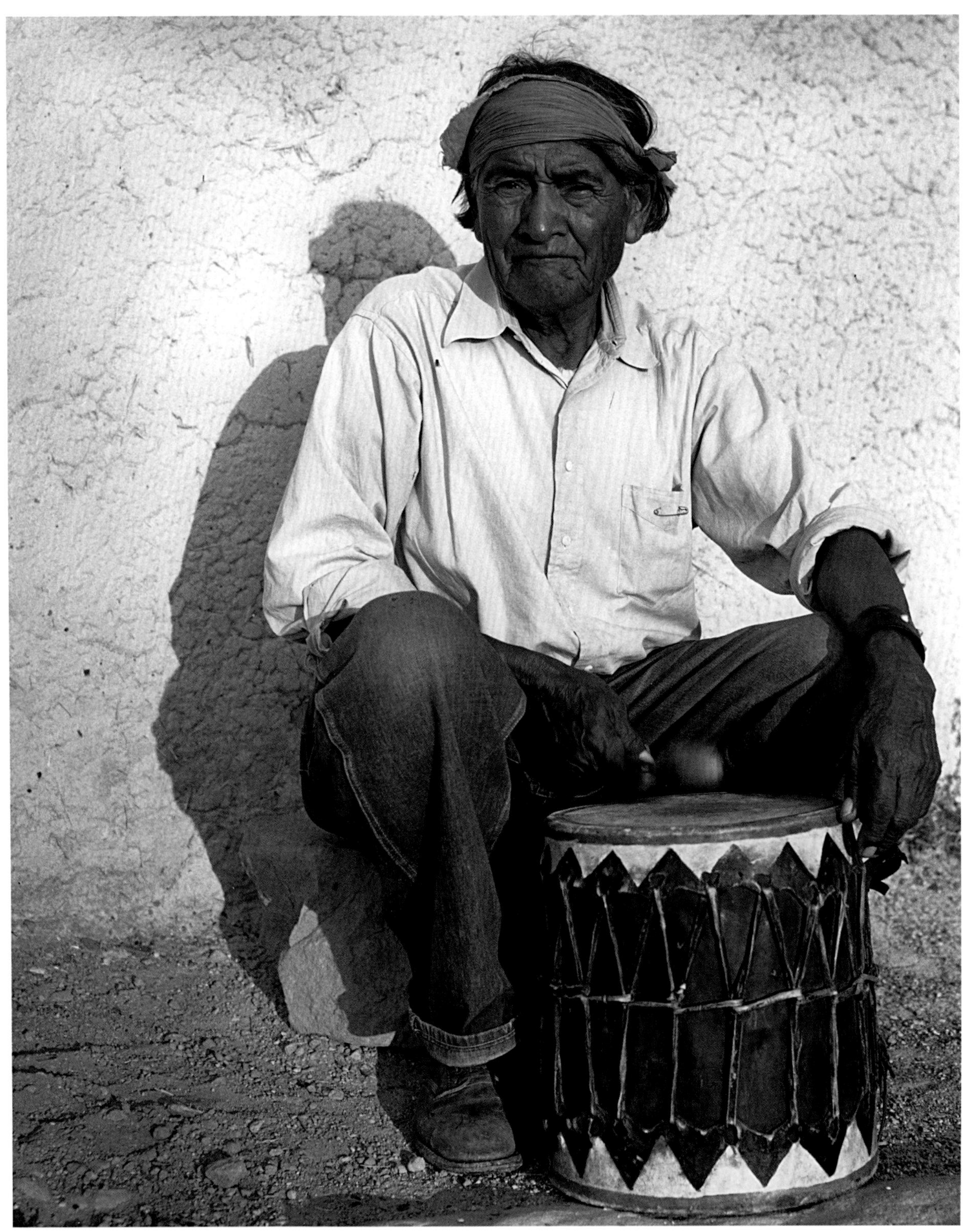

Charlie Atsye. Photo by Lee Marmon (1979).

Charlie Atsye (1979)

Charlie Atsye (1896–1986) was from Laguna village, the son of John and Marie Mariano Atsye. He attended the Laguna Day School from 1904 to 1905 and the Albuquerque Indian School from 1909 to 1912. He then attended the Carlisle Indian School from 1913 to 1914. During his summer break at Carlisle, he worked on an Amish farm.

Charlie returned to Laguna for a while and worked as a ranch hand on the Gunn brothers' cattle ranch. He later became a rodeo bareback rider, traveling the rodeo circuit around California and Nevada. He also worked at times as a longshoreman in shipyards and for the Santa Fe Railroad in Winslow, Arizona.

Charlie was easily recognized by his six-foot-two height, cowboy boots and ten-gallon hat, and good sense of humor. He married Alice Marmon in 1922 and they had nine children.

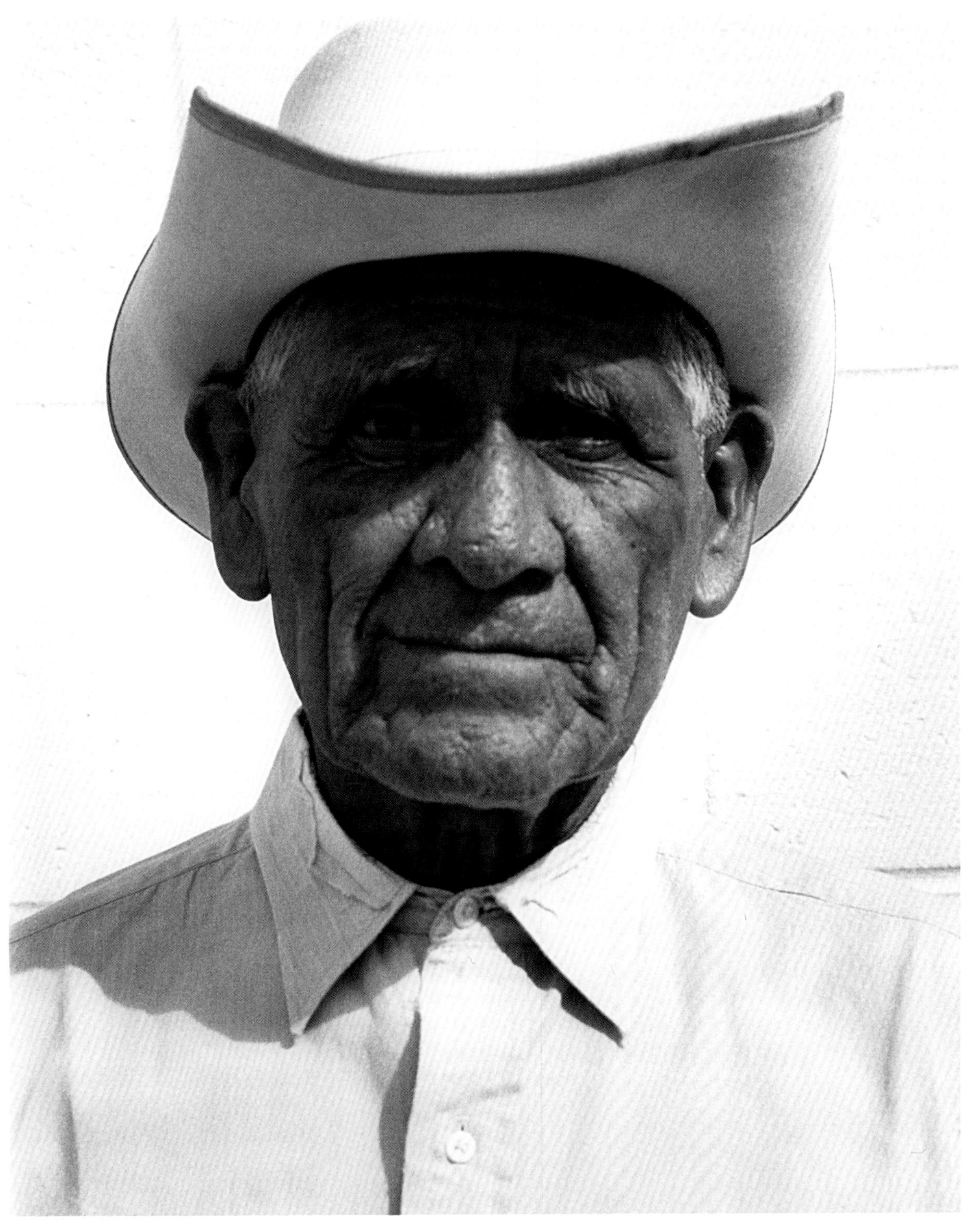

Governor Solomon with Photos (1958)

James Solomon was the governor of Laguna in 1958 when the Laguna Constitution was amended.

He was very proud that he had many sons in military service and wanted a photograph of himself with the pictures of his sons.

Governor Solomon with Photos. Photo by Lee Marmon (1958).

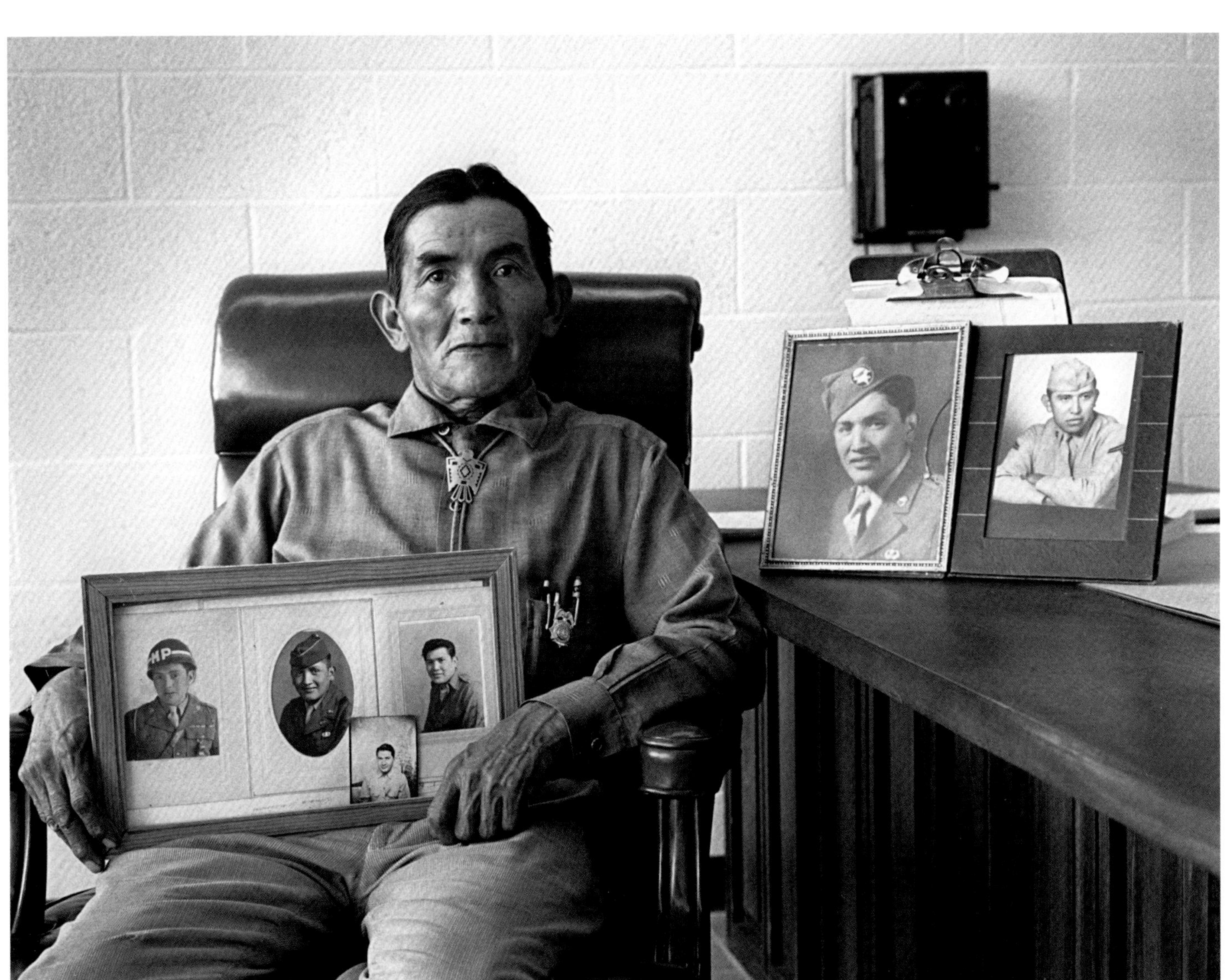
MP

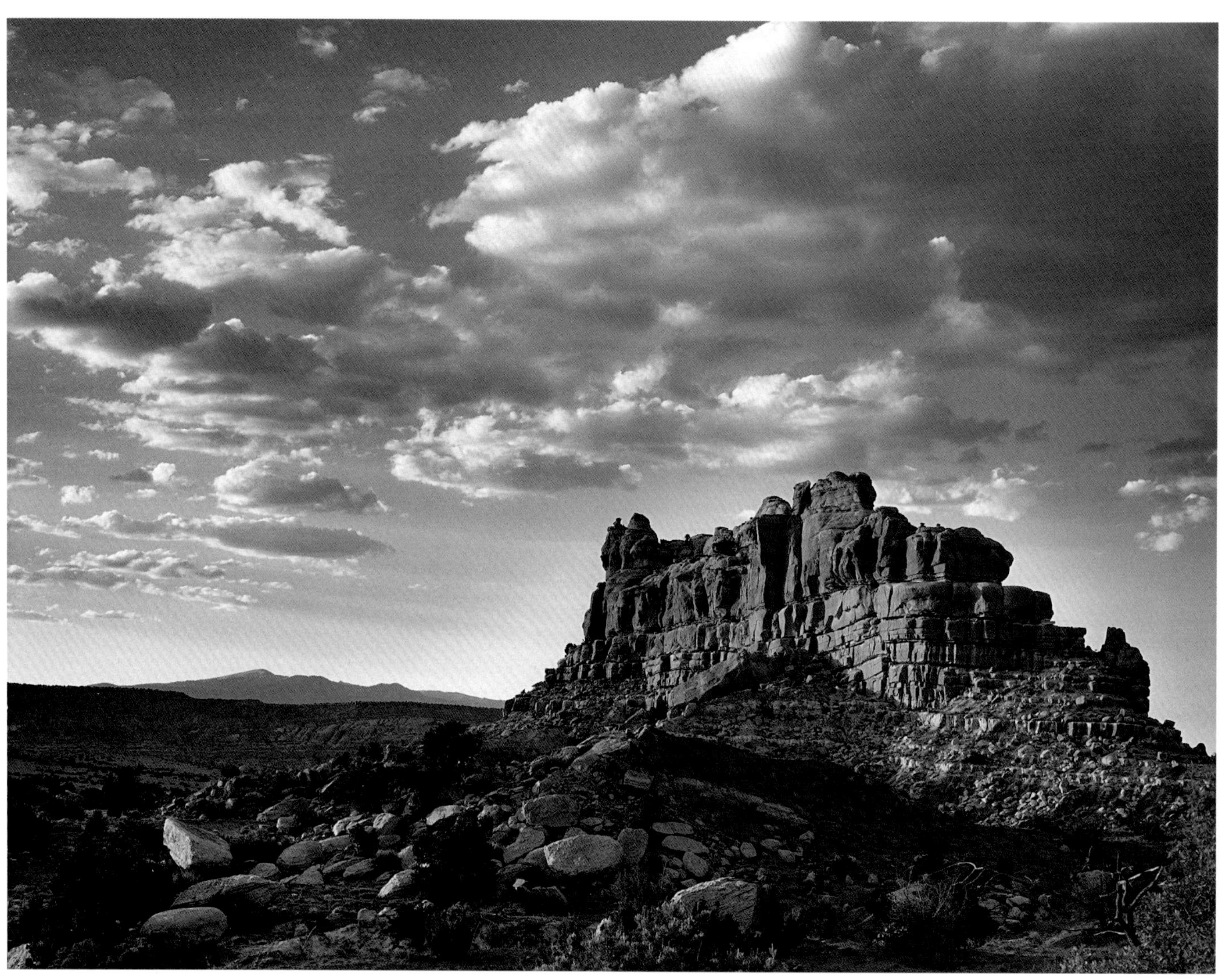

Engine Rock. This spectacular rock formation is located between Laguna and Acoma. The mystical Mount Taylor in the background and the clouds overhead make this scene synonymous with the "Land of Enchantment." Photo by Lee Marmon (1980).

CHAPTER THIRTEEN

Landscapes

Material from this chapter was transcribed by Tom Corbett from recorded interviews with Lee Marmon.

The scenery around Laguna hasn't changed much since William Henry Jackson set up his fourteen-by-seventeen-plate camera below Laguna Pueblo in the late 1880s. The change is even less apparent in the Acoma Valley where Coronado's men marched through in 1540. The only change they would notice today is Interstate 40 and the paved road from I-40 to "Sky City"—the mystical sandstone village atop a mesa that Coronado's soldiers saw for the first time over four hundred years ago. What would that have been like . . . to be an observer sitting on one of the mesas overlooking the valley and seeing Coronado's party of soldiers on horseback, coming down the valley with all their flags flying and their armor shining in the sun? What a photograph that would have made!

I love landscape photography. I consider the genre one of the most difficult photographic endeavors. Scenic photographs I consider either good or bad. There is no in between. It's very difficult to get a really, really good landscape photo. I consider the following photographs to be among my finest.

I loved to drive that old Model A truck around the reservation with my dog sitting next to me. He liked to ride, and I had my camera; when I'd see a good landscape shot, I'd stop and take a few pictures. I wish someone had taken a photo of me with the dog in that old truck.

I'm so happy to have been able to record the images of the past. I'm especially pleased to be able to pass them on so people today can look at the photographs, study the details, and remember the fine old people, the pristine landscapes, and the times when life moved at a much slower pace than it does now.

Clouds over the Malpais. Photo by Lee Marmon (1985).

Clouds over the Malpais (1985)

I always enjoyed a little time away from the trading post—getting out and being free—photographing landscapes with big clouds billowing up and finding new areas to photograph. My daughter wrote in one of her books that when the big clouds came up, I would always be away from the trading post, out taking pictures.

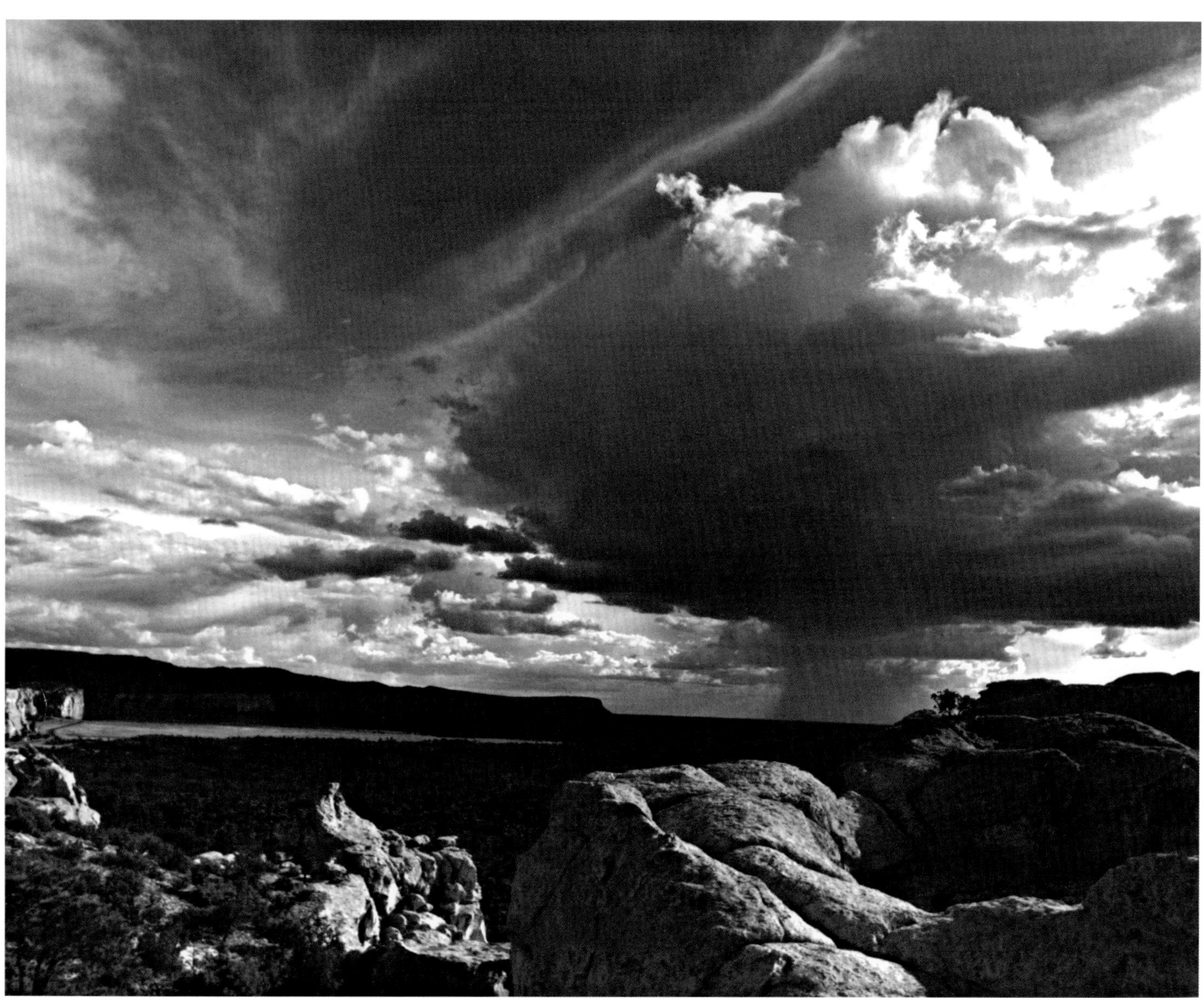

Katzimo—"Enchanted Mesa" (1990)

While traveling from the Laguna reservation to Acoma, one cannot miss Katzimo—"Enchanted Mesa"—with its walls of red and gray sandstone rising an impressive 430 feet above the Acoma plain. The sheer walls now make the flat top of the mesa inaccessible.

The legend of Katzimo has been told by Acoma oral historians for centuries. A village, accessible only by narrow steps carved in the sheer cliff, once existed on the summit. The Acomas had constructed their village on the forty acres of the plateau by carrying all the necessary materials up the treacherous pathway.

The high location offered the inhabitants protection from marauding tribes seeking their crops, livestock, and women. The village could be easily defended against an enemy trying to climb to the top, one warrior at a time. When marauding tribes were spotted in the distance, the villagers climbed to the protection of the village on the summit before the enemy arrived.

The Acomas farmed the fertile valley below, growing corn and beans, and they hunted the plentiful game on the surrounding hills and mesas.

According to legend, one day while many of the villagers were farming the fields below, a violent thunderstorm swept in, followed by flooding, and caused the east wall of the mesa to collapse. Some of the villagers, who had gathered at the base of the mesa to wait out the storm, were crushed by the falling rocks.

The stairway was gone, and those still on the mesa were trapped with no way to escape. Rather than die a slow death from dehydration or starvation, some chose to jump off the mesa. Others stayed and died a few days or weeks later.

The number of village inhabitants at the time the mesa wall collapsed varies from storyteller to storyteller but generally ranges from 600 to 1,500. The number of people trapped on the mesa varies but has been reported as high as 300—mostly children and elders.[1] The survivors moved to the adjacent mesa several miles away and built the present village of Acoma.

For many years, outsiders regarded the legend of Katzimo as questionable. In 1897, Professor Frederick Webb Hodge and his party scaled the cliffs of Enchanted Mesa and found irrefutable proof that the village did exist.[2]

Katzimo—"Enchanted Mesa." Photo by Lee Marmon (1990).

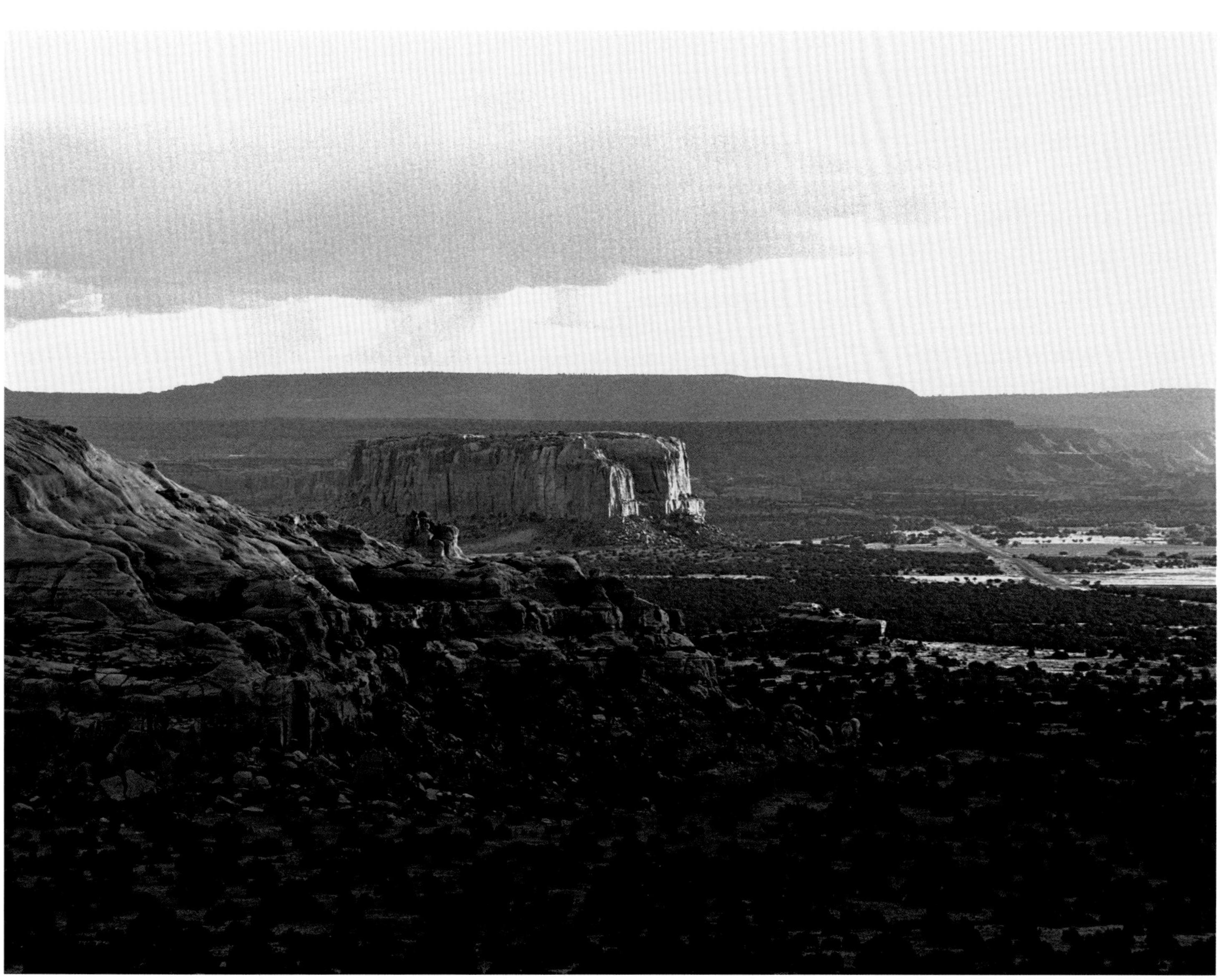

Dripping Springs (1985)

One of my favorite places to photograph is Dripping Springs—640 acres of land our family owns just southwest of Laguna, not far from Acoma Pueblo. My grandfather bought it from his father-in-law in 1880.

The property consists mostly of sandstone cliffs and mesas. It is a very scenic place, and I spend a lot of time photographing its waterholes and sandstone formations. Especially picturesque are the moments when the clouds billow up in and around the flat tops of some of the taller mesas and the light is just right; then, it is worth waiting to see the changing shadows and late-afternoon colors. I never tire of hiking there and looking for shards and arrowheads. Petroglyphs, pictographs, and ruins abound; we make new discoveries almost every time we go out there. My grandfather used to run cattle at Dripping Springs until the reservation extended too close and he had to move the cattle operations to a new location.

Two springs refresh the property. One of the springs drips down a canyon like a shower. The other emerges inside a cave; it runs out of the cave into a tank my grandfather Stagner built in 1932, during the drought that occurred through the Depression years. People have told me that no rain fell from 1928 to 1938, so the spring saved a lot of cattle and sheep. It was the only water available in that part of the country, so my family built the tank just for catching the water and piped it down to a lower level where the animals could drink.

The springs are still flowing today. And the tank is currently being refurbished so it will hold more water. The pools there in the picture fill with rainwater. It is good clean water, and we used to drink it when we were kids.

In the summertime my mother used to drop my brother Polly and me at Dripping Springs and we'd spend a week out there. We'd climb all over, even though there were rattlesnakes. We never got bit. One time she dropped us out there and the second day I ripped the seat out of my pants. I had to wear my bathing trunks for almost a week out there, and that wasn't too comfortable. I got a bad sunburn.

Polly died in 2012. We scattered his ashes at Dripping Springs.

Dripping Springs. Photo by Lee Marmon (1985).

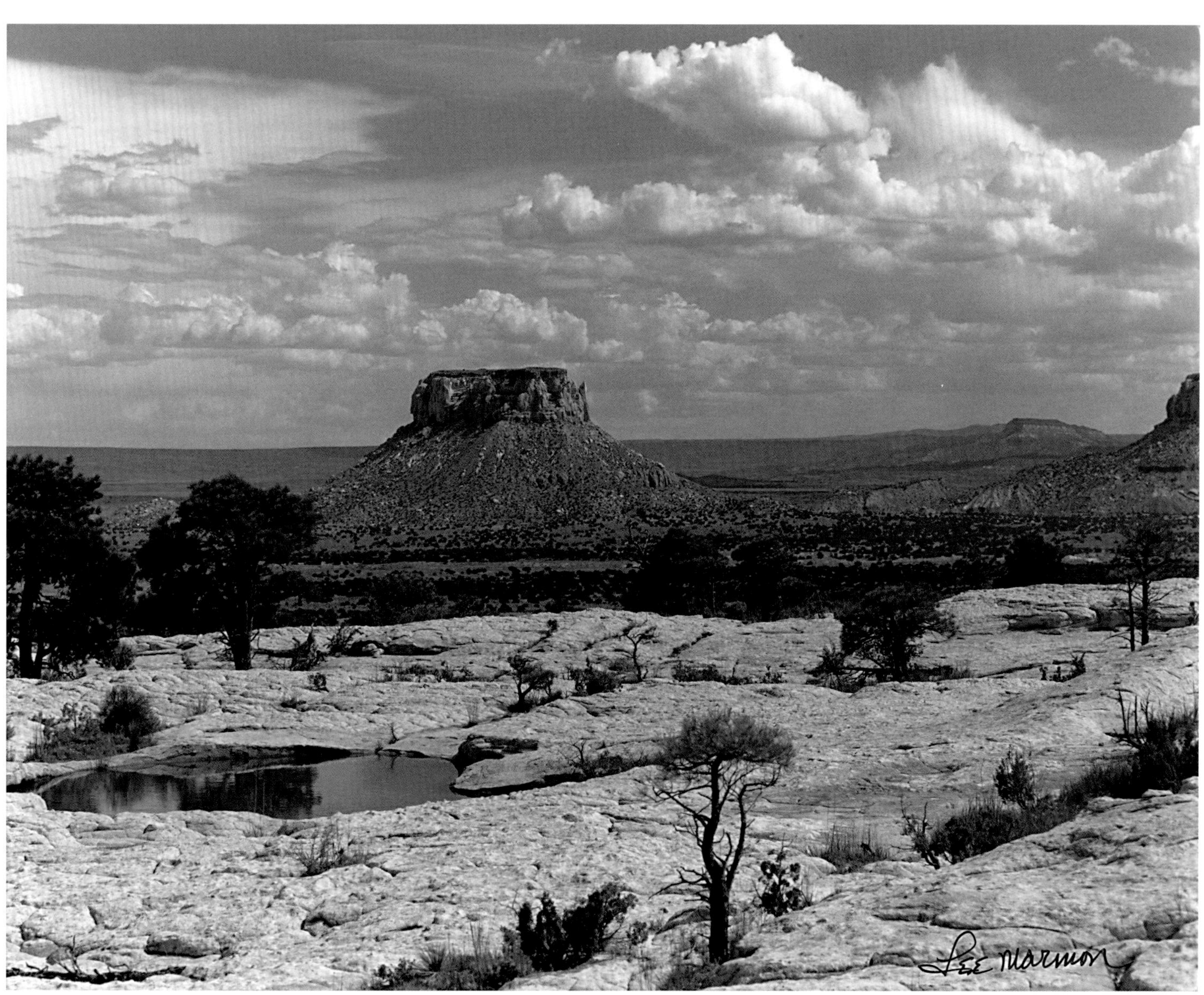
Lee Marmon

Buzzard Butte (1985)

I was out on a mesa alone, taking pictures. I had an orange backpack that held some of my equipment and a couple of sandwiches. I set the backpack down. I was trying to get set up, to decide what I was going to do that day. Just then, a buzzard started circling—a turkey buzzard—and was getting very curious about what I was doing. He kept circling and circling and getting lower and lower. I had a .32 Beretta in my back pocket. I thought, "Well, I'll just take a shot at him." The buzzard was traveling about two hundred feet above me, a moving target, but I hit him perfectly, right through the heart. He dropped like a rock.

As he was coming down, I realized he was going to hit me if I didn't move, but I couldn't move forward because I was standing right on the edge of the mesa. So I stepped back, and just as I stepped back, he hit right at my feet. Then he fell into the canyon, about 150 or 200 feet below. I thought about how ironic it would have been had he hit and killed me—knocked me into the canyon—and a search party had found the two of us, both dead at the bottom. I climbed down to the place where he fell. I modified my tripod into a makeshift travois, carried the buzzard back up, and took some pictures.

Buzzard Butte. Photo by Lee Marmon (1985).

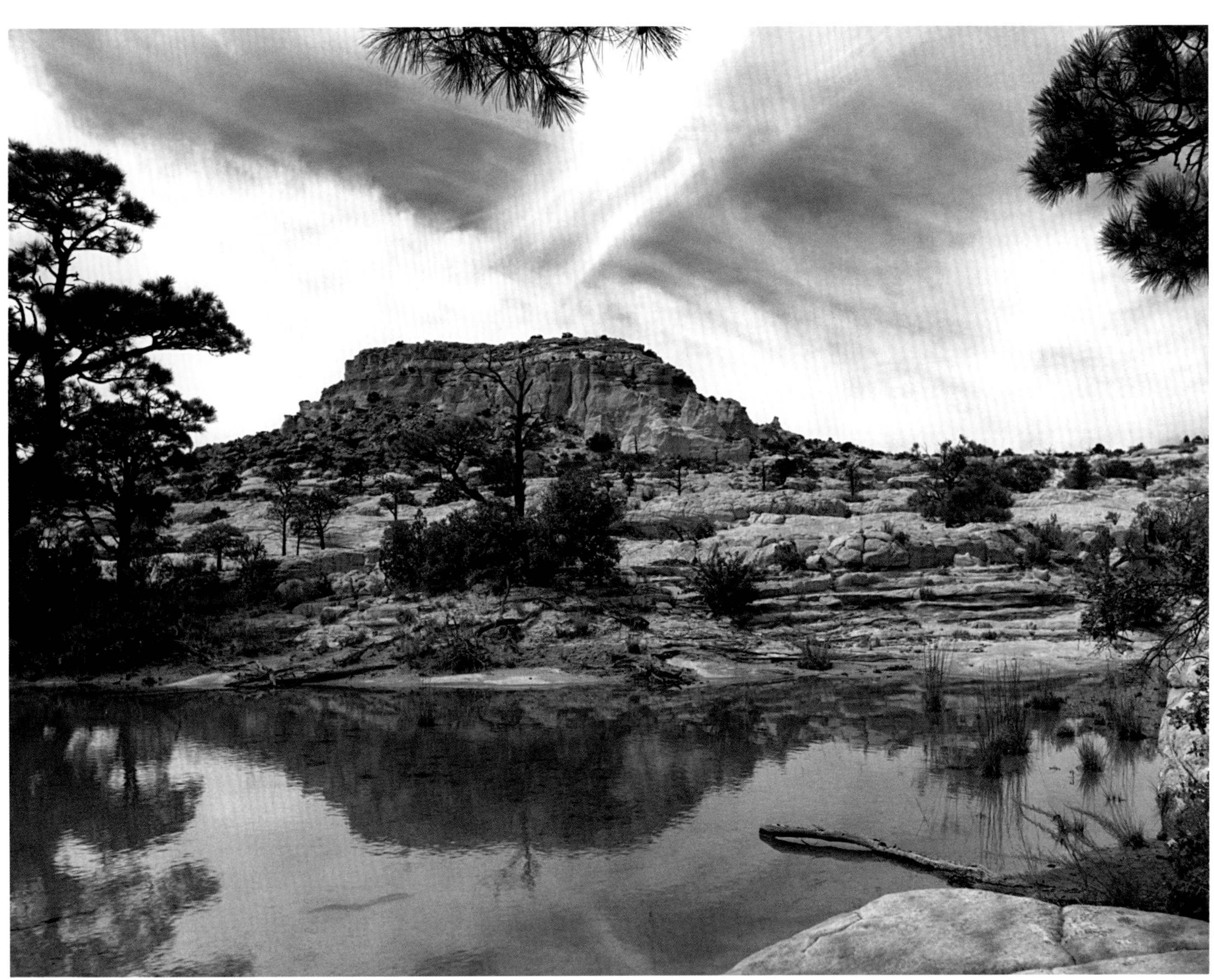

Mushroom Rocks (1995)

Mushroom Rocks. Photo by Lee Marmon (1995).

Here is another scenic shot on the road to Acoma. There is an outcropping of rocks I call Mushroom Rocks. It has some intricate sandstone formations that look like statues and shadows and things of that sort. You can pick out a shadow that looks like a person.

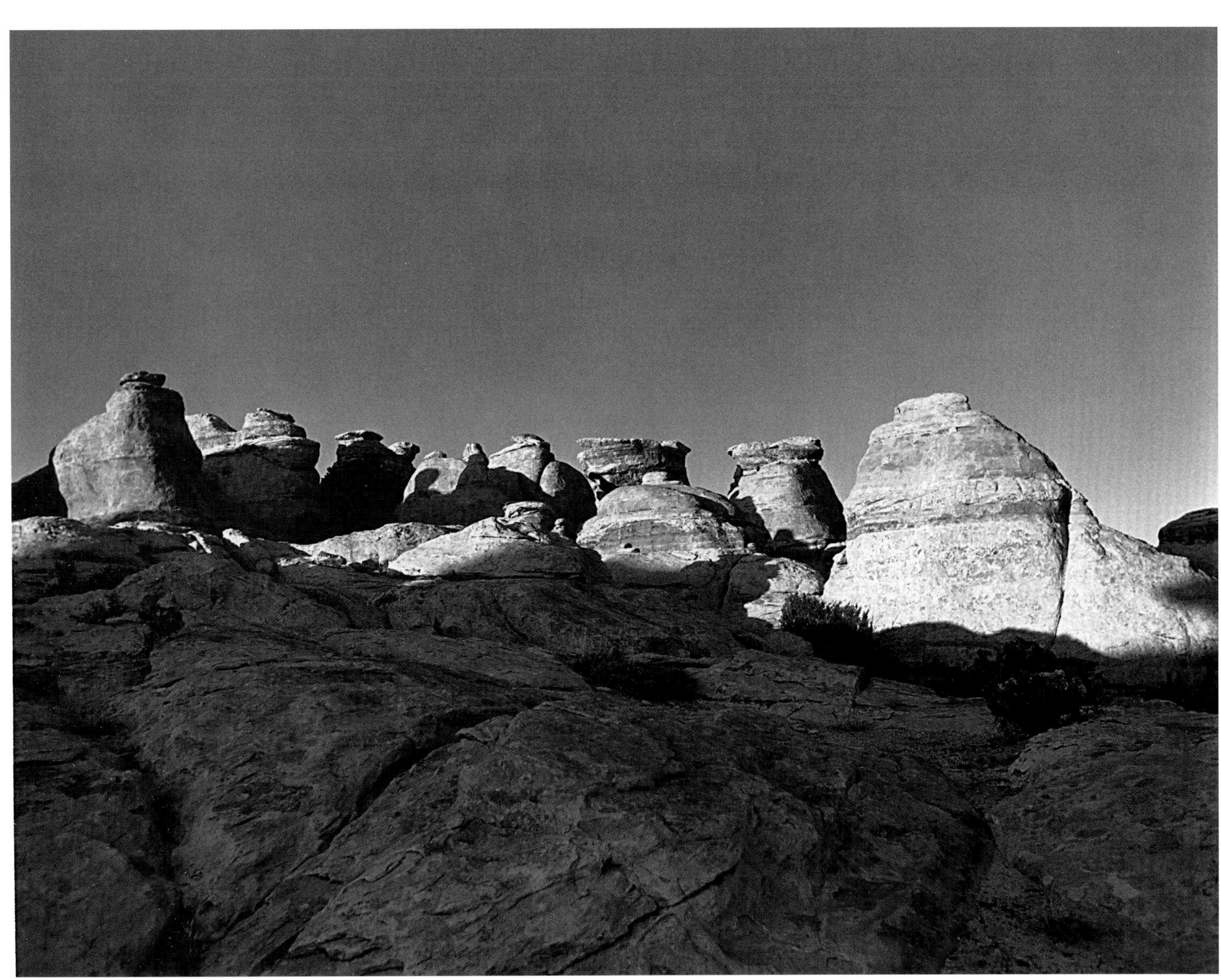

Penitente Cross. Photo by Lee Marmon (1962).

Penitente Cross (1962)

Headed north, to the L-Bar Ranch, I drove over the crest of a hill and came upon three crosses. Locals used to think they were graves, but a grouping like this is known as a *descanso*. It's a stop, a place of rest.

The Penitentes were members of a religious order often found in the small towns in New Mexico. The little Mexican village of Seboyeta is situated east of the L-Bar Ranch, and when someone died, the Penitentes would take the casket to Seboyeta for burial. The pictured descanso was one of the places along the way that they would stop and pray.

We passed through there in 1962. I took a couple of pictures—a close-up and one farther back—and the two have been very popular as a set. The smaller cross in this photo was made of metal and nailed to a wooden cross. It was worn and old. Not long after I took the picture, the cross was stolen.

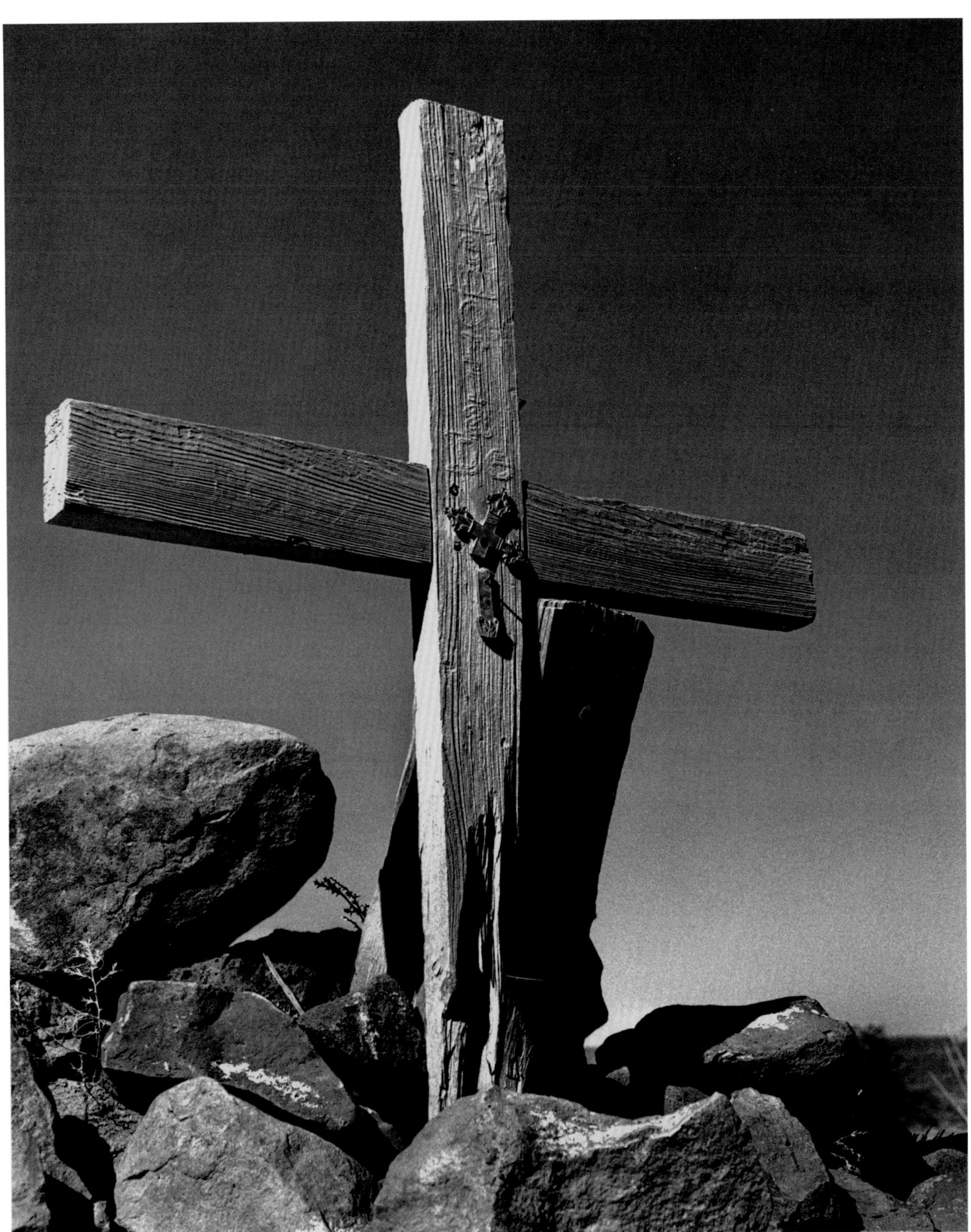

Close-up of *Penitente Cross*. Photo by Lee Marmon (1962).

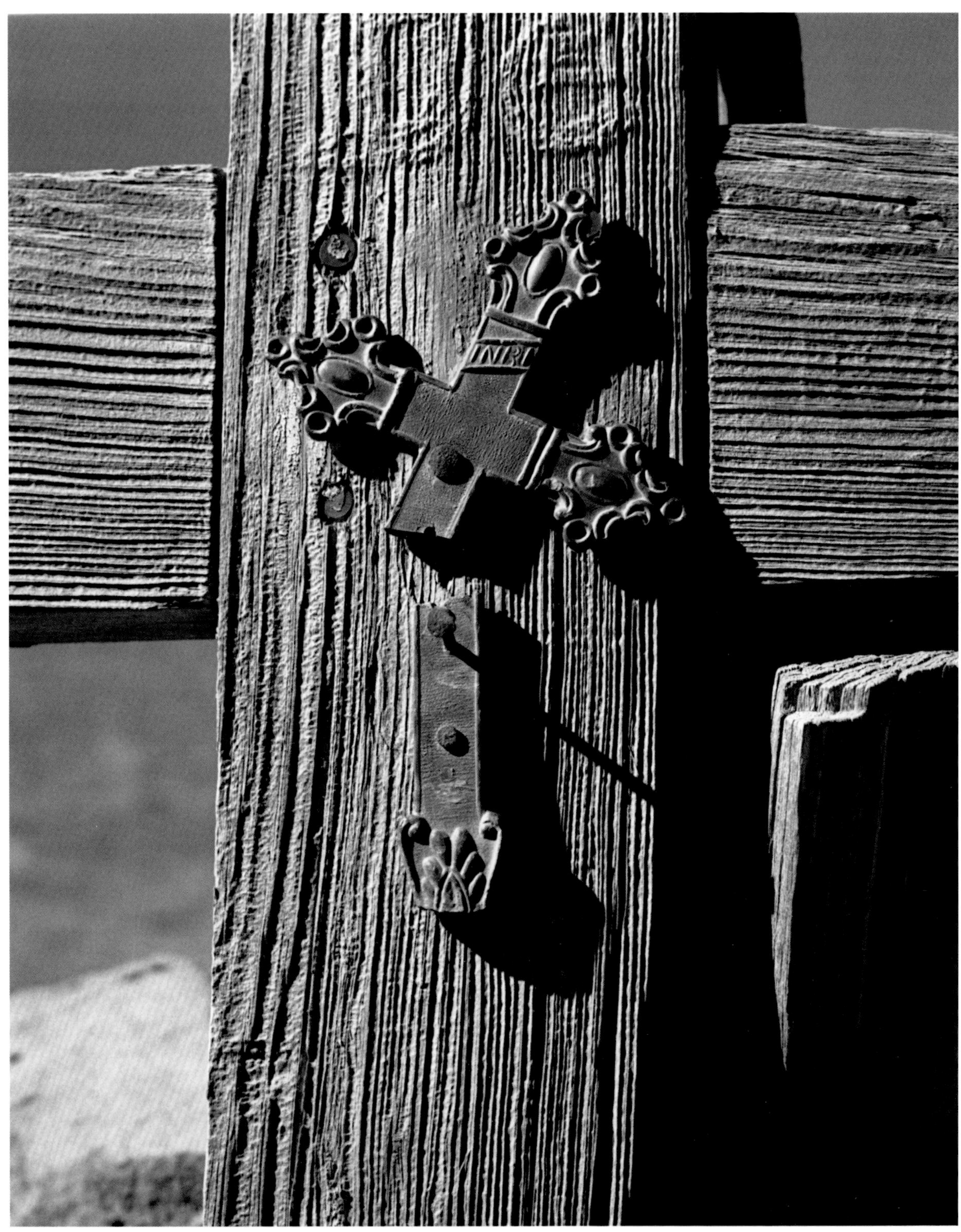
INRI

Circle of Life. Photo by Lee Marmon (1950).

Circle of Life (1950)

One day I came across this steer skull with a flower growing out of its eye. I call this photograph *Circle of Life*.

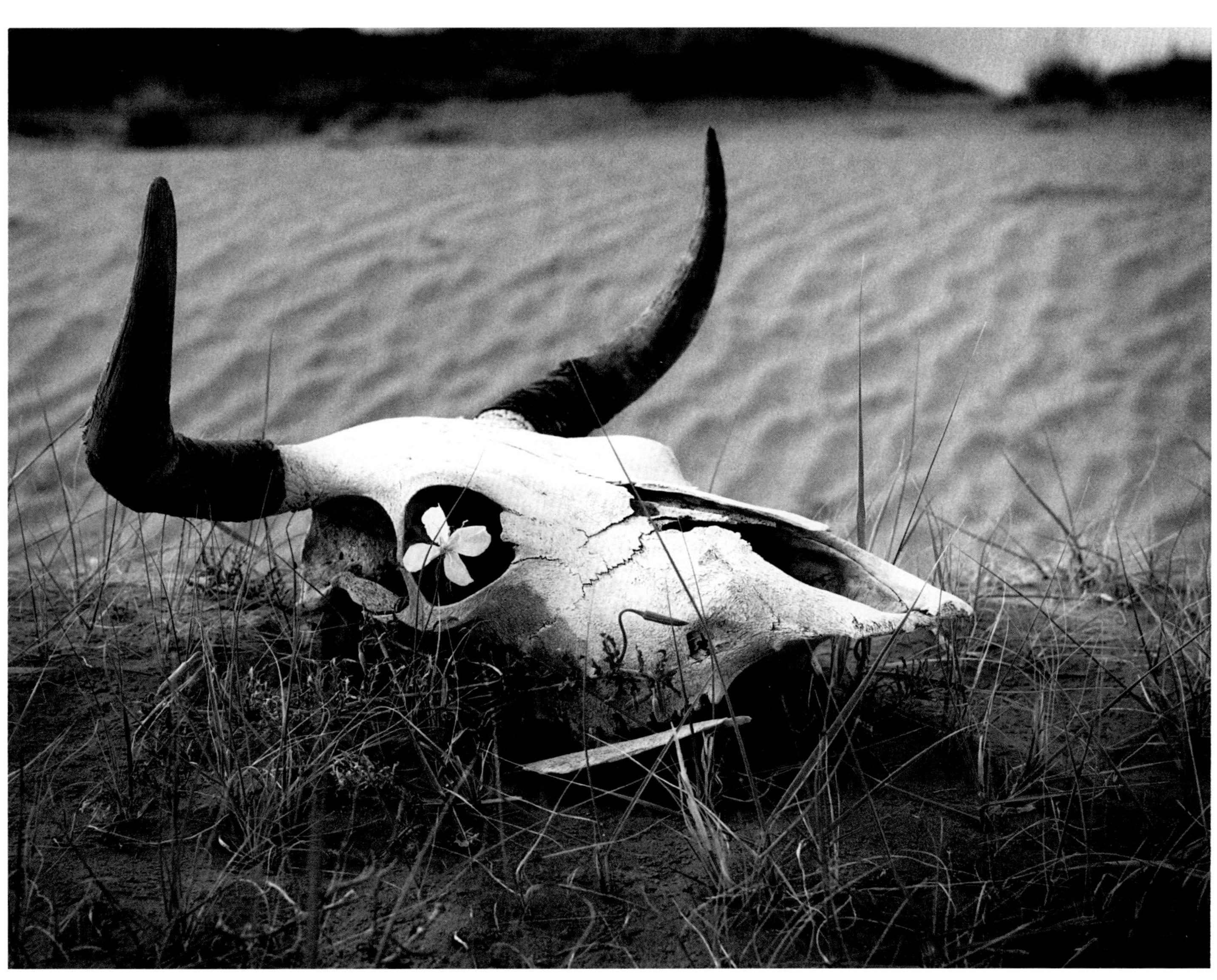

Table Rock at Dripping Springs (1980)

Table Rock at Dripping Springs. Photo by Lee Marmon (1980).

This is one of the interesting rock formations at Dripping Springs—a flat rock on a skinny pole.

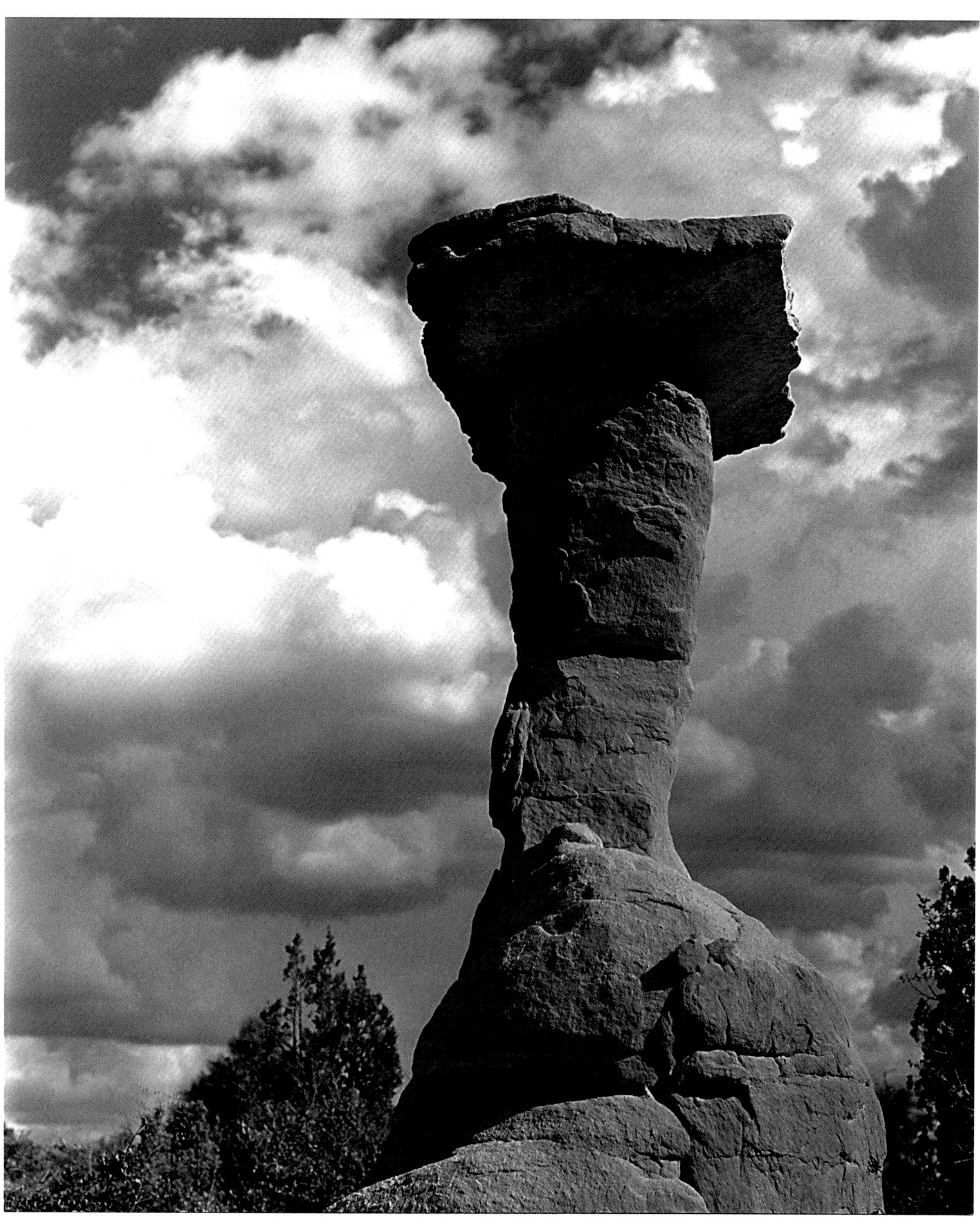

Lone Pine Tree at Dripping Springs (1990)

Lone Pine Tree at Dripping Springs. Photo by Lee Marmon (1990).

This lone pine tree was growing out of the sandstone. The butte known as Patoche is in the background.

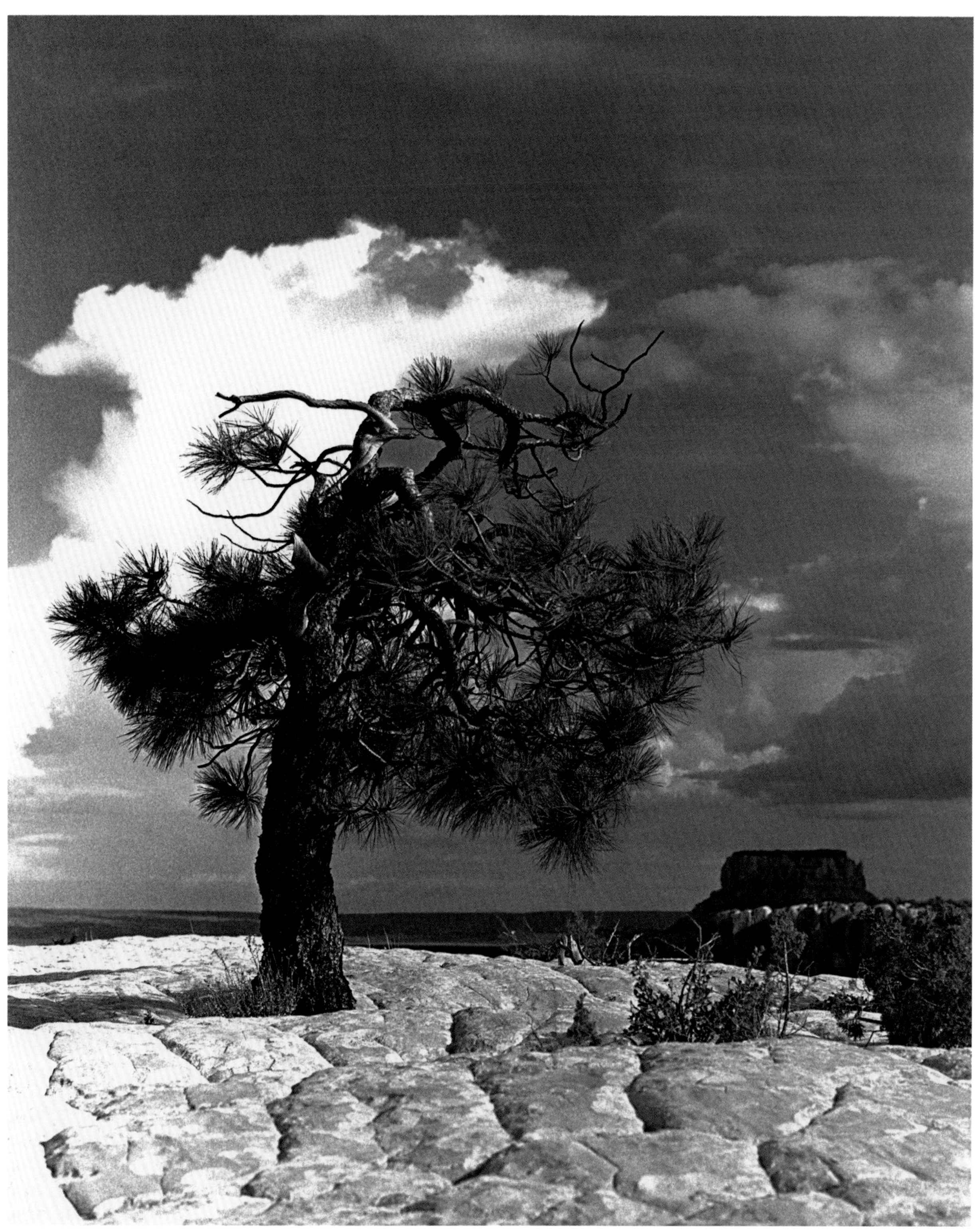

CHAPTER FOURTEEN

Health Care

Medicine men and medicine women were the sole providers of medical care for the Lagunas until the mid-1800s. Laguna oral history tells of the first medicine man. After passing several tests of courage, dedication, and endurance, he was granted special powers by the Creator and given specific instructions. He was told that he could cure people of their illnesses with prayer and songs and rituals and by touching and rubbing the body. He was told to always remember his origins in Shi-bop and the spiritual life he came from. He was to pass his skills to future generations of medicine men through apprenticeships.

The medicine man was given a basket with cornmeal and other materials, as well as two eagle feathers. The eagle feathers were his strength to send messages to the Creator. When he put his voice on the plumes, his message would be sent.

One special power he was given was the ability to resurrect selected people once they had died. If he felt that certain people needed to be brought back from the dead, he could do it with prayer and songs and rituals. He was warned to never cut into the body. Curing people could be done only through prayer and ritual. If he ever cut into the body, he would lose all his powers.[1]

The more practical aspects of medical care, such as delivering babies, setting broken bones, and treating common maladies (such as colds) with certain herbs, were done by specific women in the tribe who were commonly referred to as medicine women.

Because of the isolation of Native Americans from the rest of the world, they had no exposure to the diseases prevalent in Europe until the arrival of the conquistadores in the early 1500s. The Spanish explorers and settlers brought with them diseases to which the Native Americans had no prior immunity, including smallpox, measles, mumps, diphtheria, and tuberculosis. During the next three hundred years the Pueblo tribes were decimated by sporadic epidemics of these diseases.

The most virulent and deadly of the diseases was smallpox. It played a significant role in the fall of both the Inca and Aztec empires. Mortality rates during epidemics often ranged from 20 to 60 percent and occasionally ran as high as 98 percent in infants. Survivors were often left with disfiguring scars from the healed pockmarks.[2]

Although smallpox immunization had been discovered in the mid-1700s, it took until 1832 for Congress to direct $12,000 for smallpox immunizations for Indians.[3] Because of the great distance from Washington, D.C., and the Pueblo Indians' relative isolation, attempts to immunize the Pueblo tribes did not begin until the 1870s. When an outbreak of smallpox occurred in other pueblos in 1877, the residents of Laguna were vaccinated and spared from the disease. An epidemic hit Laguna and Paguate in 1890 and again from April 1898 until February 1899. Those vaccinated in 1877 were relatively immune to the disease. However, a total of seventy-eight cases were reported in Laguna, with twenty-eight deaths. The mortality rate was 35.8 percent. The village of Paguate endured a 40 percent death rate among smallpox patients there. The entire Laguna reservation experienced forty-eight deaths, eliminating 7.1 percent of the population.[4]

During that epidemic, Laguna had one of the lowest mortality rates from the disease, at least in part due to the efforts of Laguna Day School teacher Annie M. Sayre. Ms. Sayre administered an excellent nursing program during the epidemic, making sure patients were kept hydrated and cared for hygienically.

Lee Marmon remembers some of the survivors of that epidemic:

> Sometime in the late 1800s a smallpox epidemic occurred. My dad said it really hit hard at Laguna and many people died. I remember several people who made it through, with their faces deeply pockmarked from the disease.
>
> We also experienced deadly measles and diphtheria outbreaks. I had measles and pneumonia at the same time, so I barely survived that.
>
> As I recall, according to the 1900 census, there were only about a thousand Lagunas left. And now we're about eight thousand, and we're spread all over the reservation. But in those days most people stayed pretty close to the villages. There was no transportation other than a horse and a wagon. So they didn't wander too far till the railroad came through.

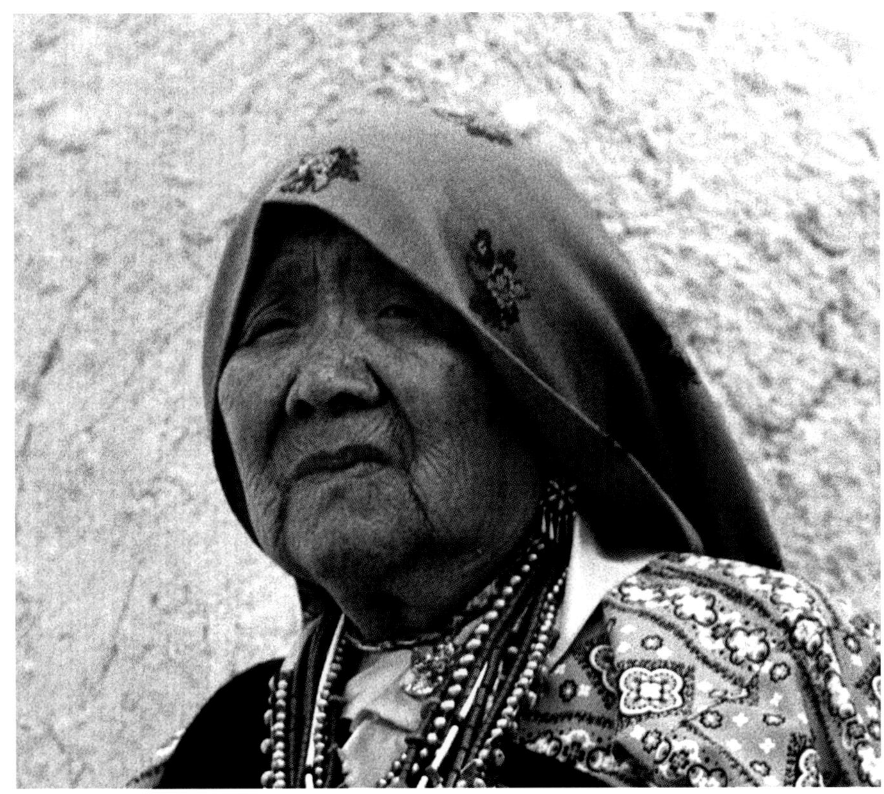

Smallpox Survivor. This Laguna woman, born in 1890, was a child when she contracted smallpox during one of the epidemics of the 1890s. She survived the disease, but like many other survivors, she developed permanent scars from the smallpox vesicles. She often wore a shawl to cover the residual scars on her forehead. Several are visible above her nose and eyebrows. Photo by Lee Marmon (1960).

The 1918 Influenza Epidemic

Laguna was not spared from the influenza epidemic that swept through the world in 1918. Father Fridolin Schuster reported about thirty deaths from the 1918 influenza epidemic among the Lagunas and about as many among the Acomas.[5]

Tuberculosis

Tuberculosis was also rampant among the Pueblo and Navajo tribes. In 1911, a two-story tuberculosis sanitorium with a capacity of twenty patients was constructed and opened at Laguna. It was located on the northeast edge of the village between the railroad tracks and the Rio San José. The facility consisted of the main hospital, used primarily as a tuberculosis sanatorium, doctors' and nurses' quarters, and a clinic building. The hospital was in operation until 1933. From 1911 to 1924, it operated under the supervision of the Pueblo Day Schools, the Pueblo Agency, and the Southern Pueblos Agency.[6] From 1924 to 1933 it operated independently and was staffed by the Presbyterian Hospital in Albuquerque.

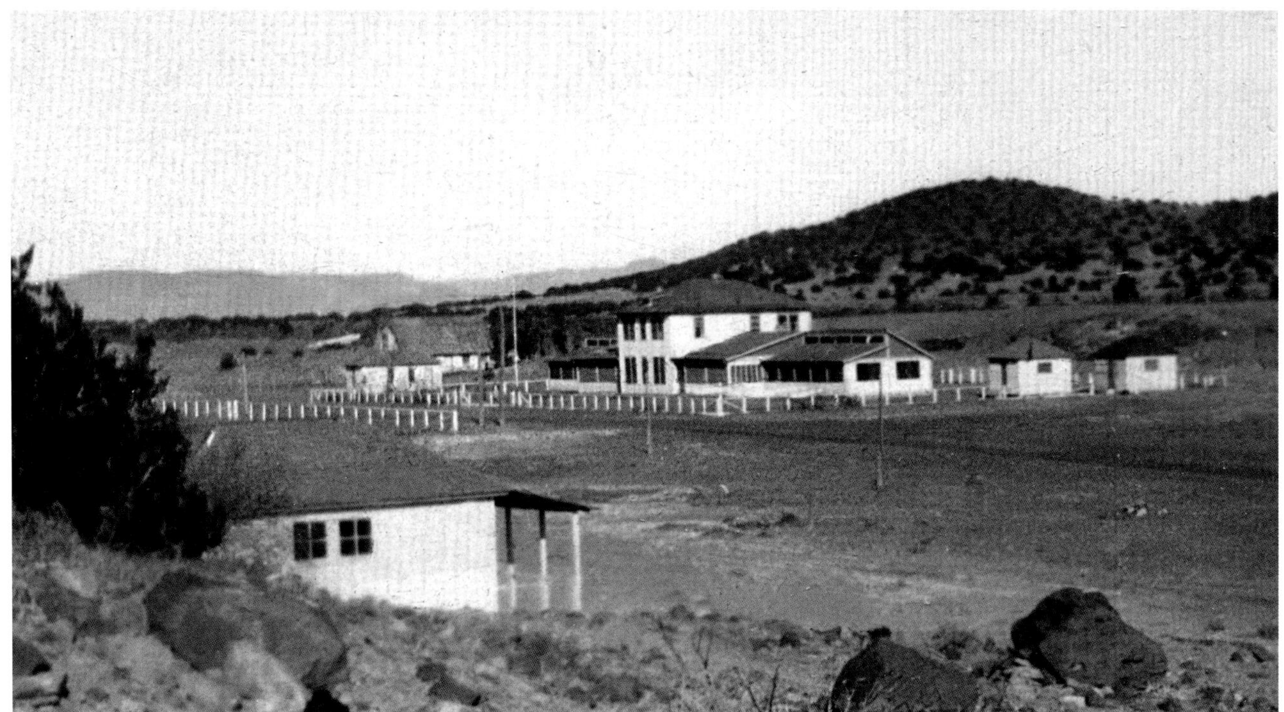

Tuberculosis hospital at Laguna, circa 1930. Although mainly a tuberculosis facility, the hospital at Laguna also functioned in other capacities. The facility closed sometime in the 1930s, but the clinic remained open. Following a major fire, the clinic and quarters were relocated to the north end of the Bureau of Indian Affairs' Laguna Day School complex. Photographer unknown. Courtesy of Ron Fernandez.

Lee Marmon recalls the hospital and a visit there:

In the early days Laguna had a TB hospital. It was built right next to the Santa Fe railroad tracks. I think that was the reason they placed it in Laguna, so they could bring other TB patients from New Mexico. From the time I was a kid, I always had the impression more Navajos than Pueblos were patients there.

Right across the railroad tracks from the hospital was a small clinic. That's where my folks took me when I had measles and pneumonia and where the doctor came out from Albuquerque seventy-five miles on a gravel road in a Model T to check on me. That was about 1927. He looked me over and said I wouldn't last through the night. Somehow, though, I lived through it.

I don't know what year officials ruled to dismantle the hospital, but I think it was in the early 1930s. They knocked down the hospital first. Of course, in those days they were very afraid of tuberculosis. They thought it was a lot more catching so they gathered up all the equipment and dumped it in the river when they left.

Anyway, some ruins can still be detected from the TB hospital.

Occupational Disease

Occupational hazards affecting uranium miners include malignant diseases, particularly lung cancer. Nonmalignant lung diseases (silicosis, pulmonary fibrosis) include a reduction in lung function from chronic inhalation of mining dust. Uranium and other heavy metals can accumulate in the kidneys and cause kidney failure in both occupational and environmental settings. Despite earlier reports of increases in lung cancer and other illnesses among uranium workers in Europe and among the Navajo miners of the Four Corners area, regulatory agencies did little to require adequate protection for Laguna miners, nor did they inform the miners or tribal officials of the risks. Evidence of disease was underplayed and even suppressed by governmental agencies, prolonging the risks to the miners. A 2010 study confirmed lung-cancer mortality to be significantly increased among underground uranium miners near Grants, New Mexico.[7]

Finally, in 1990, Congress passed the Radiation Exposure Compensation Act (RECA), which provided financial compensation to miners or their surviving families. In many cases, however, compensation was denied because the required documents to prove exposure were not available.

Tom Corbett recalls seeing two male patients with lung cancer while he was the physician on the reservation in 1965 and '66. Both men had worked in the mine since the early 1950s. One came to the clinic every week with his granddaughter, and as the weeks passed, Tom observed his deteriorating condition and tried to make him comfortable. He remembers to this day the man's distraught granddaughter helplessly watching her grandfather slowly succumbing to his malignancy. At the time Tom strongly suspected that his was an occupational disease from working in the mine and was concerned that these two cases might be the tip of an iceberg, as the mine had been in operation only thirteen years. He surmised there would be more uranium mine–related disease cases to come, but at that point, he had no solid proof or power to try to stop it.

The Indian Health Service

The responsibility of the United States government for the health care of Native Americans dates back to the Constitution, which defines the relationship between tribal governments and the federal government. That document states that federally recognized Indian tribes are sovereign nations with certain inherent rights.

In the early 1800s, the administration of Indian affairs was based in the Department of War. Indians living near military forts were provided such episodic medical care as military physicians might offer. The government gradually assumed an increasing obligation to provide health care by sending a physician and medications to selected tribes.

In 1849, the responsibility for Indian medical services was transferred from military to civilian control when the Bureau of Indian Affairs (BIA) was transferred from the War Department to the Department of the Interior. The first separate funding ($40,000) for Indian health was appropriated by Congress in 1911.

In 1921, Congress passed the Snyder Act. It provided continuing authority for federal Indian programs and is the basic authorization for federal health services to U.S. Indian tribes.

The Bureau of Indian Affairs, still a division of the Department of the Interior, continued to administer health programs for Native Americans until 1954. In that year, the Transfer Act established the Indian Health Service (IHS) as a division of the United States Public Health Service (USPHS) and transferred all functions of the secretary of the Interior, relating to the provision of health care to Native Americans, to the surgeon general of the USPHS. At that time, the USPHS was a branch of the Department of Health, Education, and Welfare, currently known as the Department of Health and Human Services.

Health care for the Lagunas and other Native Americans took a dramatic step forward after the creation of the Indian Health Service. On July 1, 1955, about 2,500 health-program personnel of the BIA, along with forty-eight hospitals, eighteen health centers, sixty-two stations, thirteen school infirmaries, and other locations, came under the jurisdiction of the newly created IHS.[8]

A regional office was established in Albuquerque with service units to provide health services in the tribal regions throughout New Mexico. The unit that services Laguna (the Acoma-Cañoncito-Laguna Service Unit) also provides services for the Acomas and the Cañoncito Navajos. The first outpatient clinic at Laguna was established in a building that was originally part of the old tuberculosis sanatorium complex. Satellite clinics were located in old adobe structures at Acomita and on the Cañoncito Navajo reservation.

The passage of the 1959 Indian Sanitation Facilities Act (Public Law 86-121) enabled the Indian Health Service to build facilities for the provision of safe water and sanitary waste disposal. This program was critical in improving living conditions and reducing waterborne and waste-borne communicable diseases.

Congress also established two major national goals in the Indian Health

Care Improvement Act (IHCIA) enacted in 1976: to ensure the health status of Indian people is elevated to the highest possible level and to achieve the maximum participation of Indian people in the Indian health programs.[9]

The 1980s were marked by great increases in funding for Indian health programs. A new facility, the ACL Hospital, was built in Acomita to provide services for the Acomas, Cañoncito Navajos, and Lagunas. The hospital offers a full range of outpatient and dental services as well as several specialty clinics. Prenatal, well-baby, medical, and diabetes clinics are scheduled regularly. Laboratory and X-ray facilities are on site. Field health programs have been initiated or expanded, including health education, public health nursing, social services, nutrition, school health programs, environmental health, and alcohol and substance abuse services.

The 1990s continued the evolution of the self-determination process and saw the conversion of the IHS director position from career public health officer to political appointee. Dr. Michael H. Trujillo, a Laguna tribal member, was the first appointed IHS director and led the organization from 1994 until 2002. He was known for his strong support of self-determination.

When Tom arrived at Laguna in July 1965, it had a one-doctor, one-dentist outpatient facility. In 1966, the Public Health Service Indian Health Division opened a new outpatient facility on Route 66, several miles west of Laguna. It was a state-of-the-art facility for its day. Beginning in July 1966, a second physician was added to the staff.

Today, the Acoma-Cañoncito-Laguna Service Unit consists of the ACL Hospital in Acomita and health centers in Laguna and Cañoncito. The hospital is meant to provide general medical, pediatric, and obstetric inpatient care with twenty-five beds. There is a dialysis unit to care for the numerous patients with kidney failure from diabetes and hypertension. The complex also houses the New Sunrise Regional Treatment Center, a residential program for adolescents.

In keeping with the Laguna tradition of revering and caring for their elders, the Laguna Pueblo Tribal Council chartered the Laguna Rainbow Corporation in 1979 for the purpose of providing comprehensive services to the tribal elders. The corporation maintains a nursing and assisted-living facility at Casa Blanca. Tribal culture is incorporated into services and activities offered to the elderly population in this facility.

Although many diseases once prevalent among Lagunas and other Native Americans have been eliminated or controlled (smallpox, TB, and other contagious diseases), new health problems have emerged and present new challenges. The radical change in lifestyle over the past few decades has resulted in obesity and an accompanying group of health problems not seen in prior generations. The most devastating of these new diseases is diabetes with its related complications: arteriosclerotic blood vessel disease, cardiovascular disease (heart attack and stroke), and kidney failure. The rate of kidney disease from diabetes among Lagunas has increased so dramatically that a dialysis center was instituted at the ACL Hospital.

Diabetes was rare among Lagunas as late as the 1960s. However, Laguna lifestyle, including both dietary and exercise patterns, changed dramatically with the onset of increased incomes from uranium-mine employment and other sources. The traditional diet was gradually replaced with high-sugar-content processed foods and drinks. To compound the risk, the average amount of daily exercise decreased dramatically with the purchase of automobiles and pickup trucks, along with television sets. The Lagunas, who used to farm and walk great distances almost daily, now have sedentary jobs and drive back and forth to their destinations. In many of the Pueblo tribes, the incidence of diabetes in adults is 35 percent or higher. Among non-Indians, the incidence is 4 percent.

Since the 1960s diabetes has become epidemic not only among the Lagunas but among American Indians and Alaska Natives in general. In order to combat the ravages of this disease, Congress established the Special Diabetes Program for Indians in 1997, including grant programs to establish diabetes prevention and treatment services for Native Americans throughout the country.

Alcoholism, drug addiction, depression, and suicide continue to be problems among most Native Americans, but with the programs instituted by the Indian Health Service, it is hoped that incidence of these conditions will decline.

However, recent changes in government policy encourage Native American tribes to become the primary providers of health services to tribal members. With less support from government subsidies and without sufficient guidance, Native Americans across the nation face cutbacks and deterioration or elimination of many health-care services.

CHAPTER FIFTEEN

Present Concerns and the Future

She-ake, the Pueblo medicine man and prophet who many generations ago accurately predicted the coming of the Spaniards, the Anglos, and the railroad, is not here to tell us confidently what the future holds, so we must rely on our own educated predictions.

Laguna is one of nineteen Pueblo tribes, all with certain common cultural traits but each distinctly different from the rest. The Pueblo peoples have survived for centuries as non-nomadic, agrarian tribes. Although they have three separate, distinct languages (Keresan, Tanoan, and Zuni), they have a common religion with tribal variances. The Pueblo tribes are survivors and adaptors, having persisted despite natural disasters, foreign and local invaders, and major epidemics of disease.

The Lagunas are unique among the Pueblo tribes, in that they have been the most heavily exposed to outside influences. They have also been the most accepting of outsiders and most willing to consider compromises in order to maintain their culture. In the late 1600s, the Lagunas became allies of the Spanish in order to protect themselves from Apache and Navajo raiders. At the same time, they accepted, to a degree, the Roman Catholic faith and combined it with their own beliefs where similarities existed. Their native religion survived and remains among their strongest cultural traits. In the 1870s, the Laguna people accepted white men who married into the tribe and adopted several of their political and religious ideas—however, not without causing some division in the tribe. In the early 1880s, the Lagunas negotiated a contract with the railroad to build tracks across Laguna land in exchange for salaried jobs and an increased standard of living for the people. The agreement was life changing for many Laguna families, who relocated off the reservation and for the first time experienced life away from their ancestral home. Contact with the outside world increased dramatically in the 1920s with the building of highways across the reservation, bringing even more tourists as well as more goods and services to the people. The discovery of uranium on the Laguna reservation led to the development of the Jackpile Mine. Even more men left agricultural and ranching activities for salaried jobs and an elevated standard of living.

In order to predict the future of the Lagunas, we must review the past and understand the problems and concerns of the present. The main concerns of the present include maintaining traditional values, religion, health care, and education.

Traditional Values

The Pueblo tribes, as well as the Apaches and the Navajos, came under the jurisdiction of the United States following the Treaty of Guadalupe-Hidalgo in 1848. That treaty transferred the New Mexico Territory from Mexico to the United States.

By the 1880s, politicians and educators decided the best long-term solution to resolve the countrywide "Indian problem" was to destroy their culture by taking the children from the reservations and "reeducating" them. In theory, through early education, the children would come to realize the primitive nature of their religion and culture and understand that the "white man's" way of life was vastly superior to their own.

The Carlisle Indian School, located in Carlisle, Pennsylvania, was the first off-reservation Indian boarding school designed for this purpose. In existence from 1879 until 1918, it enrolled up to one thousand students each year. Nearly twelve thousand students attended Carlisle during its operation.

The school was founded by Captain Richard Henry Pratt, who had served in the Civil War and later led the 10th Cavalry Regiment, known as the "Buffalo Soldiers."

The Carlisle experiment had the working hypothesis that taking children out of their original culture at an early age and immersing them into a new culture would strip the children of their original teachings and permanently instill in them the new culture's values and way of life. The goal of this government program was to "civilize" the children and give them a new identity.

Indian children from tribes throughout the country attended the school. Although some parents voluntarily sent their children to Carlisle, other children were forcibly taken from their families and shipped to the school in Pennsylvania. They were stripped of their cultural background. While at Carlisle, the children were given English names. They could not speak their native language, practice their native religion, or wear their native dress, and their hair was cut. They were forced to eat "white man's food" and attend "white man's churches." Students caught speaking their native language or practicing traditional ways were harshly punished or abused. They were taught English (speaking, reading, and writing), math, and history, as well as industrial and farming skills. They were not allowed to return home for summer vacation. Instead, they were employed by local families for domestic and farm work.

Hundreds of children died while attending the Carlisle Indian School, mostly from tuberculosis and other infectious diseases. Some suffered physical, emotional, and sexual abuse or malnutrition. Beatings were a common form of punishment for disobeying the strict rules.

The Carlisle experiment only partially met the goals of its founders. Many of the children, upon graduating and returning to their families and tribes, reverted to their old customs and ways. The Carlisle experiment did, however, instill in many of the children the value of education to live successfully in the white man's world. The school experience also made the students realize that the white man's culture was here to stay and Indians would have to learn to live with it. They would have to adapt if they were to survive. Many of the students returned to the reservations and promoted education within their tribes.

At Laguna, the Carlisle students' efforts produced a split in tribal ideology. The traditionalists were determined to continue unchanged in the old ways, while the progressives thought education was key in the struggle to survive in the changing culture. The latter faction's efforts have resulted in a current generation of highly educated tribal members with degrees in medicine, law, and other professional areas.

Notable Laguna attendees of the Carlisle Indian School include Susie Rayos Marmon, Yamie Leeds, Meta Atsye, Seichu Atsye, Charles Atsye, Marie Anaya Marmon (Grandma A'mooh), and Robert Brown.

Over the years, the Laguna on-reservation schools forbade the speaking of Keresan in school or on school buses, and physical punishment was frequently administered to those who broke the rule. As a result, many younger members of the tribe could not speak the language. That trend has been reversed more recently by the teaching of the Keresan language in the school system.

Religion

Efforts on several fronts to eradicate the native religion failed. The Lagunas' religion is a cohesive force that holds them together as a tribe, giving them a sense of belonging and purpose. The young people today, even though they may live off the reservation and have very different daily lives from their forebears, still return to Laguna for special ceremonial and feast days, to join in the dances and open houses of full-time residents. Close family ties are maintained, and special reverence is given to the tribal elders.

The Lagunas accepted the Roman Catholic Church because they were able to combine similarities in the two religions. Stories passed down through the generations foretold of the coming of the Catholics and that the people should accept this new church and combine it with their own.

The Laguna religion is rooted in something concrete, something people can see every day, every season, and every year: the cycles of nature. The cycles are represented on the walls of the mission and on the ceiling of the sacristy, the highest and symbolically most important position—above all else. The floor of the mission has never been covered with wood or cement for a reason—so the feet of the dancers, who come into the church to dance on special occasions, are in direct contact with the earth.

In 1965, Tom and his wife attended midnight mass at the mission on Christmas Eve. The mass ended and the priest left, yet when they turned to leave, someone told them to stay. They both sensed that something special was about to happen. The pews were quickly removed and the lights were turned off. They stood against the wall, totally unaware of what was about to happen. Then in the darkness they heard the faint *ching, ching, ching, ching* of the dancers approaching the church—the mesmerizing sound increasing in intensity as they drew nearer. Dim lights were turned on, and suddenly they could see the figures entering the church, dancing on the earthen floor. This very moving and spiritual experience remains burned in their memories to this day.

Those early politicians and educators were wrong to think they could destroy the "Indianness" and assimilate the people totally into Anglo society. Their programs did change the culture, but they could not destroy deeply ingrained religious beliefs. Like those of other religions, the Laguna beliefs are a powerful cohesive force—based on natural, visible, and reproducible occurrences.

Health Care

Health care for the Laguna tribe has improved dramatically. Gone are the epidemics of smallpox, measles, diphtheria, and other infectious diseases that killed so many young people. Tuberculosis, once a scourge especially among Native Americans, is rare today. Laguna people who survived the infectious disease epidemics of earlier times often lived on into their eighties and nineties—some even became centenarians. Many of Lee Marmon's photographic portraits, taken from 1947 to 2000, were of tribal elders in that age range. These people survived on a healthy native diet of corn, beans, deer, and mutton. However, the lifestyle changes since the 1950s have resulted in a high incidence of obesity, hypertension, diabetes, and related conditions (particularly renal failure) as well as occupational lung disease among the people.

These diseases, relatively new to the Lagunas, will require continued extensive preventative care programs as well as intense clinical patient care. Morbidity and mortality are and will continue to be significant. The people who have developed these conditions will not live as long, on average, as their elder counterparts. Cutbacks in health-care programs will result in a considerable increase in morbidity and mortality in this group.

Education

Indian reservations are considered sovereign nations within the boundaries of the United States. Under the treaties set forth at the time the reservations were formed, the United States agreed to provide certain benefits to the tribes in return for their agreement to live within the confines of the reservation. Included in these benefits are health care and education. Primary and secondary educational facilities are currently funded through government programs.

The Indians were given jurisdiction over their lands and at the same time were given United States citizenship. The lands given to the tribes, however, were generally considered unproductive and unable to sustain the tribes independently. By accepting the agreement to live on reservations, the tribes gave up their ability to be self-sufficient. Most tribes lost their best lands for hunting and agriculture. In the case of the Lagunas, they later lost their best farmland in the 1930s with the construction of the Bluewater Dam, which greatly reduced the flow of water across Laguna land.

Throughout the Lagunas' dealings with the government, and more recently with outside consultants on business and investment ventures, treaties, contracts, and promises have been broken. Dishonest business consultants and investment scammers have cheated the Lagunas of significant amounts of the wealth they acquired over the years. As a result, the progressive faction of the Lagunas realizes even more acutely the necessity of having their own educated professionals to look out for their interests.

The number of Lagunas prepared to meet the demands of self-reliance has not yet been achieved. Yet government cutbacks on programs dealing with education and health care are threatening to undermine the progress already made.

The future of the Lagunas and other Native American tribes will be largely influenced by the future of the United States. The support of the United States government for Native Americans throughout the country will depend on the economy, which is currently in a state of severe decline. Cutbacks in these government-supported programs are highly likely. Politicians will argue that casinos give sufficient income to tribes to allow cutbacks, but certainly in the case of Laguna, the revenue from the casinos is used to pay the mortgage and operating and other expenses. The tribal income is minimal and insufficient to pay for the Lagunas' own education and health care.

The effects of the economic decline are already becoming evident to the Lagunas and other tribes. Education has not yet brought the Lagunas to the point of economic self-sufficiency in a technological and business-oriented world, but the government is already cutting back on the programs necessary to obtain these goals. To compound the problem, agriculture and farming, once the economic base for the Lagunas, have dwindled due to the lack of both interest and skills of the people and to the elimination of potential farmland by the Bluewater Dam.

If government support for the necessary programs is cut, the economic future of Laguna is bleak. On the other hand, if these programs continue, the outlook is much brighter.

Historically, the Lagunas have survived many adversities and difficult living conditions. They are experts at adaptation and, over the past hundred years, have been able to increase their population and standard of living steadily. The culture has survived but with changes. Through his photography, Lee Marmon has documented the changes over the past sixty-five years. His work, combined with historical images, has allowed us to produce this photographic documentation of Laguna history since the 1860s.

What changes will the next hundred years bring? The future not only for the Lagunas but for the entire world is uncertain. We long for She-ake or his twenty-first-century counterpart to tell us where we all are headed—so we can prepare for and survive what is yet to come.

NOTES

CHAPTER ONE

1. Victor Sarracino, Laguna oral historian, personal communication, September 20, 2011.

2. *Report on Indians Taxed and Not Taxed in the United States (Except Alaska) at the Eleventh Census: 1890* (Washington, D.C.: Department of the Interior, Census Office, Government Printing Office, 1915), 420.

3. George B. Anderson, *History of New Mexico: Its Resources and People*, vol. 1 (Los Angeles, CA: Pacific States Publishing, 1907), 360.

4. *Thirteenth Census of the United States, 1910: Population by Counties and Minor Civil Divisions, 1910, 1900, 1890* (Washington, D.C.: Department of Commerce and Labor Bureau of the Census, Government Printing Office, 1912), 345.

5. *Indian Population of the United States and Alaska: 1910* (Washington, D.C.: United States Bureau of the Census, Government Printing Office, 1915), 86.

6. "Census 2000: American Indian and Alaska Native Summary File," United States Census Bureau, accessed February 7, 2014, http://factfinder2.census.gov/faces/tableservices/jsf/pages/productview.xhtml?pid=DEC_00_AIAN_DP1&prodType=table.

7. "Census 2010: American Indian and Alaska Native Summary File," United States Census Bureau, accessed February 7, 2014, http://factfinder2.census.gov/faces/tableservices/jsf/pages/productview.xhtml?pid=DEC_10_AIAN_AIANDP1&prodType=table.

CHAPTER TWO

1. Victor Sarracino, Laguna oral historian, personal communication, September 20, 2011.

2. Gussie Fauntleroy, "Railroad Days for the Pueblo of Laguna," *National Museum of the American Indian* (Spring 2012): 44–49.

3. Adolph Bandelier, *Keres Language of New Mexico* (Los Angeles, CA: Braun Research Library Collection, Autry National Center, circa 1883).

4. Franz Boas, *Keresan Texts*, vol. 8, parts 1 & 2 (New York: The American Ethnological Society and G. E. Stechert, 1928).

CHAPTER THREE

1. Stuart L. Udall, *To the Inland Empire: Coronado and Our Spanish Legacy* (Garden City, NY: Doubleday, 1987), 11–12, 75, 100.
2. Ward Alan Minge, *Acoma: Pueblo in the Sky*, rev. ed. (Albuquerque: University of New Mexico Press, 2002), 4–6.
3. George B. Anderson, *History of New Mexico: Its Resources and People*, vol. 1. (Los Angeles, CA: Pacific States Publishing, 1907), 360–61.
4. J. Manuel Espinosa, *The Pueblo Indian Revolt of 1698 and the Franciscan Missions in New Mexico. Letters of the Missionaries and Related Documents* (Norman: University of Oklahoma Press, 1988), 3–58.

CHAPTER FOUR

1. John M. Gunn, *Schat-chen: History, Traditions and Narratives of the Queres Indians of Laguna and Acoma* (Albuquerque, NM: Albright & Anderson, 1917), 46–47.
2. George B. Anderson, *History of New Mexico: Its Resources and People*, vol. 1 (Los Angeles, CA: Pacific States Publishing, 1907), 360–63.
3. "Historic American Building Survey," Library of Congress, accessed February 6, 2014, http://www.loc.gov/pictures/resource/hhh.nm0069.photos.114198p/?co=hh.
4. LeBaron Bradford Prince, *Spanish Mission Churches of New Mexico* (Cedar Rapids, IA: Torch Press, 1915), 202–13.

CHAPTER FIVE

1. *Amended Constitution and Bylaws of the Pueblo of Laguna in New Mexico, November 10, 1958* (Washington, D.C.: United States Government Printing Office, 1959).
2. Ibid.
3. Kim Coco Iwamoto, "Pueblo of Laguna Tribal Government Profile," ed. Frank Cerno, Tribal Law Journal, University of New Mexico School of Law, Volume 2: 2001/2002, accessed February 7, 2014, http://tlj.unm.edu/tribal-law-journal/articles/volume_2/laguna/index.php.

CHAPTER SIX

1. John Malcolm Gunn, *Schat-Chen: History, Traditions and Narratives of the Queres Indians of Laguna and Acoma* (Albuquerque, NM: Albright & Anderson, 1917), 93–108.

2. Rev. Henry Mason Baum and Frederick Bennett Wright, eds., *Records of the Past* (Washington, D.C.: Henry H. Wilkens Printing, 1904), 342.

3. Dwight P. Lanmon, Lorraine Welling Lanmon, and Dominique Coulet du Gard, *Josephine Foard and the Glazed Pottery of Laguna Pueblo* (Albuquerque: University of New Mexico Press, 2007), 43–51.

4. Fred Roeder, "The Marmon Brothers of Laguna," *American Surveyor*, April 5, 2009, http://www.amerisurv.com/content/view/6017/136.

5. "Pueblo Indians of New Mexico and Their Customs," Access Genealogy, accessed February 7, 2014, http://www.accessgenealogy.com/native/pueblo-indians-of-new-mexico-and-their-customs.htm.

CHAPTER SEVEN

1. Shawn Kelley and Kristen Reynolds, *Route 66 & Native Americans* (Albuquerque, NM: NMDOT and FHWA, 2010), 53–65.

2. Irvin W. Schiose, Laguna oral historian, personal communication, 2011.

CHAPTER EIGHT

1. Annie Heloise Abel, ed., *The Official Correspondence of James S. Calhoun While Indian Agent at Santa Fe and Superintendent of Indian Affairs in New Mexico* (Washington, D.C.: Office of Indian Affairs, Department of the Interior, Government Printing Office, 1915).

2. John Malcolm Gunn, *Schat-Chen: History, Traditions and Narratives of the Queres Indians of Laguna and Acoma* (Albuquerque, NM: Albright & Anderson, 1917), 93–108.

3. Fred Roeder, "The Marmon Brothers of Laguna," *American Surveyor*, April 5, 2009, http://www.amerisurv.com/content/view/6017/136.

CHAPTER NINE

1. Shawn Kelley and Kristen Reynolds, *Route 66 & Native Americans* (Albuquerque, NM: NMDOT and FHWA, 2010), 53–54.

CHAPTER TEN

1. Philip Sittnick, *Uranium Mining and its Impact on Laguna Pueblo: A Study Guide for an Interdisciplinary Unit* (Laguna, NM: Laguna Middle School, 1998), accessed February 9, 2014, http://www.miningwatch.ca/sites/www.miningwatch.ca/files/umine_0.pdf.

CHAPTER THIRTEEN

1. George B. Anderson, *History of New Mexico: Its Resources and People*, vol. 1 (Los Angeles, CA: Pacific States Publishing, 1907), 372.

2. Charles F. Lummis, *Mesa, Canon and Pueblo* (New York: The Century Co., 1925), 213–31.

CHAPTER FOURTEEN

1. Victor Sarracino, Laguna oral historian, personal communication, 2011.

2. Alfred W. Cosby, "Conquistador y Pestilencia: The First New World Pandemic and the Fall of the Great Indian Empires," *Hispanic American Historical Review* 47, no. 3 (August 1967): 321–27.

3. Stefan Riedel, "Edward Jenner and the History of Smallpox and Vaccination," *Proceedings (Baylor University Medical Center)* 18, no. 1 (January 2005): 21–25.

4. Richard H. Frost, "The Pueblo Indian Smallpox Epidemic in New Mexico: 1898–1899," *Bulletin of the History of Medicine* 64, no. 3 (1990): 417–45.

5. *The Franciscan Missions of the Southwest*, official organ of the Franciscan branch (Cincinnati province) of the Preservation Society, published annually by the Franciscan Fathers at Saint Michael's, Arizona, vol. 1 (1913), 39–40.

6. "Laguna Indian Sanatorium (New Mexico)," Family Search, accessed February 10, 2014, http://familysearch.org/learn/wiki/en/Laguna_Indian_Sanatorium_(New_Mexico).

7. John D. Boice, M. T. Mumma, and William J. Blot, "Cancer Incidence and Mortality in Populations Living Near Uranium Milling and Mining Operations in Grants, New Mexico, 1950–2004," *Radiation Research* 174 (2010): 624–36.

8. "The First 50 Years of the Indian Health Service: Caring and

Curing," Indian Health Service IHS Gold Book, part 1, accessed February 10, 2014, http://www.ihs.gov/newsroom/includes/themes/newihstheme/display_objects/documents/GOLD_BOOK_part1.pdf.

9. "The First 50 Years of the Indian Health Service: Caring and Curing," Indian Health Service IHS Gold Book, part 2, accessed February 10, 2014, http://www.ihs.gov/newsroom/includes/themes/newihstheme/display_objects/documents/GOLD_BOOK_part2.pdf.

INDEX

Page numbers in italic text indicate illustrations.

Abraham, Seigfried, 57, 59, *59*
ACL (Acoma-Cañoncito-Laguna) Hospital, 181
Acoma Hotel, 31, 43, *46*, 47
Acoma Pueblo, 15, 17, 19, 36, 156
Acomita village, 181
agriculture: beginning of, 10; and Bluewater Dam, 187, 188; Fernando, Santiago, 144; and the railroad, 82; and Route 66, 62
Albuquerque Indian School, 148
Albuquerque-Wingate Wagon Road, 57
All Indian Pueblo Council, 134
de Alvarado, Capt. Hernando, *14*
Anaconda Copper Company, 65
Anaya, Agness, 37
Anaya, Marie. *See* Marmon, Marie Anaya
Anglo cultural infusion, 33–38, 183–86
Antonio, Lee, 120, *121*, *123*
Apache campaigns, 36. *See also* Marmon Battalion
Apache raids, 51–55, 130
archaeological findings, 10–11, 156
archaic period, 10
architecture, 11, *12*, *13*, 72, *73*
Arny, Maj. William F. N., 35
Atchison, Topeka and Santa Fe Railway (AT&SF), 41, *44*, *49*. *See also* railroads
Atlantic and Pacific Railroad, 41. *See also* railroads
Atlantic Richfield Company, 66
Atsye, Charlie, 148, *149*, 185
Atsye, John, 148
Atsye, Marie Mariano, 148
Atsye, Meta, 38, 57, 185
Atsye, Seichu, 185
auto camp, 60, 62, *63*
automobiles, 58, 70. *See also* Route 66

Bandelier, Adolph, 7, 36
Baptist Missionary Society, 34
Baptist Mission compound, 43, *63*, 116
Barstow, CA, 47, 78
Beale Wagon Road, 57
Beecher, Henry Ward, 118, *119*
Bibo, Simon, 58
Bibo Family, *44*
Billy the Kid, 36
Bluewater Dam, *3*, 82, 187, 188
Bluewater Lake, *3*
Bluewater village, 1
Boas, Franz, 7, 10
boundaries (Pueblo of Laguna), 1
boxcar colonies, 47, 78
Broken Prayer-Stick, 9. *See also* Prayer-Stick Boy
Brown, Robert, 8, 185
Buffalo Dancers, *89*, *90*, *91*, *93*
buildings, 11, *12*, *13*, 72, *73*
Bureau of Indian Affairs (BIA), 27, *178*, 180
burial ground, 20
Buzzard Butte, 160, *161*

cacique, 19, 38
Calhoun, James S., 51
campo santo, 20, *20*
canes, *26*, 27–28, *29*, *30*, *31*
Carlisle Indian School: attendees, 30, 37, 134, 148; cultural identity, 38, 184–85; names, 8, 118
Casa Blanca village, 5, 58, 63, 181
casinos, 5, 63, 188
Cather, Willa, *46*, 47
Catholicism, 17, 20, 185. *See also* religion
cattle drive, *4*, 78, *79*

cavalry, 36, *50*, 51–55, 118
censuses, 5, 37, 128, 156
ceramics: beginning of, 10; potters, 102, 128, 136, 138; and the railroad, *44*, *45*; and Route 66, 63
Certificate of Indebtedness, *53*, 54
Chaco Canyon, 11, *12*, *13*, 57
Chetro Ketl (Chaco Canyon), 11, *12*
children, 38, 47
Chinatown (Paguate village), 110
Circle of Life (Marmon), 168, *169*
citizenship, 187
climate, *4*, 78, 158
clothing, 70, *71*
Clovis spear points, 10
coal chute, *42*, 43, *44*
Colorado Plateau, *4*, 10. *See also* landscapes
conquistadores, 15–18, 27, 33, 175
Constitution, Pueblo of Laguna, 28–29
convento, 21
Corbett, Thomas, 179
corn, 82, *83*, 110
Corn Mother, 8
de Coronado, Francisco Vásquez, 15, 33
Correa, Gov. Floyd, *31*
Council, Pueblo, 28–29, 34, 69. *See also* government
Coyote, Antonio (Kum-mus-tche-kush), 19
Creator, 8, 175
crosses, 164, *165*, *167*
cultural identity, 38, 118, 184–85
Curtis, Edward, 36

dances, 86–97, 112
Dancing Eagle Casino, 63
Darling, Ehud N., 35
Dawa-Go-Mai-Tsa, 134
de Córdoba, Diego Fernández, 27
Deer Dancers, *94*, *95*
de Niza, Fray Marcos, 15
de Oñate, don Juan, *16*, 17, 27
descanso, 164, *165*, *167*
de Vargas, don Diego, 19–20. *See also* conquistadores
diabetes, 182
diphtheria, 175–76
disease, 128, 173–78, 182, 185. *See also* health
Disney, Walt, 110
dress, 70, *71*
Dripping Springs, 158, *159*; Lone Pine Tree, 172, *173*; Patoche Mesa, *xxi*; Table Rock, 170, *171*
drought, 78, 158

Eagle Dancers, 86, *87*, *88*
Early, Harry, *26*
Earth Mother, 8–10
economy, 47, 58, 59, 62–63. *See also* employment
education: and cultural identity, 8, 38, 118, 184–85; higher, 134; and Marmon, Robert, 37; and missions, 34, 36; modern, 187–88. *See also* Carlisle Indian School
Elderly Code, Pueblo of Laguna, 29–30
elders, xix, 7, 29–30, 181, 185–87
elevation, 1
El Morro National Monument, *16*
employment: economy, 47, 58, 59, 62–63; mining, 65–66, 78; railroads, 47, 78, 80, 144; and Route 66, 62–63
Enchanted Mesa (Katzimo), *14*, 156, *157*
Encinal village, 1
Engine Rock, *152*
environment, 66
Esteban, 15
Evans, T. K., *63*

feast days, 74, *75*
Fernandez, Ron, xix
Fernando, Romero, 140, *141*
Fernando, Santiago, 144, *145*
Fifth World, 8
firewatcher, 116
"Flower of Friendship," 41
Franciscan friars, 17
future, 33–34, 183, 188

gas pumps, *61*
gas station, 59, *60*, *61*

Gorman, Rev. Samuel, 34
government: cacique, 19, 38; canes, *26*, 27–28, *29*, *30*, *31*; Council, Pueblo, 28–29, 34, 69; Pueblo of Laguna Constitution, 28–29; and the railroad, 41; sovereignty, 27
governors: Anglo, 36; Beecher, Henry Ward, 118, *119*; Correa, Floyd, *31*; Johnson, Paul, 130; Sarracino, Walter, 30–31, *30*; Solomon, James, 150
Governor’s Palace (Santa Fe, NM), 17
Grandma A’mooh (Marie Anaya Marmon), xx, 37, 53, 185
graveyard (mission), *20*
Great Depression, 55, 60, 62–63
Gunn, Jessie, 57
Gunn, John Malcolm: biography, 37–38; flour mill, 58; Gunn Trading Post, *56*, 57, 59, *59*; his book, 33; Marmon Battalion, *52*, *54*
Gunn, Kenneth Colin Campbell, 38, 57
Gunn, Meta Atsye, 38, 57
Gunn, Mrs. Isabel S., 36
Gunn Trading Post, *56*, 57, 59, *59*

health: disease, 128, 173–78, 182, 185; Indian Health Service, 179–82; medicine women, 124, *125*, 175; and mining, 66, 179; modern, 70, 186–87
history. *See* oral history
Hodge, Frederick Webb, 156

Indian Health Care Improvement Act (IHCIA) (1976), 181
Indian Health Service, 179–82
Indian Sanitation Facilities Act (1959), 180
influenza epidemic, 177
Inscription Rock, *16*
Interstate 40, 5, 63. *See also* roads
irrigation, 82

the Jackpile Mine, 31, 65–68, 78, 82, 182
Jackson, William Henry, 36
Jeff, Old Man, 100, *101*
Johnson, Eulojia Martin, 130, *131*
Johnson, Frank, 136
Johnson, Paul, 130
Johnson, Rosita, 136, *137*

Kashana (Medicine Woman), 124, *125*
Katzimo (Enchanted Mesa), *14*, 156, *157*
Keresan language: and education, 134, 185; Marmon Battalion, 52; and names, 8, 118; oral history, 69–70; Pueblo languages, 183; written form, 7
Keresan tribe, 8
kivas, 11, *12*, 35
Ko’t^{y}e, 8
Kum-mus-tche-kush (Antonio Coyote), 19
Kycero, Etta, 138, *139*

Laguna colonies, 47
Laguna Construction Company, 66
Laguna Day School, 148, 176
Laguna Rainbow Corporation, 181
Laguna section gang, *48*, 126
Laguna village, 1, 126, 136, 148
lake, 15, 17
landscapes, 1, *4*, *79*, 152–73
languages, 183. *See also* Keresan language
Leeds, Yamie, 185
legends. *See* oral history
Lincoln, President Abraham, 27–28
Lincoln canes, *26*, *29*, *30*, *31*

Maase’eewi, 9
Malpais, 154, *155*
The Man to Send Rainclouds (Silko), 106
Marmon, Alice, 148
Marmon, Annie Bell Gunn, *35*
Marmon, Henry, 132
Marmon, Lee: 1931, *63*; on changes, 69–70; home of, *42*, 77; on the hospital, 178; on photography, 99–100, 153; on smallpox epidemic, 176; as treasurer, 31
Marmon, Marie Anaya (Grandma A’mooh), xx, 37, 53, 185
Marmon, Polly, *63*, 158
Marmon, Robert Gunn: 1883, *35*; at Acoma, *32*; biography, xix–xx,

Marmon, Robert Gunn (*continued*) 35–37; buildings, *44*; certificates of indebtedness, *53*, 54; Marmon Battalion, *52*, *54*
Marmon, Solomon, 35–36
Marmon, Susie Rayos, 53, 134, *135*, 185
Marmon, Walter Gunn: 1883, *34*; biography, 34–35; governor, 36; Marmon Battalion, *50*, 51, *52*
Marmon, Walter K., 134
Marmon Battalion (New Mexico Cavalry), 36, *50*, 51–55, 118
Martinez, Edwin, *26*
McCook, General, 51
measles, 175–76
medicine men, 124, 175
medicine women, 124, *125*, 175
men: medicine men, 124, 175; mining, 78; railroads, 41, 47–48, 78, 80; traditional clothing, 70, *71*
Menaul, Rev. John, 37
Menaul School, 134
de Mendoza, don Antonio, 15
Mesita village, 1, 58, 132, 140, *143*
Mexico, 27
Miguel, Eulogia, 37
military, 36, *50*, 51–55, 118
mill, 58, 59, *59*
Miranda, Padre Antonio, 20
Missions, *3*, 17, 18–25
Mother-Father, 8
Mount Taylor, 1, 2, 68, *152*
mumps, 175–76
Mushroom Rocks, 162, *163*
myths. *See* oral history

Navajos: Old Man Platero, 108, *109*; raids, 51, 52, 130; wagons, 74, *75*, 76, *77*
New Laguna Village, 43, *45*, 58
New Mexico Cavalry. *See* Marmon Battalion
New Mexico Territory, 27, 34, 51
New Sunrise Regional Treatment Center, 181
North American Indian Women's Association, 134

Old Laguna Village: 1955, 72, *73*; and the railroad, 43; and Route 66, 5, 58; view of, *2*
oral history: Acoma, 156; emergence and migration, 7–10; and Gunn, 33, 37–38; and Keresan language, 69–70; Pueblo of Laguna Constitution, 28–29; Shiosee, Irvin W., 144

Pacheco, Bennie, 80, *81*, 104, *105*
Pacheco, Mariano, 104
pacification, 17
Pacific Railway Act, 41
Padilla, Fray Juan, 15
Paguate village: the Jackpile Mine, 65–68; Laguna Pueblo boundaries, 1; residents, 110, 130, 134; smallpox epidemic, 176
Paleo Indians, 10
Paraje village, 1, 58
Parsons, Elsie Clews, 7
Patoche Mesa, *xxi*, 172, *173*
Penitente Cross, 164, *165*, *167*
photography, 99–100, 153
Pino, Juana Marie, 110, *111*
pit houses, 11
plaster, 72, *73*, 84, *85*, 136
Platero, Old Man, 108, *109*
plazas, 11
Popé, 17
population, 5, 37, 128, 156
post office, 36, *59*
potters, 102, 128, 136, 138
pottery, 10, *44*, *45*, 63
Pradt, Bill, 116, *117*
Pradt, George H., 36, 37, *37*, *52*, 116
Pratt, Capt. Richard Henry, 184
Prayer-Stick Boy, 9
Presbyterian Church, 35, 37, 134. *See also* religion
Pueblo Bonito (Chaco Canyon), 11
Pueblo culture, 11, 183. *See also* oral history
Pueblo revolts, 17, 19

Quicero, Henry José, 102
Quicero, Juanita, 102, *103*

Radiation Exposure Compensation Act (RECA), 179. *See also* the Jackpile Mine
railroads: arrival of, 41–49, 106; boxcar colonies, 47, 78; employment, 47, 78, 80, 82, 144; Laguna section gang, *48*, 126; surveys, 35; train station, *40*, *42–45*, 47, *49*
ranching, *4*, 78, *79*, 80, *81*
Read, Rev. Henry W., 34
religion: and the Anglo infusion, 38; archaeological findings, 11; Baptist Missionary Society, 34; Catholicism, 17, 20, 185; dances, 86–97; medicine men, 124, 175; oral history, 7–10; Presbyterian Church, 35, 37, 134; symbols, 21, *24*, 186; today, 185–86; war chiefs, 126
Richmond, CA, 47, 78
Riley, Bruce, 126, *127*
Riley, John, 146, *147*
Rio Puerco, 5, 15, 17, 57
Rio San José: and Blue Water Dam, *3*, 82, 187, 188; bridge, *61*, *62*; course of, 15, 17; and the railroad, 41, *44*; and trade, 57
roads, 5, 57–63
Route 66, historic, 5, 57–63
Route 66 Casino, 5, 63
Royal Ordinances of 1573, 17. *See also* conquistadores

Sanchu, José, 132, *133*
Sanchu, Raphelita, 132
San José de la Laguna Mission, *3*, 18–25
San Juan Pueblo, 17
Santa Fe Indian Band, 126
Santa Fe Railroad, *48*. *See also* railroads
Sarracino, Gov. Walter, 30–31, *30*
Sarracino, Luis, 31, 35
Sarracino, Mary Mollie, 35
Sarracino, Victor, 8
Sayre, Annie M., 176
Schat-Chen: History, Traditions and Narratives of the Queres Indians of Laguna and Acoma (Gunn), 33, 38
Schuster, Father Fridolin, 177
Seama village, 1
Seboyeta village, 1, 164
Seven Cities of Cibola, 15
She-ake, 33–34, 183, 188
sheep camps, 80, *81*, 102
Shi-bop, 7–8, 175
Shiosee, Irvin W., 144
Siow, Lupe Garcia, 128, *129*
smallpox epidemic, 128, 175–76, *177*
Snyder Act (1921), 180
Solomon, James, 150, *151*
sovereignty, 27
Spain, 15–18, 27, 33, 175
Special Diabetes Program for Indians, 182
Stagner, Grover, 62
Stagner, Jack, 62
Steck, Dr. Michael, 27–28
Steele, Lola, 142, *143*
St. Joseph's Feast Day, 74, *75*
Susie Rayos Marmon Day, 134
symbols, Lagunan, 21, *24*, 186

Table Rock at Dripping Springs (Marmon), 170, *171*
Tanoan language, 183
Teofilo, José, 106, *107*
Tewa Pueblo, 17
Thomas, Santiago, 112, *113*, *115*
topography, 1, *4*, *79*, 152–73
tourists: and Old Man Jeff, 100; and pottery, 102, 128, 136, 138; and the railroad, 43; and Route 66, 62
trade routes, 57
trading posts, *56*, 57, 59–60, 62, 99
trains. *See* railroads
train station, *40*, *42–45*, 47, *49*
Treaty of Guadalupe-Hidalgo (1848), 27, 51, 184
Tri-Centennial Marksmanship Competition (Santa Fe), 52
Trujillo, Dr. Michael H., 181
tuberculosis, 176–78

underworld, 7. *See also* religion
United States, 27, 34, 51, 58, 184
uranium mine, 31, 65–68, 78, 82, 182

U.S. Forest Service, 116
Uyuuyeewi, 9. *See also* religion

villages: Acomita, 181; Casa Blanca, 5, 58, 63, 181; Laguna, 126, 136, 148; Mesita, 58, 132, 140, *143*; New Laguna, 43, *45*, 58; Old Laguna, 2, 5, 43, 58, 72, *73*; Paguate, 65–68, 110, 130, 134, 176; Paraje, 58; Pueblo of Laguna, 1; Seboyeta, 164
visions, 33–34, 183, 188

wagon trails, 57, 58
Wallace, General Lew, 36
war chiefs, 126, 132. *See also* religion
Ward, John, 5
water, 15, 17, 41–43, 72, 82. *See also* Rio San José
"Watering the Flower," 41
water tower, *42*, 43, *44*, *49*, 58, *59*
Weiss, Gus, *44*, 58
White Hands, 9
White House, 9
White Man's Moccasins (Marmon), 100, *101*
Winslow, AZ, 47, 78
Wittick, George Benjamin, 70
women: and the economy, 63; medicine women, 124, *125*, 175; plasterers, 72, *73*, 84, *85*, 136; potters, 102, 128, 136, 138; traditional clothing, 70, *71*
World War II, 76, 104, *123*

Zaldivar, Juan, 17
Zuni language, 183
Zuni Pueblo, 15